D0378914

Praise for *The Empathy Effect*

"Everyone who cares about others will benefit from Dr. Helen Riess's book. An important contribution in these challenging times."

PAUL EKMAN, PHD
professor emeritus, University of California Medical School,
San Francisco; author of *Unmasking the Face* and *Emotions Revealed*

"Empathy has always been a secret strength of the healer's art. In *The Empathy Effect*, Dr. Helen Riess, a compassionate physician herself, updates this ancient tool, making it a practical and accessible skill for anyone in the healing professions—and everyone else too."

DANIEL GOLEMAN
New York Times bestselling author of *Emotional Intelligence*

"This wonderful exploration of a vital topic, coming from a world-class scientist, reads like a page-turning novel with heart-touching stories, fascinating research, and tons of practical takeaways. At a time when the fabric of human society seems to be fraying, this book offers hope and help for individuals, couples, families, organizations, and communities to mend it together."

RICK HANSON, PHD
New York Times bestselling author of *Resilient*,
Buddha's Brain, and *Hardwiring Happiness*

"*The Empathy Effect* offers us a deep dive into one of the most important human capacities—to sense, understand, and care about others. In a time when compassion is often in short supply, our eloquent guide reveals the science of how empathy and compassion overlap and shows us the key ingredients to cultivating both in our lives. Built upon years of practical applications and scientific studies, this book is a timely gift for humanity."

DANIEL J. SIEGEL, MD
New York Times bestselling author of *Aware:*
The Science and Practice of Presence and *Mindsight*

"In this remarkable book, Dr. Riess dissects empathy with rare insight, offering us all a path to examining our own hearts by listening carefully to those whom we serve."

JIM O'CONNELL, MD
president of Boston Health Care for the Homeless Program and
assistant professor of medicine at Harvard Medical School

"Through story and science, Dr. Helen Riess describes an understated but pivotal emotion: empathy. We learn how our glances, posture, and tone of voice can envelope or isolate—can create healthy children, great workplaces, and inspiring political leadership, or promote cyber-bullying, lawsuits, and social disorder. *The Empathy Effect* is a must-read for anyone interested in understanding relationships, from the personal to the political."

BARBARA BRADLEY HAGERTY
New York Times bestselling author of *Life Reimagined:
The Science, Art, and Opportunity of Midlife*

"A fast and interesting read, full of big *aha* moments about what actually happens when we experience another's pain."

SUZIE REIDER
managing director, advertising sales, Google

"This book had me at hello. As a faculty member and teacher trainer at the Kripalu Center for over thirty years, and an ongoing movement and yoga teacher for the Parkinson's community and those with special needs, I have learned a thing or ten about empathy. Reading this book is teaching me much more about the topic. The authors carefully analyze and 'dig deep for empathy,' while offering readers seven critical components of empathy. As I read these wise, wonderful words, I only wished this book had been written three decades earlier to help me navigate the often-treacherous path of training people to be compassionate and empathetic. I am so grateful *The Empathy Effect* came to me and hope it will be read around the world."

MEGHA NANCY BUTTENHEIM, MA
chief joy officer, Let Your Yoga Dance® LLC;
author of *Expanding Joy: Let Your Yoga Dance*

"Everyone knows that empathy is an enormously powerful asset in the work of healing. But few knew that it could be developed through systematic training. Now, this book puts the development of the skillful practice of empathy fully in the reach not just of health-care professionals, but—frankly—anyone who wants to be a better listener and carer."

DONALD M. BERWICK, MD
president emeritus and senior fellow,
Institute for Healthcare Improvement

"What's at the intersection of neuroscience research, masterful storytelling, and practical application? *The Empathy Effect*. Yes, empathy can be learned, and medical schools are leading the way thanks to Dr. Riess. Business schools should make *The Empathy Effect* required reading!"

MARGARET H. GREENBERG, MAPP, PCC
coauthor of the bestselling *Profit from the Positive:
Proven Leadership Strategies to Boost Productivity
and Transform Your Business*

"Any effective middle school teacher understands that kids learn more if they know you love them. We're not going to be their best friends—nor should we be—but if kids know we care, they can soar. Dr. Riess has done a huge service articulating the science behind what good teachers know. She supports this science with concrete examples and pragmatic advice that will help fundamentally change the trajectory for many children."

THE REV. DR. JOHN H. FINLEY IV
cofounder and head of Epiphany School, Boston

"Dr. Riess operationalizes the word 'empathy,' honing it from an often-proclaimed but poorly defined modern cliché to a tool that will help readers connect, grow, and flourish."

JOSEPH LEE, MD, ABAM
medical director of Youth Continuum at
Hazelden Betty Ford Foundation

"In an age of epidemic meanness, the media catalog daily events that shock us with their rudeness, even cruelty. How will we relearn civility? In this wonderful, accessible new book, Helen Riess weaves the story of her discoveries and their implementation to raise our levels of empathy. From 'shared mind intelligence' through the seven keys of empathy to the politics of empathy in leadership, Dr. Riess describes in the simplest terms the neurobiology of empathy and why it is critical to health care and every other service offered to humans. She succeeds brilliantly in the challenge of her title—to transform life, love, work, and human connection."

RICHARD I. LEVIN, MD
president and CEO, The Arnold P. Gold Foundation;
professor emeritus, New York University and McGill University

The
Empathy
Effect

The Empathy Effect

SEVEN NEUROSCIENCE-BASED KEYS
for Transforming the Way
We LIVE, LOVE, WORK, and
CONNECT Across Differences

Helen Riess, MD

with Liz Neporent

Foreword by Alan Alda

SOUNDS TRUE
BOULDER, COLORADO

Sounds True
Boulder, CO 80306

Published 2018

Book design by Beth Skelley

Printed in Canada

Library of Congress Cataloging-in-Publication Data
Names: Riess, Helen, author. | Neporent, Liz, author.
Title: The empathy effect : seven neuroscience-based keys for transforming the way we
    live, love, work, and connect across differences / Helen Riess with Liz Neporent.
Description: Boulder, Colorado : Sounds True, 2018. | Includes bibliographical
    references and index.
Identifiers: LCCN 2018005382 (print) | LCCN 2018025370 (ebook) |
    ISBN 9781683640295 (ebook) | ISBN 9781683640288 (hardcover)
Subjects: LCSH: Empathy. | Compassion. | Affective neuroscience.
Classification: LCC BF575.E55 (ebook) | LCC BF575.E55 R56 2018 (print) |
    DDC 152.4/1—dc23
LC record available at https://lccn.loc.gov/2018005382

10 9 8 7 6 5 4 3 2 1

This book is dedicated to all who know the feeling of being "othered" and to faith that empathy and our shared humanity will one day unite us.

Contents

Foreword by Alan Alda

Down the road, headlights askew, a mangled car sat crosswise in an intersection. A man sat in the road, covered in blood. My friend George saw this and stopped his car. Someone said the police were on the way. George got out of his car, but he didn't stand by, watching in silence, as a few others did. He sat on the pavement and held the man in his arms, pressing him to his chest and whispering words of comfort and encouragement as the man's scalp leaked blood onto his clothes. What gave George the strength to do this? He went toward trouble, not away from it.

Years earlier, my friend Bert was in a hotel room in Chicago. It was 1968 and the Democratic Convention was in an uproar of protest. Young people were shouting slogans in the street just outside Bert's hotel. Suddenly violence erupted, and the police responded with violence of their own. Some of the protestors ran into the hotel, hoping to escape the police. Within minutes, there was knocking on Bert's door, and when he opened it, there were several young men who were bloodied. Bert let them into the room, but after another few minutes the police were at the door. They removed the protestors, dragging some by the hair.

When they were gone, Bert felt an undeniable urge to do something. He put on a tie and jacket and went down to the street, walking cautiously through the mob. He made his way to the police station where the young men had been taken.

Bert walked up to the desk sergeant and pretended to be a lawyer from New York (he was, in fact, an actor). He claimed to be representing the young men who had just been brought in. He was taking the risk that at that late hour the police would not be able to call New York and check his credentials. And it worked. He got the students out of jail and to a hospital, without being arrested himself.

I've often thought about these two friends and wondered where they got the courage to perform these acts of kindness.

I've come to believe the source of their courage was what this book is about: empathy.

For more than twenty-five years I've been trying to understand what makes people relate in the most positive way to one another, to communicate clearly, without snags and misunderstanding, and it's been increasingly clear to me that I've really been on the search for empathy.

Helen Riess is an expert on the subject, and when I met her, I felt I had finally found a deeper understanding of my friends' courageous behavior. They had experienced a moment of empathy and had acted on it.

But what exactly is empathy? Trying to define it, people say all kinds of contradictory things. Some say empathy is compassion, while others say that it could be a *stepping stone* to compassion but doesn't in itself lead to good behavior. Others say that whatever it is, you're born with a certain amount of empathy and you'll never have any more. No, say others: you have to be taught empathy as a child. And, of course, there are those who declare emphatically that empathy *can't* be taught.

Helen Riess steps into this cacophony of assertions and quiets the crowd. Helen knows that empathy can be taught because she teaches it and studies it. Her teachings have reached thousands of medical professionals. She has seen levels of empathy increase, and she's documented the results of her studies.

She's dealing in a fundamental way with a fundamental human trait.

Scientists who have studied what makes us stand out among the other animals have told me that empathy plays an awfully big part in making us who we are.

It gives us the ability to read another person's mind, or, put less dramatically, to take their perspective and see the world as they see it. And this ability may be to a great extent what makes life possible for modern humans.

Empathy not only allows conversation to happen; it allows commerce to take place and even makes politics possible. (How can you convince someone that what you're proposing is in their self-interest unless you have the ability to figure out what interests them?)

It's not surprising that we've been wondering about this trait of ours for centuries.

The word "empathy" has only been in use in our language for about a hundred years, although writers and philosophers have been exploring it for a long time.

Walt Whitman was thinking of the effect another person's suffering can have on us when he wrote, "I do not ask the wounded person how he feels. I myself become the wounded person." He was discovering the idea that we understand what another person is feeling when we experience those feelings in ourselves. In a way, our own feelings are the lens through which we see another's feelings.

As David Hume said, "The minds of men are mirrors to one another."

And the thought goes at least as far back as Homer, who in the eighth century BC wrote: " . . . taught by time, my heart has learn'd to glow for others' good, and melt at others' woe."

Empathy is not the same as compassion, but it's hard to think of compassion taking place without empathy. It seems to be central to our humanity, to the risks my friends took on those nights long ago for the safety of people they didn't even know.

What allows us to connect to others? What helps us to build things together? To collaborate unselfishly? What is this powerful force that can push us over into our best selves?

If the question is *how can we get hold of that very fundamental thing that helps us thrive?*—the answer is in the book you're holding in your hands.

Introduction

Why Empathy?

In my first year at Boston University School of Medicine, my psychiatry professor, Dr. Richard Chasin, arranged a collection of chairs on a stage in a circle that represented a family system in which members had endured trauma. Each chair represented a family member. Rather than focusing exclusively on a traumatized individual, he demonstrated that the entire family was involved in expressing and managing the emotions of those who suffered. Each time a chair was removed from the system, the family had to grapple with what would happen without that member playing his or her role.

This was the first time I realized that my own family was not as unique or even unusual as I had always thought. It was a relief to recognize that the themes that had shaped my early life were recognizable and shareable—the basic elements of empathy.

My parents came to the United States after losing nearly everything in World War II. When my father was just fourteen years old, his parents were executed by a dictator's regime. In that moment, he and his two sisters were ripped from a life of privilege and sent off to a starvation camp. My mother's family was also forced to leave their home and all their belongings to work in labor camps, where her own father died. These grim stories hung around the edges of our home like curtains around a window; plenty of light came in, but the drapes were always there, casting a shadow.

Further complicating their story, my parents were of German heritage and Protestant. Their ancestors moved to the Danube Valley in

Yugoslavia in the 1800s, where they lived peacefully until near the end of World War II. Under the Tito regime, they were suddenly swept up in the ethnic cleansing involving the removal of Germans and other "undesirable" groups. In a sad twist of fate, the Tito regime drove these Germans from their homes and sent them off to concentration camps, just as the German regime under Hitler was doing to millions of Jews and others in Europe, and ruthless regimes had done to millions of others throughout history whose own stories remain untold.

My parents escaped from the camps with the help of their faith and transformative empathy from people in their church community. Later they met and married in Austria and immigrated to America. People who didn't understand or want to know about their story instantly judged them because of their background and German accents. Many assumed because they were German they must be complicit in the very horrors that they themselves had been subjected to.

The pain of being judged and associated with the horrific crimes of the war, compounded by receiving little empathy for their own experience, had a profound effect on them. On top of the tragic losses of family, home, and homeland, being misjudged was difficult for them to bear. And these misconceptions affected me deeply too.

As a child, I got very upset when my classmates ridiculed others because of things they could not control, such as the color of their skin, where they lived, or their family situations. The unfairness of judging a book by its cover roiled inside of me. It led to a preoccupation with social justice that has stayed with me to this day. It was this desire to heal the emotional pain of others that led to my career in psychiatry. Now as a professional, I listen to my patients tell stories about being stigmatized for having mental illnesses, or being grilled about why they "take so many psych meds," and I chafe at the lack of empathy for their struggles.

I was already involved in empathy research by the time headlines started appearing about a decade ago in the *New York Times*, *Wall Street Journal*, and *Washington Post* that consistently called for greater empathy in health care. In my work in the Department of Psychiatry at Massachusetts General Hospital (MGH), we investigated whether physiological parameters between patients and doctors matched up during visits when doctors behaved more empathically. We were interested to see whether we could find physical evidence to show when two people were "in sync."

By way of a simple technology known as galvanic skin response, which measures changes in the electrical resistance of the skin and is one of the most sensitive measures of emotional arousal, a former student of mine, Dr. Carl Marci, obtained physiological tracings that revealed when doctors and patients were in sync with one another and when they were not. The tracings revealed electrodermal activity that measures the amount of sweat secreted on the skin, and indicates the degree of physiological and emotional activity in real time. Then we asked patients to rate their doctors on an empathy scale. It turned out that the doctors in the patient-doctor pairs with the greatest physiological concordance received the highest empathy ratings.

The big breakthrough here was that we had discovered a biomarker that seemed to quantify this elusive trait called empathy. One woman who saw her own tracing representing her inner state of anxiety and her doctor's response to it gasped, "I feel like I'm looking at an x-ray of my psyche!" She had lived with anxiety for most of her life but felt no one had ever seen her pain. The value of seeing this connection helped her go on to make enormous strides in her treatment. Here we note the power of empathy while refining our ability to identify and measure it.

As an educator at Harvard Medical School, I was fascinated by the fact that we could make invisible emotions visible, and I began to think about how to use this tool to improve the empathic response in medical professionals. I was very fortunate to obtain a postgraduate medical education fellowship at Harvard and to take courses at the Harvard Macy Institute to learn the neuroscience of empathy, incorporate new tools, and develop an empathy training intervention and test it in a randomized controlled trial.

This led to my founding the Empathy and Relational Science Program at MGH, the first research program of its kind. When we first began, many experts believed empathy was something you were either born with or you weren't. In research conducted with my colleagues in the Empathy Program, we recruited doctors in training from six different specialties to investigate whether a brief training in empathy skills could teach them to better perceive patients' emotional cues and respond to them more effectively. Patients were asked to rate the doctors before and after the training period, and those who had been assigned to the training group consistently received significantly higher ratings on empathy scales than the untrained group. Yes, we saw, empathy could in fact be taught and learned.

We know that when patients are treated with greater empathy and respect, they have a better experience and as a result are more likely to trust their doctor, stick to medical recommendations, and have better health outcomes. Doctors benefit too. Our research showed that increasing empathy in their interactions gave them greater job satisfaction and left them feeling less burned out. They reported that by learning to sit down and notice the whole person before them, and not just the illness or injured body part, they felt more connected to their patients and their profession.

The demand for my empathy training grew so fast that I couldn't keep up with it through live training. A course at the Harvard Macy Institute called Leading Innovations in Health Care & Education taught me how to scale my program to reach the widest audience possible, and I subsequently cofounded Empathetics, Inc., an empathy training company that provides e-learning and live empathy training solutions around the world.

Soon requests for empathy training started coming from other professions, and I realized that the methods I had developed for teaching medical professionals can be applied to everyone, no matter who they are, what they do, or where they come from. In fact, the very first organization that implemented our empathy training was a large bank in the Midwest. Its executive vice president of organizational development, Lauris Woolford, recognized that empathy was a key competency that her executive teams needed in order to bring about the success of the organization.

In this book, I hope to demonstrate how showing greater empathy toward your fellow human beings can enhance your own life and society as a whole. Through empathy, parents see their children for who they are and help them realize their potential. Teachers connect with students in ways that help learners discover and expand their talents. Businesses are more likely to thrive because they invest in the people working for them. Politicians start to represent the needs of all of their constituencies. The arts have always been a connector for people from all walks of life to learn more about one another, find common ground, inspire curiosity rather than judgment, and provide shared mind empathic experiences that remind us that all people are part of the fabric of humanity.

The seven keys of empathy that I've developed in my research and refined in my training can help you lead a better life. You will learn what they are and how you can use them to improve every facet of your life, from your most intimate relationships to family life, school, business, community life, and leadership roles in organizations. By becoming more attuned through the rich neural networks of shared mind intelligence, the subject of our next chapter, we enhance the lives of others, and the world can become a more tolerant and inclusive place.

Any resemblance of those mentioned in this book to actual patients and their families is coincidental and not intentional. For readability, when referring to individuals, I have used the singular pronouns "he" and "she" rather than use the more awkward "he or she." This is not to suggest any generalities based on gender. The opinions discussed in this book are mine and do not necessarily reflect those of the institutions with which I am affiliated.

Part I

1

Shared Mind Intelligence

Sandra dropped into the chair in my office with a heavy sigh. The expression on her face was foreboding.

"I don't know how I'm ever going to get over what happened," she said.

I felt my throat tighten and my heartbeat quicken. Without knowing the details, I had caught her emotion as a sense of dread and fear spread through me. She had been a first responder at the Boston Marathon bombing. While she was trying to remove the shoe from an injured runner's leg, his entire leg came off in her hands.

Perhaps this story made you gasp or left you feeling uncomfortable. Maybe you reached unconsciously for your own leg. If so, you are having a shared mind experience.

Even though nothing has physically touched you, your brain has registered the emotional and physical pain of both Sandra's and the victim's story through specialized neural circuits that deliver an approximation of what Sandra felt, and you probably don't feel quite the same as you did before you read it. This is empathy at work. We temporarily imagine someone else's thoughts and feelings and experience their discomfort. Typically, this leads to *empathic concern*, a caring feeling toward the other person that motivates a compassionate response.

In many cases, empathic concern prompts our motivation to help. Believe it or not, an entire field of psychology and neuroscience research has developed to study empathy, and the results are fascinating. Empathy scholars believe that empathy had its origins in parental care, to ensure the survival of offspring by motivating caring behaviors. Because caring behaviors for others have helped ensure the survival of our species, the circuits for empathy in our brains have been preserved for millennia.

There are many definitions of empathy, and this has caused confusion even among the many different types of scholars who study it, including philosophers, psychologists, scientists, and educators who have attempted to define it as a single trait. Empathy is best understood as a human capacity consisting of several different facets that work together to enable us to be moved by the plights and emotions of others. I prefer to use the term "empathic capacity" rather than "empathy" because this conveys that empathy is made up of many different psychological and physiological facets.

Our empathic capacity requires specialized brain circuits that allow us to perceive, process, and respond to others; remember my own reaction to Sandra's experience at the Boston Marathon. The integration of these three very human activities predicts how "empathic" a person will be. When people show empathy for others, they are usually good at *perceiving* what others feel, able to *process the information*, and able to *respond effectively*. So it is important to broaden the definition as a capacity that encompasses the entire empathy loop from perception *of*, to response *to* someone else's experience, and finally to check with that person for accuracy, if there is any doubt. This last part of the loop is called "empathic accuracy." Throughout the book I will use the scientific term "empathic" rather than the term "empathetic" because the information is based on the neuroscience of empathy.

Let's go back to Sandra. I caught her feelings by perceiving her facial expression, her posture, and her tone of voice and by imagining what it was like to be motivated to help a wounded man and to find herself holding his entire leg, now loose from his body and in her hands. Her story was overwhelming. I had to check my feelings so I could fully listen to her account without being overwhelmed by the horror. I did this by taking slow, quiet, deep breaths to steady myself. I also didn't know exactly which emotions *she* was feeling, but I knew they were tremendously uncomfortable and I needed to learn more. I needed to take care of my own human emotional reaction before I could really help her. I used my "ABC" technique that's a foundation for the empathy training I developed. By registering my own tension and racing heart, I (A) *acknowledged* we were entering an emotionally difficult conversation. I took (B) deep *breaths* to manage my reaction, and I engaged my (C) *curiosity* to learn more. I imagined her emotions included terror and grief. When I asked her what *she* was feeling, she said she was terrified and grief stricken and then added that she was also feeling guilty.

"I should have been able to do more for him," she told me.

I then had to imagine what it was like to try to help someone and feel that my efforts had actually made things worse. (This was obviously not true. His leg was tragically and permanently damaged by the shrapnel in the bomb and could not have been saved.) This was an exercise in perspective taking and imagination since I had never been in the same situation. In my therapeutic role, I could not linger in the shared distress of the moment, which had initially let me resonate with her horrifying experience. I had to move to a more thoughtful mode to engage my curiosity and professional skills as a psychiatrist in order to understand what she had been through. Sandra needed to heal, and she needed someone to bear witness to what had happened and assist her recovery from her psychological trauma.

How empathy is ignited in the brain has been demonstrated by neuroimaging studies that take pictures of the brain while people are in scanners watching images or videos that activate structures involved with empathy. Researchers have identified different regions of the brain that become activated when people feel empathy for others. One of the most important contributions made by neuroscientists who study empathy has been to prove that the capacity has both emotional (affective) and cognitive (thinking) parts. Putting these together, we now know that empathy is triggered when people understand the plight of others and respond appropriately even if they do not themselves feel the exact same emotion but are able to access an experience cognitively through imagination.

Empathic capacity is an essential human trait that we carry into every aspect of our lives, from parenting to education systems, health care, the workplace, business, legal practices, the arts, the environment, the digital world, and in leadership and politics. We will explore why and how empathy helps us consider possibilities and outcomes that we could never achieve on our own, but can achieve because of the power of our shared brains when we understand one another and cooperate with each other. Because empathy evolved to ensure parental care and survival of their offspring, the parental care model forms the basis for understanding empathy in other contexts.

In the past, people believed that you were either born with empathy or not, and there was not much that could be done about it. It is very important to those of us who study empathy's applications that empathy *can* be taught. Research done in my lab has proved this hypothesis. We showed that patients rated their doctors more highly on empathy scales after empathy training. Specific interventions can increase perception, perspective taking, and self-regulation skills to ensure that we aren't overwhelmed by the suffering of others, leading to our own personal distress. Empathy is a delicate balance of appreciating the feelings of others and learning how to manage our own feelings so we can be helpful. We need to learn to manage our empathic responses so that we ultimately deliver caring responses even when we can't immediately find the words on our own.

Einfühlung

The word "empathy" did not come into existence until the early twentieth century. It is derived from the German term *Einfühlung*, which means "feeling into" and was introduced by German aestheticians in the mid- to late nineteenth century, who used this word to describe the emotional experience that was evoked by viewing a work of art and feeling one's way into an emotional experience. It originated from the early twentieth century Greek *empatheia* (from *em* "in" + *pathos* "feeling"). This phenomenon, that an artist whom the viewer may never meet can project emotions that inspired the painting (or music, or play), was the first attempt to describe how we can "feel our way into" the emotions of others. The original meaning described a kinesthetic connection with a painting or sculpture. It also included a sense of being moved by art and a profound emotional resonance with it.

The word empathy is often confused with other similar terms. You may use the words sympathy and empathy interchangeably, but for researchers and scientists they are not the same. Sympathy is the older of the two words. Its ancient Greek root *sún* means "together" and *pathos* means "suffering." The word sympathy evolved from the observation that humans have similar feelings and we can identify the feelings of others because we share them to some extent. As used today, sympathy aligns with feeling bad *for* others or taking pity on others and doesn't imply the fully shared sense of feeling personally *with* someone's plight.

You may, for example, sympathize with someone's desire to find a new job when he is miserable at work even if you are content with your own. With sympathy, there is agreement that someone's unhappiness or suffering is undeserved. Sympathy can be described as the feeling you have when you look out your window and see someone shivering in the cold rain. You feel bad for this person. Empathy is as if you're going out in the rain and standing next to this person, through your imagination, and experiencing his discomfort and distress *as if* it were your own, but, as psychologist Carl Rogers pointed out, not losing the "as if" quality. This distinction is important because it allows you to consider the best way to help this person without focusing solely on your own discomfort. Empathy is a dynamic capacity that allows you to share experiences with others, feel concern, take the other's perspective, and motivate a caring response. The full empathic circle leads to an empathic response. You go back out in the rain in reality and offer the unfortunate freezing person a warm raincoat and umbrella.

By the early twentieth century, psychologists began to view empathy as a way to understand essential components of interpersonal relationships. Rosalind Cartwright, working at Cornell University in the mid-twentieth century, conducted some of the first tests measuring interpersonal empathy. In doing so, she ignored the earlier meaning of empathy emphasizing "projection of the perceiver's feelings" and redefined it as "feeling the feelings." In the process, she deliberately rejected empathy's early meaning of imaginative projection, and instead emphasized interpersonal connection as the core of the concept. It's easy to relate to the difference between "projective empathy" and true empathic concern. In projective empathy people springboard from what you've shared and overlay their own experience onto you. Rather than creating a connecting experience, the projector often upstages your distress with her own story without offering understanding and comfort, often placing you in the position of now comforting her.

With a flurry of experimental studies of empathy that followed, psychologists began to differentiate "true" empathy, defined as the accurate appraisal of another's thoughts or feelings, from what they called "projection." Then in 1955, *Reader's Digest* introduced the term to the general public as the "ability to appreciate the other person's feelings without yourself becoming so emotionally involved that your judgment is affected." This definition was the precursor to our more complete understanding of empathy today. It indicates that empathy has cognitive appreciation of others' feelings, an emotional resonance, and the ability to distinguish the other person's experience from our own so that we perceive accurately and aren't in danger of becoming emotionally overwhelmed by their feelings.

Empathic capacity requires a sophisticated integration of many brain regions. The psychoanalyst Heinz Kohut defined empathy in 1959 as "vicarious introspection" and emphasized the ability to consider the feelings of others as if they were our own, but then consider them objectively. In the field of psychotherapy, he considered empathy to be "psychological oxygen" and a necessary component of every therapeutic relationship.

Empathy as we now use the word broadens beyond sympathy, or *feeling bad* for others in discomfort, into an understanding of how others actually feel emotionally and seeing the world from their perspective. By definition, empathy is not detached or abstract. It requires intimate comprehension of others' inner lives, the context in which they live, and their resulting actions. To experience empathy, you need both perceptive channels that take in the experience of others (as a researcher I call this the "afferent" or incoming route) and responsive channels that have been motivated to respond (with "efferent" or outgoing signals, words, or nonverbal behaviors such as facial expressions and body language).

This new meaning has been validated by neuroscientists over the past few decades. By conducting numerous neuroimaging studies, they have identified that we share neural circuits with others while simultaneously understanding what they are going through on an intellectual level. Thus empathy has both emotional and cognitive, or thinking, components. Therefore, it feels easy and natural to empathize with someone who is like you, who has lived through a similar experience, or who shares a common purpose. For example, you probably empathize much more with the person who has a child with learning disabilities or an elderly parent with physical impairments if your own relatives have similar struggles.

Today we view sympathy as a less emotionally intense phenomenon compared to empathy. You feel bad for someone in discomfort but not intensely enough to become emotionally upset. When hearing about an acquaintance's favorite teacher passing away, you may send a sympathy card as a polite gesture but not necessarily because you feel that person's pain. If a close friend loses a loved one whose deep attachment you have witnessed, your feelings—and actions—are more likely to cross over into empathy. The more you experience in life and come to realize that all human beings share comparable emotions, the greater is your empathic capacity for all mankind, not just those closest to you.

Artist Patricia Simon provides a good example of the difference between sympathy and empathy. In 2010, she and her family took a vacation in what now seems like an unthinkable place: Syria.

"We fell in love with the beauty of the country and the rich culture, and especially the people," she recounts. But within a year after their return home, the political situation began to deteriorate. Soon images of historic towns and bombed-out, abandoned villages began to appear on her TV and computer screens. These were the very places she had just visited, and she grew so concerned for the Syrian people that she and her husband, Dick, signed up with a nongovernmental organization called Karam Foundation, which sends Americans to teach refugee children on the Turkish-Syrian border.

When I asked Patricia, or Patty as she's known to her friends, why she was motivated to wade into the dangerous war zone and essentially risk her life for a place that was not her home and for people she didn't really know, her answers revealed a great deal about the different types of empathy we experience as humans.

"I grew up moving every few years," she said. "I was always the new kid on the block, the outsider. I became very sensitized to what it feels like to be the marginalized and invisible person. They were experiencing this on a much larger scale, but I could relate to them. I also had met the Syrians. I had gone there, so I felt connected to them."

Empathy takes more imagination and relatable identity than sympathy does. Patty and her family experienced this deeply. She had personal experiences of feeling displaced that felt related to the Syrians' plight, and she also felt she knew the people. When you empathize, you can imagine others' suffering through your ability to see things from their point of view. You may also be able to imagine what others are thinking, what motivates them, and what they desire. The average person may feel sympathy for what Syrian refugees are going through, but people like the Simons, who have witnessed what is happening in this war-torn country firsthand, or people who have survived other genocides, will likely feel empathy related to their own experience of living through a war and losing loved ones and a homeland. What's even more amazing is that Patty and her close friends have organized groups of women who send care packages and other forms of support to the children in Syria through the Karam Foundation. The empathic response of one person has expanded to a community that may never have been moved to act without Patty's inspiration. Her perception of the suffering of others, processing it partially through her own experience, has led to a ripple-effect response, a compassionate response that is made possible through emotional and cognitive empathy. When we witness compassion, we know the circle of empathy has been completed: from perceiving another person's suffering, to feeling empathic concern, to being motivated to soothe another's pain through an act of compassion.

2

How Empathy Works

In this chapter we will take a closer look at how the brain works to make the experience of empathy possible.

This was an actual experiment: Imagine yourself watching as my finger is being pricked by a needle. Scientists first viewed the brains of their subjects in a brain scanner as the subjects had their fingers stuck by needles to determine the precise neurons involved in pain perception. In this same experiment, another set of subjects in scanners viewed a video of the pin prick.

The researchers discovered that the nervous system of the watchers essentially duplicated the experience of the people who felt real pain, responding as if they were feeling the pain themselves. Interestingly, the same neural networks light up during actual pain felt by those being pricked as during observation of the pinprick. When a part of your brain called the insular cortex fires, you experience the pain because there are neurons whose job it is to physiologically respond to pain. It turns out that a similar subset of neurons will also fire when you are a mere witness to an action that produces pain. By simulating how the prick would feel, the brain activates the neurons in the same areas of the brain as the person who experienced the pain itself. It is like a mirror image of the pain, albeit to a lesser degree. And that is remarkable, and useful because if you were to experience the full and complete degree of pain as the victim, empathy would be thwarted, because guess whose pain you'd be focused on then? Your own! This is a remarkable feature that allows us to vicariously experience others' pain without becoming so overwhelmed that we are rendered unable to help them.

There are two important reasons why your brain is primed to experience the pain of others: to teach you what to avoid and to motivate you to help the injured person, whether their pain is physical, psychological, emotional, or some degree of all of these. One byproduct of helping others is that it also inspires others to help in return. Helping others feels good. This is considered the basis for collaboration, cooperation, and reciprocity in human relationships. By feeling the pain of others, we are motivated to help them, which brings about a good feeling in others, ensuring that helping behavior is likely to be reciprocated and ultimately ensuring the survival of our species by completing the full circle of empathy. We have specialized neurons that help us know what's happening in the brains of others, which form the substrate of what I call our "shared mind intelligence."

Mirror neurons are specialized brain cells in specific areas of the brain called the premotor cortex, known as the F5 area and the parietal cortex. They were first discovered in the 1990s by Italian researchers doing experiments with primates. These specialized brain cells fire up both when an action is performed by one primate and when another primate observes that action. These unique neurons were named "mirror neurons" because they essentially mirror and map what is going on in one brain onto the brain of an observer. Although mirror neurons have been observed only in our primate relatives among nonhuman species, their discovery spawned an explosion of neuroscience studies that subsequently identified shared brain circuits for touch, pain, and specific emotions such as disgust in brain regions that include the somatosensory cortex, the insula, and the anterior cingulate cortex, respectively.

Researchers examined the motor cortexes of macaque monkeys, and their discoveries were the first indication that observers' brains map the same actions they observe others doing. Before their discovery, scientists generally believed that our brains used logical thought processes to interpret and predict other people's actions. We now believe these neurological "mirrors" and shared circuits give us the ability to *understand* not just what another is thinking but to *feel* what they are feeling as well.

Why did the brain evolve this amazing network loop? If you ask a group of scientists this question, some will say it was for the self-protection of the witness who observes someone else getting hurt; if you see someone getting stuck with a sharp object, you're more careful when handling sharp objects. Other experts say it evolved so we would be motivated to help others as a direct benefit for the community at large, extending to family, society, and the whole of mankind. Dating back to our tribal heritage, watching someone eat something and make a disgusted face maps a feeling of disgust in the observers and teaches the whole group what to avoid. I believe both motivations are true; we have to survive long enough as individuals by learning how to avoid danger, which in turn helps to ensure that our species survives.

Increasing evidence suggests that empathy is partially hardwired into the brain and splits into three different aspects: emotional (or affective empathy), cognitive (or thinking empathy), and motivation for an empathic response. For some highly sensitive people and empaths, feeling empathy is natural and automatic. Some people must turn down the dial on their emotional empathy to become objective enough to do their jobs. Think of firefighters, or surgeons who must focus on the technical tasks to complete a successful operation and not be distracted until the operation is complete. Those who are not highly sensitive may need to hone their empathy skills. Most people have at least some natural empathy, as it does play a role in our evolutionary history and can be traced to the mirror neurons in our ancestors' brains. To fully understand how we can best take advantage of empathy to improve our relationships and our lives, we need a more complete understanding of these facets. Empathy is produced not only by how we perceive information, but also how we understand that information, are moved by it, and use it to motivate our behavior.

Some scientists have posited that empathy is our default mode and that we must suppress it so we are not constantly attending to and being distracted by the feelings of others. There are people on both ends of this spectrum, including those who have not learned to suppress empathy at all and those who have become all too skilled at suppressing empathy. Most people are somewhere in between.

Emotional Empathy

As a child, Patty Simon, whom you met in the last chapter, moved frequently because of her father's work. Even at a young age, she became sensitized to feeling ignored and unwelcome. She is quick to point out that life wasn't so tough for her and that she's never been a refugee of a war-torn country like Syria. Nevertheless, those early experiences shaped her emotional brain so that when she saw what was happening in the news, she felt connected to what Syrian refugees must be feeling. Not that she could put those feelings into words the moment she decided she wanted to help. Reflecting on it now, she says that she felt a wave of empathy as she watched the images of bombs and crumbling buildings flicker across her TV screen. In psychological terms, her response was what we researchers refer to as affective empathy, but in simpler terms we can call it "emotional empathy." This is the first aspect of empathy I'd like to describe for you.

The emotional side of empathy is familiar. It's that sense that you can feel what other people feel. When you see others having a hard time or in pain, you can instantly imagine their inner experience based on either your own personal familiarity with the pain or from past experience. For Patty and Dick, it was seeing the expressions of sadness, fear, and loneliness etched on the faces of Syrian mothers and children every night on the news. Millions of people watch those same stories, but for whatever reason it doesn't rise to the level of emotional empathy for many.

That said, the majority of people have a capacity for emotional empathy. For example, most of us have, at one time or another, witnessed somebody cutting their hand on a piece of glass. And you will remember that when you saw something like this, you caught some of the bad feeling yourself, both an emotional and physical resonance. You may physically flinch as you vividly imagine the slicing sharpness of glass cutting through your skin. It's possible you conjured up a little bit of that feeling simply by reading about it just now. Remember, there is another practical reality to the emotional empathic response. You might flinch when you see someone in pain, but recall: you don't actually have exactly the same experience. If you did, you would be focused on your own pain, and this could render you unable to help someone else in distress. This sophisticated neurological system allows you to observe others hurting and gives you just enough of a taste of the pain to consider helping them out.

Just as importantly, emotional empathy teaches you what to avoid. If there were no internal representation of pain based on an external observation, you could observe what was happening but wouldn't learn from it. The only way to understand that dragging a piece of glass across your skin is a bad idea would be to personally experience the shock of it yourself. We'd be a species eternally surprised by jagged cuts on our hands.

Emotional empathy must also be kept in balance with self-regulation to help manage excessive levels of emotional arousal that can lead to blurred boundaries and personal distress. If you are exposed to too much pain and suffering every day, such as a day in the life of an oncologist or social worker or prison guard, excessive emotional empathy can lead to depression, anxiety, and burnout. The sharp edge of empathy would soon become dull, and you'd start to distance yourself from the human experience. In the medical profession, we call this "compassion fatigue."

Emotional empathy flourishes more readily when someone is most similar to us, or when we at least feel a connected similarity, as Patty does with Syrian refugees. Instinctively we are more likely to reach out and support our relatives and people who live in our neighborhoods, or who attend the same house of worship, or whose children play on the same hockey team. Empathy, as most people practice it, is often alive and well and on its best behavior when something happens to a person with whom you share much in common. By contrast, emotional empathy can be weak or absent when someone is from a different neighborhood or a different ethnicity or race. We aren't all like Patty and her husband, our hearts aching for a country and a people not our own. And this is where another type of empathy comes in to play: cognitive empathy.

Cognitive Empathy

Somewhere along the line Patty and Dick went from feelings of emotional empathy to a cognitive shift that worked to spur action, which for her and her husband was to stay and teach the children who no longer had schools to attend. They didn't speak Arabic. The kids didn't speak English. Yet as an artist, Patty could prepare art lessons and projects that provided learning experiences.

"The trauma these kids held inside themselves was so masked by their incredible resiliency. They just wanted to be kids, to laugh, draw, learn, play ball," she says. "I wanted each one of them to know that I was from America and we do care."

Cognitive or thinking empathy is a way of managing all the perceptive information that lands in your own conscious feelings. Before you can experience cognitive empathy, you need several components from your psychological development as well as your behavioral capabilities. The very first step required for cognitive empathy is the ability to appreciate on a basic level that another person has thoughts and feelings separate from your own.

This is called "theory of mind" and is considered a milestone of psychological development that starts in children by age four or five. Very young children cannot make the distinction that each person has a separate brain, mind, thoughts, and feelings. One evening when my daughter was three, she was speaking with her grandmother on the phone while eating a piece of apple pie. She asked her grandmother if she'd like a bite. Her grandmother, who was in another city at that moment, had no idea what she was eating. My daughter, who had yet to develop theory of mind, had no idea that her grandmother didn't share her immediate experience and reality. As adults, we take theory of mind for granted, but when it's highlighted, you can see it at work. You've probably seen someone run to catch a flight or a bus and miss it, the doors slamming shut. You don't need to know the details or anything about the person who misses the bus to instantly access the range of feelings he experiences. In the same way, you need only look at a photograph of people on a zipline to tell by their facial expressions whether they're feeling exhilaration or terror.

Theory of mind is not the same as "mind reading," but on a certain level it is the ability to understand what is going on in another person's brain at that moment while also understanding that their decisions, intentions, and beliefs may be different from your own. In fact, depending upon the person, the situation, and your mood, you might even feel empathy for that person who's a total stranger because you understand how it feels to miss a bus or have vertigo on a zipline. Without the cognitive foundation of theory of mind, empathy does not come easily. We know this from research on autism, where the neurocircuitry in the regions of the brain related to cognitive empathy are not well developed. We also know that theory of mind can be interrupted in cases of dementia or other types of brain trauma.

Theory of mind allows us to infer the thoughts, intentions, emotions, and desires of other people, which leads us to the next step of cognitive empathy, known as "perspective taking." This is the active component of cognitive empathy in which we are seeing the world through the eyes of another person. Perspective taking requires focused attention, imagination, and curiosity. In neuroscientific studies, when people adopt the perspective of another, the brain areas that are active in the first person also become activated in the observer. We must understand the situation from the other person's physical, psychological, social, and spiritual perspectives.

As with other facets of empathic capacity, taking the perspective of someone who is like you or is a member of one of your in-groups (people with whom you have things in common) comes easily. It becomes much harder to take the perspective of an out-group member, such as someone in another social group; it requires much more attention and working memory. It is cognitively demanding. It takes mental work to see the world through the eyes of someone who is quite different from you. When you do manage to break through and understand the world from a foreign point of view, it usually helps break down stereotypes and leads you to a more favorable judgment about an individual, as well as for the "tribe" they come from. We have many stories in history of how concern for a specific individual who elicited compassion from a perceived enemy led to iconic examples, such as the abolitionists who helped set the slaves free and the rescuers of Jews during World War II.

Empathic Concern: Why We Need This to Show Compassion

After cognitive and affective empathy, empathic concern is the third facet of empathy. It is the inner motivation that moves people to respond and express the urge to care about another person's welfare. This is what most people generally think of when they think of the word "empathy." The main benefits of cognitive and affective empathy are that they spark empathic concern, which can motivate action and compassion. When thinking and feeling blend together, you are primed for empathic behavior. First you feel with others, then you understand their pain, and then you truly care and offer a compassionate response. Compassion is the outward expression and evidence that empathic concern has been motivated; it is the warmhearted response to another's suffering. You may think this behavior is the norm, but compassion is not always where it winds up.

I sometimes refer to empathic concern as leading to "behavioral empathy" because it may lead to compassionate acts, but it may also lead to personal distress. I think we've all had the experience of seeing something bad happening but not having the motivation, energy, or skill to do something about it. Every week we pass by homeless people on the street. You may feel disturbed and yet don't always do something to help. At other times a switch may be flipped, and your empathic concern leads to a compassionate behavior; you offer a proximal response such as money, food, or a blanket. And empathic concern can show up as a more distal way of helping: writing to your Congressman and asking why there aren't more shelters, or giving to programs that provide support and mental health services to the homeless. Many people

I know struggle with feeling helpless about seeing homeless people on the streets every day. The concept of "proximal empathy" versus "distal empathy" is important because different people are moved to act in different ways at different times. A compassionate behavior could be something as small as a caring look in your eye. Even that brief moment of connecting as a human to another human lifts a person from the anonymous masses to the status of an individual. It doesn't have to be something big. But when you choose to embark on any of these actions, you are most likely doing so because your empathic concern has been motivated by your perception of what is happening around you.

To me, one of the most perplexing phenomena of our time is how much more aware we are of pain and suffering around the world through news broadcasting and daily alerts, and how much remains to be done to ameliorate the struggles of those in need. We are wired to help, yet those in the most powerful positions to help on a grand scale are often more preoccupied with personal power, helping the rich, and expanding their spheres of influence among their supporters than marshaling efforts to decrease suffering around the world. Scientific studies have shown there is an inverse relationship between power and empathy. This distance often insulates the rich and powerful from the suffering of the everyday person. However, thanks to thousands of grassroots efforts, many in need are helped because the hardwired empathy loop is in play. We must be careful to notice when our own empathy perceptions fail to lead to empathic concern and compassionate responses. As we will see, empathic capacity is not a static state. It fluctuates considerably, and our empathic concern is a good barometer of when our empathic skills have become blunted.

3

The Empathy Spectrum

L oneliness and the feeling of being unwanted is the most terrible poverty."

Take a moment to absorb this quote from Mother Teresa carefully. How moved are you when you read it? What picture do you form in your mind? Do you see a desperate, orphaned child living in poverty? Or what about an elderly, homeless person begging on a corner?

Depending on the current context your own life provides, and even your mood when you conjure this image, you are likely experiencing at least a twinge of empathic concern. We relate to loneliness, hunger, and isolation even if we never experience them at the level of an orphan or a homeless person. However, some of us will muster up very little emotion when we read Mother Teresa's words. Does this mean you don't care? Maybe. Or it could be that you're having a really bad day and have no more energy to devote to the misfortune of others.

The truth is there are times when our empathic capacity is activated and other times, even when the circumstances are similar, when it is suppressed. We all come to empathic concern differently. Some of us tend to feel waves of concern often. Others are tougher nuts to crack emotionally. Just as with every other human emotional and neuro-logical capacity, there is a continuum for empathy, with most of us clustered around the center. Each day, depending on a host of factors including mood, hunger, sleep, and the level of responsibilities you carry, you slide a notch or two up or down this scale.

Imaging Individuality

How, why, and when you feel empathy is unique to you, though the neurobiological activation works roughly the same way for everyone, with specific and recordable activity taking place in your brain. Scientists can see the electrical impulses spread through the brain using fMRI (functional magnetic resonance imaging) brain-scanning technology. The more we find, the more we learn about the fluid nature of empathy and how we are indeed hardwired—I like to think "endowed"—to empathize and connect with each other from the very beginning of life. Yet it is only relatively recently that Italian neuroscientists at the University of Parma made a breakthrough discovery that opened an exciting new door to the true nature of what's going on in the brain when we feel empathy.

In 1996 an Italian research team was studying the motor cortex of macaque monkeys during hand-to-mouth movements while the animals grasped peanuts and placed them in their mouths. The monkeys were hooked up to cleverly built fMRI scanners they wore as hats. While they were eating, an area called the F5 premotor cortex, mentioned in chapter 2, lit up every time they reached for a nut. At one point a researcher picked up a handful of nuts and started eating them himself. The research team noticed that when the monkeys observed the scientist reaching for peanuts, that same F5 area lit up again. Interesting.

Next, the research team gently restrained two of the macaques to keep them calm while they watched their friends snack on bananas. Once again, the monkeys' premotor neurons lit up in exactly the same way as if they themselves were the ones enjoying a piece of fruit. In effect, the restrained monkeys' brains "mirrored" the experience of the banana-eating monkeys. Though they didn't set out to discover these "mirror" neurons, the Italian team could document the brain's monkey-see-monkey-do activation down to a single neuron.

Since then, hundreds of studies have substantiated this original research, and we now know that mirror phenomena, or shared neural circuit mechanisms not directly involving mirror neurons but other circuits in humans, are activated by much more than peanuts and bananas. They're also sparked by others' facial expressions and postures—the neural basis of the empathic response. Thanks to specialized neurons, a smiling face makes you feel happier, a scared face stirs up fright, and an angry expression puts you on the alert.

In the last decade, researchers have explored the role of "shared neural networks" in the empathic response. Neuroscientist and psychologist Tania Singer of the Max Planck Institute for Human Cognitive and Brain Sciences in Leipzig, Germany, has focused intently on the area of empathy and our understanding of the brain's processing of others' emotions. In 2004, she and colleagues invited married couples to participate in a study to measure empathy. Singer placed the female partners in fMRI scanners. She then attached electrodes to both the female and male partners' hands. The electrodes delivered painful shocks to the hands of the female partner in the couple. After each female received the shocks, she then received a signal just as her partner received similarly painful shocks to his hands. An fMRI scanner recorded the brain activity of the females both when they were receiving shocks and when they knew their loved one had received a similar shock.

What Singer and her team observed after analyzing the resulting data was that very similar areas of the brain's pain matrix were activated in the female partner whether she received the shock or her partner was receiving similar shocks, except that when it was the partner they were activated to a lesser degree. This demonstrated that the human brain has shared neural circuits with the brains of others, which helps us relate to other people's feelings of pain or suffering. That Singer found that humans feel the pain of others who are experiencing pain but to a lesser degree than their own makes sense for these reasons: we feel another's pain but don't become overwhelmed by it; by knowing what causes pain to others, we learn to avoid those situations to protect ourselves to the extent that we can; and we are also motivated to help others, because through empathy, we feel their pain and experience empathic concern.

Singer's paper was the first neuroscientific study to report the results of two responses to the experience of pain—one when we experience "self-pain" and the other when we observe "other pain." Her novel findings led to a new line of research into the emotional reaction of others versus exclusively measuring the emotions of the study participants themselves. This was also the first neuroimaging research that showed how powerful the wiring in our brains is for pro-social, or helping, behavior. Rather than a "survival of the fittest" model, our personal experience of the pain of others motivates us to engage in cooperative and reciprocal facilitating behaviors that are necessary for the enhancement and survival of our species.

"Before I conducted the study, some people even predicted that I would find an 'empty brain,'" Singer has said. "I think this was the beginning of a bigger change in the overall consciousness about the importance to move from an exaggerated egoism and individualism toward altruism and the notion of interdependence." This brain interdependence is the foundation of what I refer to as *shared mind intelligence*.

Empathy Triggers

What all this fascinating science shows is that we are all more profoundly connected on a neurobiological level than we have previously realized. Consciously or not, we are in constant, natural resonance with one another's feelings. When we are engaged in shared mind awareness, the possibilities for mutual aid and collaborative problem-solving abound. But this resonance can be emphasized or blunted by many factors.

Think for a moment about all the letters you receive during the holiday season from those many charities looking for your donations. They're all worthwhile causes, and they all help people, animals, and the environment. But you often get an immediate sense of which causes will lead you to reach for your checkbook, which are "maybes," and which others you'll discard. Something from your own life experience dictates which issues are closest to your heart and deserving of your financial contribution. Let's try a quick exercise to demonstrate what I'm talking about.

Take a look at this list of organizations that follows. Say you had about $1,000 to divide among them. Which causes get $100 of your money? Which get $50? And which get zero? Or would you give all the money to a single charity?

National Wildlife Foundation

Save the Children

Muscular Dystrophy Foundation

Habitat for Humanity

LDAMF

UNICEF

Susan G. Komen

Greenpeace

Smile Train

ASPCA

Doctors Without Borders

Make-a-Wish Foundation

This task can be very challenging for some people. After all, who doesn't want to help all these groups do their good works? But I'll bet there was one you didn't consider contributing to. Fifth on the list is an organization called LDAMF. Since LDAMF started as a local fund in my community, chances are great that you didn't know what it was. Your lack of familiarity with its very existence and the fact that its name gives nothing away about what it does, most likely didn't motivate you to select this choice.

The point of this is to show you how the more you identify with a cause, the more empathy you feel, and thus the chances increase for you to be charitable. Perhaps you know someone who has had breast cancer, or you have a lot of pets and love animals. These are going to be the organizations that attract your attention and your empathy. If I told you that the LDAMF stands for the Lauren Dunne Astley Memorial Fund, established to provide grants for relationship education, you may still not be moved to give. However, if I told you that Lauren Dunne Astley was my daughter's childhood friend who was killed at the hands of her high-school boyfriend in an act of violence after she had broken off their dating relationship, it may command your notice. This small fund got the attention of the Massachusetts State House and put relationship education at the top of its agenda. By tragically learning, much too late, that women and men should never meet alone with former partners after a breakup, the Dunne Astley family is committed to supporting educational efforts that educate young women and men about the emotional complexity of dating relationships and steps to prevent violence. These educational efforts span every race, creed, religion, age, and gender and apply to all members of society.

On a person-to-person level, how we prioritize our trust, empathy, and resources is no different. The more we relate directly to others and their lived experience, the more we can empathize. As we noted in chapter 1, the people we relate to the most are those we consider our "in-group." This group is not hard for you to identify. These people are usually those with whom you share your ethnicity, religion, class, level of education, and political affiliation. In-groups can reach into the realm of sports teams and school identification, neighborhood, car club, or any self-identifying group of which you are a member. Can you think of five in-groups you already belong to?

Psychologists call our preference for those who are familiar to us "in-group bias." For thousands of years humans lived primarily in tribes and small communities. Our survival depended upon aligning ourselves with our in-groups—people who looked like us, spoke the same language, ate the same foods, worshiped the same god, and much more. Even today, in a connected, digital world, we humans still act tribally: sometimes unconsciously but at other times with great pride. (If you're a fan of professional sports, you know this very well.)

The in-group legacy becomes a problem when it limits our capacity to experience empathy for people who don't match up to any shared characteristics—the so-called "out-groups." You may not even realize you have out-grouped whole segments of society, but all of us do. Homeless people, for example, generally fall into the out-group category for most of us, so much so that for some people they cease to be considered human beings. Some people automatically consider anyone with a skin color different from their own an out-group. Other people automatically out-group people of other nationalities, political affiliation, gender, lifestyle, and religion—the list goes on.

In-group bias is so ingrained and often so subliminal that most of us struggle to be objective. A recent study at Lehigh University in Pennsylvania found that when white subjects are confronted with an image of a black face, they experience a brief time delay in their brains as they *consciously* process how to react to someone with a different skin color from their own. Other studies show that it takes more time for white subjects to accurately identify the emotional expression on a black face, and that it is easy to confuse fear with anger. When the subjects were made to feel anxious and then shown faces of black men, their time perception slowed down even more, and they perceived that they were exposed to the images longer than they were. The discovery of this racially biased time-lapse has extremely serious implications for how police respond to an emotional expression on a black face. It could mean the difference between life and death if a fearful face is mistaken for an angry or aggressive expression. Such differences in face perception may influence everything from how law enforcement treats a suspect to how much time educators spend with students to

33

how employers react to job applicants. Our society cannot afford to continue making these devastating mistakes, and empathy training is desperately needed to change this trajectory.

In my own work, I've seen how empathy training can help doctors and other health-care workers relate to each other and communicate with patients from unfamiliar communities. I've seen for myself that opportunities to walk in the shoes of diverse people make these patients seem less like numbers or objects and more like fellow human beings. In addition to my own research, we can see the positive effect empathy training has in programs like the one at Missouri State University. There, students studying to be orientation and mobility specialists must learn to navigate local streets with blindfolds on so they can better comprehend what a blind person experiences on a day-to-day basis. The course, called "the blindfold class," requires 160 hours in the blindfold. New technologies are also enabling people to gain a deeper understanding of others' experiences. After a life-threatening accident left theater artist Jane Gauntlett with a traumatic brain injury that resulted in occasional seizures and disorientation, she developed a virtual reality simulation of her experience in a project called In My Shoes. People don goggles and can more closely experience what happens when a person has a seizure. You will read more about this later.

While no exercise or simulation can give you the full experience of being disabled, they enlighten us about the challenges other people face as well as how they feel. Most of us can't conceive of what it's like to get on a bus in a wheelchair and how agonizing it must be to overhear the hushed tones and hostile mutterings from other passengers annoyed at being held up for a few extra minutes. To feel like an inconvenience to others is a tremendous burden to bear on top of the disability itself.

Empathy Killers and Imposters

For some people, especially those in the caretaking professions, running low on empathy can become an occupational hazard. I'm sure you've heard of it—compassion fatigue. Some can create self-protective boundaries to distinguish their own feelings from those of others. Others may become increasingly more upset when witnessing other people's pain and may require skill building in self-regulation to avoid blurring the lines between the needs of others and their own emotional responses.

Brain-based empathic capacity has a genetic and neurophysiological basis. The empathy training program I developed incorporates enhanced perception skills of others' emotions and self-regulation and self-management techniques. These techniques and strategies help manage what's known as "emotion contagion," the experience of catching someone else's experience almost instantly, like having someone sneeze on you before you can duck out of the way. One of the ways we teach appropriate empathic responses is by strengthening the cognitive aspects of empathy while offering strategies for managing and tamping down excessive emotional responses. Some of the practices we teach include guided imagery, diaphragmatic breathing, and mindful meditation techniques.

One of the easiest practices to implement self-regulation at a moment's notice is to take several deep breaths while saying the following words to yourself: as you breathe in, "I am breathing in to the full extent of my breath," and as you breathe out, "I am breathing out to the full extent of my breath." Many individuals in my classes find this simple technique more useful than the traditional advice of counting to ten before you speak. Counting without breathing deeply does not lower heart rate and blood pressure the way full diaphragmatic breathing does. When you take deep, slow breaths, they activate pressure sensors in the carotid arteries of your neck called "baroreceptors" that decrease your blood pressure. Slowing your physical response helps avoid the fight-or-flight response, whereas counting may simply delay an emotionally unregulated response.

Some professions, like police officers, physicians, nurses, social workers, and teachers, are at risk for compassion fatigue. People who work in these vocations are often predisposed to empathy but feel ground down by all the challenges and suffering they witness. They must learn to balance a healthy quotient of cognitive (thinking) and affective (emotional) empathy and still perform their jobs.

For example, social workers and other mental health workers who are expected to be warm and empathic may become emotionally exhausted and burned out if they dwell on the negative experiences and multiple obstacles their clients face. By focusing on what they *can* control, such as getting their clients the services and resources they need, and balancing their emotionally taxing jobs with self-care practices, they can better manage the emotional overload and avoid depression and burnout. Similarly, nurses who care deeply about their work may be more effective if they concentrate on what they can control, learn to ask for help from one another and their medical teams, and take time for self-care. They are far more effective if they do these things than if they try to manage everything themselves. Institutional support is essential to provide workplace conditions that foster collaboration and decrease onerous workloads and competing responsibilities. A study in Minnesota showed that burnout was reduced when medical professionals were freed from patient care roles that extended into when they had to leave work to pick up their children from day care. Whatever the profession or situation, balancing empathy and duty is critical to conveying humanism and compassion while maintaining professional roles that are helpful, hopeful, and meaningful.

People pleasers also risk compassion fatigue. We may think that trying to make others happy is driven by empathy, but that's not always the case. Often the motivation has more to do with a need for acceptance. If you feel resentful or angry because you feel you give a lot to others without getting enough in return, you may have this tendency. I would urge caution: don't allow yourself to be taken advantage of or, even worse, to become "codependent" by habitually placing others' needs above your own and believing that you thrive on helping others. This habit leads to an erosion of self-empathy and, often, anger and resentment of others in the long term. You'll find more about this in chapter 11.

A number of other enabling behaviors also fall into the category of "feels like empathy" but is not truly empathy. The classic example is when we enable destructive behaviors such as substance abuse and gambling or fail to seek help for loved ones with mental illness.

Enablers are the first to loan money, feed, house, clothe, and make excuses for a person with a substance use disorder. While this may look and feel like empathy, in fact, it prevents loved ones from experiencing the natural consequences of their behaviors, thereby perpetuating the problem. People recovering from alcohol use disorder know this best. They, more than anyone, can empathize with what an addicted person may be experiencing, but they are generally the last to become enablers, based on their own experience that it won't do any good.

Finally, one additional empathy imposter I'd like to highlight has been dubbed "helicopter parenting." You've seen this: parents who overpamper, overprotect, and hover over their children's every act. They swoop in and come to the rescue at every turn rather than allow the child to manage the lumps and bumps of life. They say, "I have so much empathy for my child," but that is not empathy either. These parents, as much as they feel they are showing love, are impeding their children's development to manage their own lives and learn from bearing the consequences of their actions. Children who grow up like this often tend to expect the same protective treatment in the workplace. One of my colleagues once had the parent of someone she'd recently interviewed call her up demanding to know why her son didn't get the job, yelling at her for not recognizing that he was "the most qualified."

Roadblocks to Empathy

No matter how extensive or well developed your capacity for empathy may be, you cannot feel empathy for everyone all the time. Nor should you. It's interesting to think about the mechanisms that spur you into action when you read one story or to click away when you read another.

After the massacre of twenty-two elementary children at Sandy Hook Elementary School in 2012, the Connecticut town was overwhelmed by so much charitable assistance that they had to recruit more than eight hundred volunteers just to deal with all the items sent there. Stuffed animals, supplies, and millions of dollars were sent to the small yet quiet, affluent town, which didn't need material goods. Supplies arrived even while officials pleaded for the public to focus their charity elsewhere. At the same time the tsunami of goodwill poured into Sandy Hook, nearly twenty million other American children went to bed hungry.

For many who contributed, this proximal form of empathy was a completely visceral and primal reaction to the thought of losing their own children. Every parent can relate to this worst-case nightmare, made even more horrifying by the idea that someone would purposely shoot and kill so many young innocents. This primal fear is linked to our inborn empathy and love for our children and has its roots in evolutionary biology. This drive to protect one's own offspring is so strong and innate because throughout human history it has been necessary for the survival of the species. Furthermore, while most people are not consciously aware of this, our brains are concerned with preserving our own genes for the next generation. Worrying excessively about protecting our own children is a guarantee that our genes will be carried forward.

Charity, compassion, and empathic responses such as the outpouring of generosity to the victims of Sandy Hook and other tragedies are also driven by what social scientists refer to as the "identifiable victim effect." The more we identify directly with a victim—whether it is elementary-school children in Connecticut or runners and onlookers at the Boston Marathon bombing—the more likely we are to open our hearts and pocketbooks. So why don't we respond in other instances when the suffering is just as great or perhaps even greater? University of Oregon studies looking at the relative lack of public outcry for human disasters in far-off places like Darfur, Liberia, and Rwanda have shown the indifference is not due to a lack of empathy per se but a sense of hopelessness that any effort will succeed in helping. With overwhelming statistics and millions starving, what can one person's empathic response accomplish?

Confronted with massive, global needs, individuals—as empathic as we may be—simply don't have the cerebral capacity to process such large-scale suffering. So often, we don't. Experts working with policy makers, however, are beginning to find solutions. Programs that microfinance poor farmers in Africa $50 at a time, expansion of nongovernmental agency programs, and global technology-sharing cooperatives are all examples of how empathy can be scaled while remaining personal and relatable.

There are other reasons we sometimes stumble instead of run when empathy calls. For example, various traits of human nature seem to be typically associated with gender, with females naturally at the higher end of the empathic scale. Tania Singer's group has done some research into how gender may play a role in neural empathic responses. In one experiment, her research team hired actors to play a money-sharing distribution game with a group of study partici-pants. One actor was instructed to act in a consistently generous way while the other was told to be consistently unfair in his distributions. By the end of the game the participants expressed generally positive feelings toward the generous actor and generally negative and dis-trustful feelings toward the unfair actor.

Next, Singer replicated her earlier experiment with the couples get-ting electric shocks, except this time, instead of the members of the couples being linked with their loved one, they were now fed informa-tion about the two actor/players. The results were rather surprising. The female participants behaved empathically regardless of whether the fair or unfair player was being jolted by a painful shock. Her dis-trust and personal dislike of the person getting zapped played no role in the intensity of her empathic response. But the male participants showed another story. They did display empathy when it was the gen-erous actor's turn to receive a shot but showed no mercy for the actor who played the jerk. In fact, the male subjects showed marked acti-vation in their brains' pleasure-associated reward centers when they knew that the cheater was in the hot seat.

The researchers concluded that the men's empathic reactions were shaped by how they viewed people's social behavior. Unlike the women, they showed compassion toward the well-liked players but felt an unmistakable satisfaction in the punishment of those they found unlikable.

Despite the seemingly inherent gender bias in the empathic response, there is other research that supports the idea that we can modify these automatic neural responses. Whether we're talking about doctors who have never been patients, able-bodied people who have never imagined the lives of those with disabilities, or simply people who need to broaden their empathy net to others outside their immediate circle, we know that people's ideas can change, and change quickly and deeply, when trained properly. Experiencing firsthand the struggles others face appears to improve empathy significantly.

One of the most exciting findings within my own research into the malleability of empathy in the brain resulted from looking at physicians of six different medical and surgical specialties in a randomized, controlled trial, which in the medical profession is the gold standard for proving causation and measuring the success of a procedure, intervention, or medication. "Randomized" means subjects are assigned to groups by computers in no particular order, and "controlled" means we take pains to tease out factors that might influence or bias the results of the experiment.

The physicians in our study were assessed by real patients in both their perceptive skills and their empathic responses to their patients before and after an empathy training intervention. Using the E.M.P.A.T.H.Y.* acronym and techniques that we will discuss in the next chapter, we showed the physicians how to properly "read" their patients' emotional states and understand their communications by using a number of methods, including a specially selected sample of facial expression decoding tools designed by psychologist Dr. Paul Ekman, the leading expert in facial expression recognition. The physicians learned how to interpret cues such as body language and posture, and developed skills in self-regulation techniques and assessing the emotions of others. With this brief, precision training, the clinicians became more attuned to what was displayed right before them. The group that received the training also received instruction on how to manage difficult interactions; for example, learning how to manage manipulative requests for prescription drugs by steering the conversation away from procuring drugs toward

---

*The trademark E.M.P.A.T.H.Y.® is a registered trademark of, and under exclusive license from, Massachusetts General Hospital to Empathetics, Inc.

getting treatment for substance use disorders. They learned to cultivate curiosity through empathic listening rather than judging the person. By taking the time to deepen relationships and expanding care to include a team, they were able to start new conversations about drug use and explore new, healthier solutions. After the brief empathy-enhancing interventions, the training group received significantly higher patient satisfaction scores than the physicians who were randomized to the control group. This study was the first to show that empathy can indeed be taught.

The good news about our research is that it showed very clearly that there is hope for changing the culture of medicine and, really, hope for any individual or organization that prioritizes relationships. We now have evidence-based tools to accomplish this. With proper training, including skills in emotional intelligence, emotion regulation, perspective taking, self-other distinction, and other brain-based abilities that are amenable to change, we can work toward a brighter future in health care and all industries where empathic principles are learned and practiced. That's exactly what we're going to talk about in chapter 4.

4

The Seven Keys of E.M.P.A.T.H.Y.®

We learn reading, writing, math, and many other important subjects in school, but many educators have been talking about the need to teach the 4 Rs: reading, writing, 'rithmatic, and relationships. Most of us don't get a real education in two subjects I consider incredibly important: nonverbal communication and expression of empathy. We are taught to focus on "what to say" and to some extent "how to say it," but rarely do we receive instruction on "how to be" and "how to let others be." You might think such things are soft subjects that don't need to be taught in school or that most people have automatic skills in these areas, but I would argue this is not typically the case.

When you focus solely on the literal words spoken and nothing more, you overlook the essential role of nonverbal signals. The information you glean beyond the definition of the words themselves is pivotal in the communication of emotions and true meaning. The same phrases take on vastly different connotations depending on how they are delivered. When someone says, "Nice shirt," he may be complimenting your taste, insulting you, or flirting with you. It's an intricate dance of the verbal and nonverbal, honed by evolution, social factors, and each unique interaction. Some researchers have found that over 90 percent of what we communicate is nonverbal and only 10 percent of what people walk away with is based on the words we've spoken.

In my own profession, I saw an urgent need to teach the nonverbal aspects of communication to foster better understanding between physicians and patients. I've often witnessed breakdowns in communication in these relationships. Physicians sometimes believe they are saying one thing while patients are hearing something else. Doctors hear what they think patients said. Patients may selectively hear what they want to hear.

This was not my imagination. A voluminous body of literature supports my observation, including a fascinating survey of more than six hundred individuals that explored how physicians communicate cancer risks to their patients. In the survey, administered by Medscape, a news site for physicians and primary care practitioners, respondents were asked if they initiated discussions about cancer risks with their patients. More than 70 percent said they did. Yet only about 30 percent of patients remembered their doctors broaching the subject with them. This disconnection may lead to real consequences. About half of the patient respondents reported experiencing signs and symptoms of cancer, and more than 20 percent of these patients eventually were diagnosed with cancer.

When doctors and patients communicate well, symptoms are caught much earlier. Lives can be saved. Clearly, this does not always happen. There are often language barriers between doctors and patients, massive cultural differences in the appropriate way to deliver and receive information, and subtle yet important nuances in the meaning of nonverbal cues. An arched brow, crossed arms, and tone of voice can easily be missed. There is a real opportunity for miscommunication when you rely on words alone.

In a systematic review of nonverbal cultural expressions of empathy, my research team identified several universal nonverbal expressions of empathy, including open body posture, warm facial expressions, and a soothing tone of voice. Interestingly, even when people smiled and tried to be friendly, if their arms were crossed or if they took a dominant body posture, they were not perceived as displaying empathy. Unlike smiling, arm positioning requires a great deal more conscious attention to ensure it communicates a friendly rather than defensive intention.

I knew there had to be a better way for the medical profession to speak to and listen to patients. So I began to study and experiment with various methodologies. Ultimately, I came up with the E.M.P.A.T.H.Y. acronym, part of my novel teaching program for assessing nonverbal behavior. This acronym was the cornerstone of our empathy education in our randomized controlled trial of empathy training at Massachusetts General Hospital for physicians in residency programs from 2010 to 2012, and it also was used to train hundreds of MGH staff physicians during a quality improvement initiative called MD Communication. Using it as an easy-to-remember guide, we were able to demonstrate how the acronym orients medical professionals to key aspects of perceiving and responding to verbal and nonverbal communications with patients.

The E.M.P.A.T.H.Y. tool, I quickly realized, does not only apply to doctors. These same concepts translate to other types of relationships and settings. In human interactions, empathy is one of the most powerful forces we have for connecting with and helping others. And like any skill, it can be molded, fine-tuned, enhanced, and managed. I have been testing and refining the E.M.P.A.T.H.Y. tool ever since I started using it, and I've seen how it can help anyone make tremendous strides in how empathically they engage with the world. We have used the E.M.P.A.T.H.Y. tool in other sectors including business and banking, education, and all levels of mental and physical health care. I'd like to spend some time reviewing the tenets within the acronym and explaining their role in clear, empathic communication.

E Is for Eye Contact

In some African tribes, the word for "hello" is *Sawubona*, which means "I see you." Such cultures consider looking someone in the eyes the highest tribute you can pay to their humanity because it refers to seeing the light in another person's soul. This practice is much more intentional than the mere "Hi, how are ya?" that we practice in our own country. In Western society, we say, "Eyes are the window to the soul." Lock eyes with someone even for a brief instance and you gather a wealth of information about what he may be thinking and feeling.

Making eye contact is among the very first human experiences. When a mother and newborn gaze into each other's eyes, both of their brains release a shot of the bonding hormone, oxytocin. Feelings of love, connection, and empathy flood into their gray matter. The mother's eyes also serve as a kind of mirror, reflecting a confirmation to newborns of their very existence.

In fact, studies suggest maternal gaze is considered so important for development that early deprivation of eye contact can have severe detrimental effects on a child. Under these circumstances, areas of the brain that coordinate social communication, empathic attunement, emotional regulation, and stimulus appraisal tend to develop improperly. Children deprived of early parental eye contact are more likely to develop "insecure attachment" along with a subsequent loss in self-esteem, difficulty trusting others, and problems regulating emotions.

From the very beginning, eye contact is one significant way the social brain regions involved in empathy appear to be activated. As eye-tracking studies show, when you are looking at someone's face, your eyes flit to the eyes, mouth, or nose for a fraction of a second before skimming off to another point. These micro pauses allow you to take a mental snapshot to form an impression of the other person, revealing a trove of social and behavioral clues. Studies suggest that people who rate higher on emotional empathic capacity scales spend more time fixated on the eyes, even when the person they are observing is on video.

When we speak to someone face to face, a process similar to those initial maternal gazes occurs, sending information about ourselves through another person's eyes. The research shows that how we use eye gaze is important for making an emotional connection, and the brain is exquisitely tuned in to the differences between direct and indirect eye contact. Brain scan studies show that the amygdala, considered one of the brain's central areas for processing emotion, lights up differently when we encounter someone who is fearful or angry, depending on whether they look at us directly or avert their gaze.

Meeting face to face helps you internalize information and understand how it relates to you. Some scientists posit that this social evaluation inspires you to act in more positive and altruistic ways.

One reason in-person meetings are highly prioritized in important business discussions and during health-care visits is that participants can access nuanced and subtle information that can only be appreciated in person. The opportunity to assess someone else's emotional state telegraphed through eye contact is increasingly lost in today's world as we shift our interactions to texts, email, and other forms of digital communication. When billions of dollars are at stake, people in business still get on a plane and travel halfway around the world to attend a meeting or sign a paper. They want to look their future partners in the eye.

When meeting people for the first time, you can deepen the empathic key of eye contact by making a point of noticing their eye color. That extra beat you spend looking into their eyes moves beyond a simple greeting and telegraphs the notion that you truly "see" them. The medical trainees I supervise report that noting eye color makes all the difference in what follows because it strengthens the purpose of their greeting to patients—to promote trust—and helps them focus on the patient's individual humanity.

However, I don't recommend prolonged staring into the eyes of someone you just met. Taking eye contact too far can make others uncomfortable. It's also important to keep cultural and individual differences in mind. For example, in many Eastern cultures, the acknowledgment of another person's presence is conveyed quite subtly, and prolonged direct eye gaze is considered impolite. Furthermore, some people find direct eye contact difficult to receive and process, such as some people on the autism spectrum whose brains have a reduced ability to process the emotional context of eye gaze. Sensitivity to differences and knowledge about others' cultural preferences and norms are key to showing respect and demonstrating empathy.

M Is for Muscles of Facial Expression

Your brain is wired to automatically mimic the facial expressions of others. In normal situations, when someone smiles at you, you smile back. The same thing happens if you see someone pucker their lips in disgust, lift their eyebrows in surprise, scowl in frustration, or display any other facial expression representing a primary emotion. This automatic motor mimicry often elicits the same emotions by the muscle memory as the actual emotion. When you frown, it brings up feelings of sadness or annoyance, for example. This is such a powerful reflex that you may even catch yourself reproducing the facial expressions you see in a snapshot or video. It's a response that is so subconscious you may not even be aware of it, but it is one of the important processing components of our empathic capacity.

In his groundbreaking work, clinical psychologist Paul Ekman identified the facial expressions associated with basic emotions. Current research by Ekman and others suggests that decoding facial expressions for emotion is based partially in biology and, in some smaller part, social conditioning. Some emotions have largely universal interpretations while others have different interpretations depending on cultural background. For example, Easterners and Westerners tend to look at different parts of the face during facial expression recognition, which may lead them to draw different conclusions from each particular facial expression. Easterners tend to take in a more global impression of facial features, whereas Westerners tend to focus more on specific features.

The way people's faces telegraph their thoughts and emotions is as individual as a fingerprint. Most of us are fairly adept at reading the faces of others to understand what they are thinking and feeling, but it's easier to be accurate if you know a person well or if that person is of a similar background and culture. So while you can generalize the meaning of a particular facial expression, you may misinterpret the same one in strangers, especially if they are from a country foreign to yours. Studies show that neural circuitry activates differently depending on whether we encounter a familiar or unfamiliar face.

It's also true that similar facial expressions don't always mean the same thing. Slight shifts in how one shapes an eyebrow, controls the muscular group around the eyes, or arranges the delicate muscles that control the mouth are the subtle differences that vastly change the meaning of what a face communicates. Many factors influence the interpretation of the face. According to Ekman, we pay more or less attention to facial expressions depending on social status and perceived balance of power. You notice slighter shifts in the facial muscles of your boss or a professor than you might with someone else.

Take the smile. We associate this facial expression with happiness, joy, and pleasure, but is this always the case? In Ekman's studies, he could distinguish between the Duchenne smile, the genuine smile of happiness, and other types of smiles by identifying the microexpressions formed by the subtle and subconscious use of facial muscles. The Duchenne smile was named after French anatomist Guillaume Duchenne, who studied emotional expression by stimulating various facial muscles with electrical currents. It involves contraction of both the zygomaticus major muscle, which raises the corners of the mouth, and the orbicularis oculi muscles, which raise the cheeks and form crow's feet around the eyes. With a forced smile that has no true emotion behind it, the zygomaticus major hoists the lips but the orbicularis oculi remain stationary. Duchenne himself wrote that the orbicularis's inertia in smiling, "unmasks a false friend."

In fact, the smile can serve to mask other emotions, as I observed firsthand one day when my patient "Susan" came in wearing a huge grin on her face: she had finally broken up with her abusive boyfriend! Her smile of happiness at first glance appeared real, but the lack of involvement of her eyes and a rather pronounced inverted U–shaped muscle in the middle of her forehead immediately drew my attention.

This rounded inverted U, which in some people appears more like a short column depending on the normal variants of the forehead's tiny corrugator muscle group, was first described by Charles Darwin in 1872 as "the grief muscle" because it is involuntarily activated when someone is feeling true sadness. It is difficult to fake because it only stirs when a person is truly experiencing grief or agony. And there it was, featured along with Susan's upturned, grinning mouth.

"You look really upset," I said to her.

That was all it took. She burst into tears as she responded, "This is the hardest thing I ever had to do. I was ready to break up with John, but I'm *really* going to miss his family. When I came to the United States, they were all I had . . ." As she sobbed, I couldn't help thinking about the emotions she might have kept suppressed if I'd responded to her smile alone.

So how do facial expressions relate specifically to empathy? One Danish study demonstrated empathy's link with "facial reactivity" by showing a group of volunteers a set of photographs of angry and happy faces. Measuring facial expressions with a technique known as facial electromyography, the researchers found that subjects who answered a questionnaire with highly empathic responses had much more activity in their brows and eyes when exposed to angry expressions and more activity in their cheeks when viewing happy expressions. The volunteers who measured lower on the empathy scale couldn't differentiate between the angry and happy stimuli at all. The high-empathy group, as compared to the low-empathy group, also rated the angry faces as expressing more anger and the happy faces as showing more happiness. This seems to indicate that people higher in empathic capacity have a greater sensitivity to facial reactions and facial expressions and that this ability also provides them with a higher sense of empathic accuracy.

You don't have to be an expert to pick up on the minute microexpressions described by Ekman and others. You just have to pay attention. When you focus on a person's face, you may find that even if you can't put your finger on why, you get a fleeting impression of how the other person is feeling by how you yourself feel in their presence. Sometimes you unconsciously register these microexpressions by catching the feeling without even being aware of a change in your own emotional state. More about this when I discuss the "Y" in the E.M.P.A.T.H.Y. acronym.

P Is for Posture

A person's posture reveals a great deal about internal emotional states, independent of facial expression. Charles Darwin himself suggested that the evolutionary purpose of emotions is to predispose us to respond in a certain way and that postures are associated with emotional states and are designed to help identify those states. Slumped shoulders can signal dejection, sadness, even depression. Sitting up tall and erect suggests happiness or confidence. Body movements and the postures associated with emotional states may be just as important as facial expressions for understanding the neurobiology and meaning of emotional behavior. Many of the same areas of the brain involved in the perception of facial expressions also light up during the perception of body positioning.

You may have noticed that in upscale restaurants, airlines, and other service industries, servers are trained to make eye contact at an equal eye level with you. Nursery school teachers interact in the same way, squatting to look at their students squarely in the eyes, which conveys respect and listening. By comparison, a CEO wishing to display dominance may stand at the head of the table while everyone else sits. One line of research claims that taking a power pose with your legs spread apart, spine erect, and arms akimbo floods your brain with chemicals associated with status, helping you project an air of confidence and greater physical presence, although these studies have not yet been replicated.

You get a sense of just how much posture and body language reveal when you talk with another person. Imagine you are at a party and you're chatting with someone you just met. If you two are hitting it off, you may subconsciously match body postures with each other and begin mirroring one another's nonverbal cues, such as hair touching and hand gestures. If you're not clicking, you may turn slightly away from each other, stiffen your backs, and fidget nervously until one of you makes up an excuse about wanting to sample the hors d'oeuvres across the room so you can quickly exit the conversation. Pay attention to all of this the next time you're introduced to someone for the first time. You'll learn a lot about the first impression you are making and vice versa.

As a doctor, I know that subtle differences in my own posture have a significant bearing on how my patients view me and the level of empathy I project. I always try to convey my respect and openness through my body language. When I sit down with patients, I turn my body toward them, lean forward, and sit at eye level. I use mirroring and nonverbal cues. All of this conveys that I am attentive and interested on a personal level. If I find myself sitting with crossed arms, I check in with myself: Is the room too cold, or have I unconsciously sent a signal that doesn't reflect openness? I have been teaching these same techniques to health professionals all over the world for more than a decade, and it is truly amazing to hear feedback months after a class. One physician revealed to me that now when she's sitting down with her patients, she feels more connected to them and enjoys her interactions with them much more than she used to. This simple change opened a different way of relating that her patients openly appreciated. This was especially meaningful because she had been considering leaving the profession because of experiencing burnout and a lack of meaning in her work. Staring into computer screens had left her feeling more like a typist than a physician, and this simple adjustment helped her see her patients as people again.

A Is for Affect

The human face is a critical guide to knowing the emotions another person is experiencing. Every human face tells a story of emotion, and as we age, some of those emotions become etched upon the face in lines that no longer fade. "Affect" (pronounced with emphasis on the first syllable and a short "a," as in "cat") is the scientific term for emotion. In training to become a psychiatrist, I've been taught to always notice and name a patient's emotions to myself and make a note of it on the mental status exam, a vital part of every psychiatric assessment. This helps me orient myself to the key sentiments being expressed by a person, and ensures I don't lose track of the sadness, irritation, confusion, or elation that's being expressed. It's a crucial exercise for becoming emotionally attuned to my patients and, in fact, everyone I care about. It's not enough to simply notice a person's facial expression. You must also interpret what you are seeing, which, studies show, tracks through the prefrontal cortex and into the primate emotional centers of the limbic system in the midbrain.

When I speak with groups of non-psychiatric physician colleagues, I find that naming emotions is not something most of them are trained to do. Who is, really? Most people say they tend to "skip over" that part, as if it's not important. I dare say that if physicians, teachers, customer service agents, and others who work with people in a helping capacity don't know how to tune in to the emotions of others, they may not realize that the person isn't hearing a word they're saying because they have not connected on a human level.

Emotions are at the core of all challenging conversations. Without "naming the affect" (the emotion), you cannot be fully conscious of why a challenging conversation is so tricky. Is it because the person feels threatened, suspicious, helpless, angry, disgusted, ashamed, or guilty? And what emotions do these feelings elicit in you? While you may try to ignore or suppress your own emotions in response to others, they are important clues to understanding what is going on in someone else's mind and heart.

You can probably relate to the frustration of calling a customer help line with a very pressing problem that has serious consequences only to be greeted with a sharp response that includes "I need to put you on hold." Your emotions could have been kept on simmer had you heard "I understand how frustrating this must be to you, and I'm so sorry you're having this problem. I need to put you on hold and I'll be with you just as soon as possible to help you." But when a callous response doesn't include acknowledgment of your emotion, you start to boil. And sometimes you boil over onto the person who comes back on the line, making them even less inclined to help you. This is how others' responses affect us physiologically and emotionally.

I'll discuss this concept further when we get to the last letter of this acronym, the "Y" for "your response," but for now it's important to recognize that labeling the emotion to the best of your ability is the first step in trying to orient yourself to essential personal data without which you can't be fully present or attuned to the person with whom you are speaking. If you're trying to encourage, inspire, soothe, or hold someone accountable for her actions, you first must try to understand which emotional platform you are starting from; otherwise there is little chance for effective communication.

T Is for Tone of Voice

Because tone of voice conveys over 38 percent of the nonverbal emotional content of what a person communicates, it is a vital key to empathy. Linguists refer to this pace, rhythm, and pitch of spoken language as "prosody." Prosody infuses a layer of emotion to the spoken word that goes above and beyond the singular meaning of each word and the sequence of words.

We humans are exquisitely sensitive to variations in tone of voice and its prosody. When you say about someone, "He's really good at that . . . " how you say it telegraphs the meaning. Did you convey admiration, sarcasm, contempt, surprise, fear, or disgust? If your voice had a lilt to it and an implied exclamation point at the end of the phrase, you probably meant it in admiration. If your tone was lower, with each word bitten off, you probably meant it with contempt or perhaps disgust.

Tone of voice is often more important than the actual words we say and can determine whether there is an empathic communication. In one brilliant and telling study by the late Nalini Ambady, a doctor's level of empathic tone had a huge impact on the patient experience. Audiotapes of surgeons communicating with patients were filtered so that only the volume, pace, and rhythm of their conversations were audible. When the researchers played these sliced recordings for a group of volunteers, they found that listeners could determine from tone of voice alone which of the surgeons had a history of malpractice claims filed against them versus those who did not. A surgeon's voice peppered with dominance and delivered with a lower register of concern was predictive of a malpractice claims history. This suggests that a communication style sensitive to a person's emotional state, as well as one that promotes bonding with the listener, improves an interaction between two people.

I suspect the results of the empirical studies in medicine have lessons for everyone. I find it helps to match the volume and pace of my own voice when having a conversation with a friend or colleague who is having a difficult time. A soothing tone can go a long way to helping another person feel heard. By contrast, if someone is sharing a loud, upsetting story, you may do better to tone down your reflective response. Though mirroring his outrage may show you share his sense of injustice, it's not helpful to increase the agitation he is already experiencing by raising your own volume.

H Is for Hearing the Whole Person

What many people refer to as active or reflective listening, I call "empathic listening." Empathic listening means paying attention to another person, identifying her emotions, and responding with compassion and without judgment. The basic principle behind empathic listening is to first try to understand the other person's perspective and then try to have your own point of view understood. This sounds easy but is extremely difficult to do. It means setting aside your own emotions and listening with openness. Neurologically speaking, it means tamping down your own amygdala-driven threat sensors while listening to the other person. Nothing productive comes of speaking when two people are in "the red zone." This is a zone of mutual threat and fear where defensiveness is activated and no one listens. It's most helpful if both people instead agree to take turns to speak and then listen, knowing they will each have their chance to be heard without interruption. Clinical psychologists call this the "talk-listen" exercise, and it is especially helpful to couples who feel misunderstood by their partners. Each partner gets to talk for up to ten minutes without being interrupted. The other just listens. Then they switch, and the second partner speaks as if she or he is speaking first. With no interruptions, high emotions tend to deescalate and hearing each other's whole perspective is often enlightening. Empathic listening makes it possible to connect with someone on both an emotional and cognitive level.

A great many people find empathic listening difficult. They hear the "chief complaint," but miss the "chief concern." So even if a lawyer attends to a client's grievance that he is not being treated fairly by the court, she may not be addressing the client's unexpressed concern, namely—how is he going to face his employer if he ends up missing another two weeks of work and risks getting fired? By asking about her client's concerns, an attorney can create a much more trusting and caring relationship with her client, which may make his day in court less stressful. Similarly, if a teacher hears a student's gripe about a low grade, he may not realize the true concern is much bigger, that the grade may determine whether she will qualify for a scholarship she needs to attend college. Pay attention and then be curious about why the person is so upset. You may pick up not only on what the person is saying, but also what has been left unspoken and deserves further exploration, opening up possibilities for solutions that will ease the person's apprehensions.

When you listen with an empathic ear, you call upon many of the other empathic keys. With your ears, you take in not just the word, but also the prosody and tone. With your eyes, you watch the person's face and body language. You draw upon your instincts and your "heart" to uncover the emotional intent behind the words. At the same time, you communicate back to the other person trust, respect, and a sense of openness through your own body language. In two studies using my E.M.P.A.T.H.Y. tool, our research team showed that when doctors improved attention to "hearing the whole person" (the chief concern) instead of the stated complaint, their patients ranked them much higher on empathy scales. Our research shows that paying attention to the problem at hand only gets you so far. Paying attention to the underlying issues that people deeply care about is where the golden experience of mutual empathy and understanding comes together.

Y Is for Your Response

When I give presentations about empathy in the public sphere and I speak about the "Y," which stands for "your response," most people assume that I'm talking about forming a verbal response, but I'm not referring to what you will *say next*. With deep empathic listening comes an empathic response that starts on a physiological level because of our shared brain circuitry. How do you feel when you're in the presence of the other person or team? Paying attention to this is important because, whether you are aware of it or not, you resonate with the feelings of others. Numerous studies support the notion that empathy has a physiological substrate that provides an internal experience that is shared between people.

Most of us react to others' intense emotions. We can actually feel them physically, a phenomenon referred to by psychiatrists as "projective identification," which happens when patients project disavowed feelings onto their doctors, informing them of what their patient is feeling but not verbally expressing in the room. Most of us aren't trained to pay attention to our own responses as important indicators of what others may be feeling. Through shared neural networks, your feelings about others may transmit very important information about how they are experiencing what you say and do. Think about the last time you listened to a very intense and agitated person at a parents' meeting at school, a group of professional colleagues on a committee, or the local hiking club. This person was raising fears about potential threats to the school, the community, or the environment. Now try to tune in to how he made you feel. Most likely his anxiety infected everyone in the group to some degree. If you thought he was exaggerating potential threats, you may have become unsettled and annoyed; if you agreed with him, you may have become more anxious and motivated to act on the issues yourself. Either way, your internal response reflects the dysregulated alarm of the agitated person. High emotions tend to find a home in their listeners.

In a clever study at Massachusetts General Hospital, a researcher named Carl Marci set out to investigate whether there was physiological concordance between doctors and their patients during clinical visits and whether physiological concordance correlated with patients' ratings of their doctors' empathy. Physiological concordance means that markers of patients' and doctors' physiology, such as heart rate and skin conductance (also known as the galvanic skin response, or GSR), would vary in synchrony, whereas physiological discordance would indicate no relationship between their individual physiological parameters. Marci videotaped twenty doctors and their patients as they interacted with each other (with the consent of the patients and doctors). Before the visit each patient-doctor pair was hooked up to skin conductance monitoring that measured the participants' physiological responses. At the end of the visit the patients completed a questionnaire rating their doctors' empathy. He found the highest ratings of physician empathy on a standardized reliable and valid empathy scale correlated with the highest degree of physiological concordance between doctors and their patients. This demonstrated rather elegantly that heartbeat and skin conductance tracings line up like mirrors when a person feels understood by another. This study also found the opposite case to be true. Low physiological concordance correlated with low patient ratings of their doctors' empathy. When emotions aren't responded to empathically, the physiology between two people doesn't sync either.

We have all seen examples of this in the workplace. For example, let's say an unqualified person is put in charge and is now responsible for training a junior work team. The new leader feels unsure about her role and perhaps somewhat insecure and paranoid that others will discover she lacks the emotional skill set for managing her team. She uses fear and intimidation to exert her authority, and when she hears rumblings that the team doesn't think she's doing a good job, she gathers them together for a lecture.

"People are talking about you," she tells them. "They're saying you are the worst team that's come through this system in years! You'd better watch your step and watch what you say. . . ."

The team's reaction? They begin to feel as fearful and as paranoid as their leader. The "your response" experienced by the team reflects the leader's emotional state. This can poison a team's spirit and have dire consequences for engagement and productivity.

This type of failed leadership tends to spread across organizations like the plague. Eventually something gives. People leave the team or quit the company entirely. Or the so-called leader eventually resigns or gets fired. Unfortunately, when employees are dependent on their jobs, they may endure this sort of situation for a long time, stirring up unnecessary emotional turmoil, decreased morale and burnout—all reasons why people quit. The emotional toll of an unempathic leader cannot be overemphasized, and the physiological data supports this. (More about this in chapter 10.)

We've all been there—and it helps to understand why you suddenly feel so unsettled. Your "response" in this case is not about what you say. It is paying attention to how you feel. It may be a bellwether for how others around you are feeling. And it should be factored in when considering whether or not you're working in the right place. Understanding this may help you decide to speak up or leave.

Why E.M.P.A.T.H.Y. Matters

My research team and I were so intrigued by the importance of empathic communication and relational factors in health care that we sought to answer a question often posed to us: "Does improving the patient experience with empathic care also lead to better health outcomes?" Our intuition was that the answer to this question was yes, but we decided to focus our research efforts on a systematic review and meta-analysis of the medical literature to examine the evidence. We looked at all randomized controlled trials published since 1990 that investigated the link between relationship factors and improved health outcomes. And indeed, we found that strong relationship factors in health care led to significant improvements in many common conditions, some of which are among today's most important health problems, including obesity, arthritis, asthma, obesity, lung infections, and the common cold, as well as meaningful improvements in our most vexing widespread health challenges including diabetes and hypertension. By examining relationship factors, we can now say with confidence that *how* physicians treat patients is as important as *what* they treat.

Although my research focuses on health care, I've learned lessons that can be applied to nearly every profession, personal relationship, and human interaction. When we stop to consider what distinguishes a great teacher, professor, business leader, lawyer, tutor, mentor, or coach, intellect is often what jumps to mind. The true "greats" that we've encountered in our own lives also shine interpersonally. A teacher may be an expert in her subject, but when she conveys understanding of a student's situation, and is even moved by it, a bond of openness, trust, and respect is formed. We will see in the education chapter that empathic concern and understanding is an essential ingredient for students to succeed.

Every person alive who has touched your life meaningfully and positively in some way has conveyed and/or received these seven empathic keys in your interactions. We've also felt the void during those times when they were absent. And if we follow these original empathic threads, we may be surprised to learn that they play a part in the reasons we choose our jobs, our hobbies—and the people we choose to love. All parties are equally enriched when we perceive and respond to each other with empathy and compassion. After all, it's the human bond that adds the music to the words in life.

5

Who's In, Who's Out

O n April 5, 1968, the day after Martin Luther King Jr. was assassinated in Memphis, a young third-grade teacher in Riceville, Iowa, named Jane Elliott asked her students if they wanted to learn what racism felt like. They all agreed, so she embarked on a now-famous experiment to divide the class by eye color—blue and brown. On the first day, the blue-eyed kids got preferential treatment: seconds at lunch and longer recess, among other perks. The blue-eyed kids sat in the front of the room, and the brown-eyed kids sat in the back.

To more easily identify the different groups, the brown-eyed kids were made to wear an armband made of construction paper. They couldn't drink from the same water fountain and were not allowed to play with the blue-eyed kids. They were told that the blue-eyed kids were superior and the brown-eyed kids inferior. At first, there was some resistance from all the children, but Ms. Elliott persuaded them little by little that those with blue eyes were superior.

"The blue-eyed people are the better people in this room," Elliott told them. "They are cleaner and they are smarter."

Quickly, the blue-eyed kids adapted to their "superior" status and went out of their way to display this discovery by exhibiting both bossy and cruel behavior toward their darker-eyed peers. The brown-eyed group responded with retreating behaviors such as isolating themselves at recess, as well as performing more poorly on tests despite having performed well previously on similar material.

The following week, the experiment was reversed, and the brown-eyed group placed the armbands on the blue-eyed kids. However, this time, Elliott noted that the now "inferior" kids were treated less harshly by the new "superior" group.

The exercise showed the children how it feels on a stark emotional level to be separated by an innate physical trait you can't control and be told that you are superior or inferior because of it. As the kids acted out and experienced both the positive and negative emotions attached to racism, they got a firsthand taste of how it feels to be in a preferred in-group and a nonpreferred out-group. A pretty powerful lesson for those young people living in a small town in Iowa.

At the same time Elliott set out to teach the children about how discrimination feels, she also helped them learn about empathy. Now they knew what it felt like to be in an out-group where certain traits made them inferior. It didn't feel good.

Elliott's racism experiment put her in the national spotlight with an ABC documentary called *Eye of the Storm* in which she repeated the experiment on film, and later she even made an appearance on *The Tonight Show Starring Johnny Carson*. She went on to pioneer the new field of diversity training and since then has lectured and coached the original exercise around the world to much acclaim. To this day, she continues her valuable work helping people intrinsically understand the fundamental experience of discrimination.

In and Out

While most of us have never had the opportunity to participate in the eye color exercise, it's quite possible that more than a few of us have had direct experience with what it feels like to be actively discriminated against because of the group we belong to—or have been assigned to. And while we all like to think we know what it feels like to be the out-group underdog, most of us surely do not when compared with anyone who belongs to a truly oppressed minority or reviled segment of society. We live our lives from within, and view our world primarily from the perspective of the various clans to which we belong.

As we've suggested, you are less likely to feel empathy toward others who do not fall into your naturally selected in-groups. When you share the same color skin, culture, nationality, religion, school, team, or whatever grouping you identify with, you feel a familiar bond. You seek out those bonded relationships because it's been hardwired into your brain through centuries of evolution that this is what is safe and comfortable.

When people were asked to rate what was going on in the mind of someone talking about a dating experience, for example, they tended to have the greatest accuracy about someone from the same ethnicity. Chinese Americans had a closer psychological link with other Chinese Americans, and the same was true for Mexican, African, and European Americans. As this research indicates, both cognitive and emotional empathy flow more naturally for someone who has had similar experiences, teachings, and values because it is easier to "read their minds" and then relate to what they are thinking and feeling. Tribally based perceptions and preferences don't automatically confer hatred on members of those who don't belong in our cliques or clans, real or perceived, but they do tend to make us less likely to empathize with the plight of people with whom we don't closely identify; we're also less likely to feel empathy in the absence of personal experiences with that group or person.

Lacking experience and bonding with those who are not like you is also part of the reason you may feel little emotional connection to scenes of war and unrest in faraway countries. If you click through such scenes taking place in the Middle East on an internet news site and you've never met someone from that region, you may not be moved. But if you happen to be close to someone from Syria, Palestine, or Israel, those images are more likely to tug at your heartstrings.

There is no end to these divisions. Something as basic as the kind of car you drive can create a perceived separation among people. Studies show that drivers of expensive cars cut other drivers off more often at a four-way stop than do drivers of more economical vehicles. Drivers of high-end autos also fail to stop for pedestrians in crosswalks far more often than the drivers of lower-cost autos. Why are the rich so reckless on the road? The speculative answer is that it comes down to wealth and power and an internalized belief that they are more deserving of the space they occupy on the road compared to others. People with money and status also don't feel as vulnerable as those with fewer resources and seem to perceive less risk in committing driving infractions even if they do get caught. In a way, they feel they have a right to put others in danger because they are in the in-group of expensive car drivers.

Empathic indifference toward an out-group, taken to its furthest conclusion, can have life-or-death implications. You may never have considered how a person's ethnic and racial background can affect his or her chances of receiving an organ donation—but the influence is dramatic. Our research team's investigation of empathic communication during the organ donation conversation found that despite African Americans having a much higher incidence of end-stage kidney failure than most other groups, they are among the least likely to receive organ donations. This is due in part to the fact that fewer African Americans are made aware of the need to donate their organs and the importance of finding organs with a tissue match. Research also shows that requests for organ donation are less likely to result in consent if the transplantation coordinator is not of the same ethnic or racial background, showing again the important role alikeness plays in connecting with and trusting strangers.

The flip side of this is that when you feel a connection to another person, it can lead to extraordinary and heroic acts. For my friend Vicky Shen, it was a series of events and an unexpected association with someone she knew that inspired her to magnanimous acts of empathy.

When Vicky had to exit the course of the 2013 Boston Marathon early because of police barricades, she knew something very bad had happened but not the full magnitude of it. Later, as she stood in her kitchen watching details on the news about how terrorists had planted two bombs near the finish line of the race, killing 3 people and wounding 269 more, she recognized one of the victims.

"I saw the picture, the little eight-year-old boy, and I cried out, 'Wait a second, that's Martin!'" she recalls. "I pulled out my phone because I volunteer coach for a kids' cross-country team and I had a picture from the fall of 2012. There he was."

Vicky's personal connection to eight-year-old Martin Richard, tragically the youngest victim of the Boston Marathon bombings, led her on a personal journey that can teach us so much about the power of empathy to effect good in the world. Though she didn't know him well, she kept thinking about her connection to Martin and what she could do to make right the wrongs of the horrific bomb attack that killed and wounded so many—including Martin's sister, who lost her leg in the attack. By January, Martin's parents had formed the Martin Richard Foundation, and Vicky decided she would help them raise money for its mission, "No more hurting people, peace" inspired by a photo of Martin holding a homemade sign he had made for a school project. The sign with those words depicted his sweet and kind character and a remarkably prescient moment, considering what ultimately claimed his young life.

As an avid marathon runner, Vicky realized she could put her feet to work to help the cause. She ran the 2014 Boston Marathon on behalf of the foundation and has continued to run marathons, raising over $68,000 for the foundation to fund sports programs for kids with mental and physical disabilities. And in what she describes as one of the biggest compliments of her life, Martin's parents asked her to join the board of the foundation, which has already raised over $7 million to help promote inclusivity, including sports programs that are open to kids of all abilities.

This story shows the power of empathy when a tragic event becomes personal and touches the heart. Vicky came to consider Martin, his family, and their charitable cause as a cherished in-group. While some argue that personal empathy steers us away from the big picture, Vicky's example shows just the opposite. Her personal connection helped her lean into a cause and make an investment in the Martin Richard Foundation because it touched her heart. It has given her marathon career new meaning and purpose and positions her as someone who can inspire thousands of others who have felt helpless to do anything in the face of similar acts of violence. The Martin Richard Foundation has raised funds to build, next to the Boston Children's Museum, the only fully inclusive playground where kids can play regardless of their abilities.

The Ripple Effect

If you throw a pebble into a pond, circles ripple outward through the water, with rings moving farther and farther away from the center. As a simple analogy, this works to show how empathy's reach stretches away from the central core of our in-groups. The more distant the group, the less empathy the average person tends to feel for that group and the individuals who are part of it. This explains why you are naturally going to feel less direct empathy for a tribe across the world caught in a drought than for someone in your hometown whose well has dried up. Distance and division aren't necessarily geographic. What ripples into those outer rings may have as much to do with how you see the world and how you think other people should live.

Your level of empathy may change for the same person or group under different circumstances. I find this is especially true when people base these decisions on perceived morality. For instance, if you have two neighbors who happen to look like you and live a life similar to yours, you may consider them both part of your in-group. But if you learn that neighbor X has been arrested and has a police record, you might immediately "out-group" him due to lack of trust. In an alternate universe where you've also got a record, you might be quicker to empathize with that same neighbor because you relate to how hard it is to rebuild a life following time in prison. It may even draw you closer to him. We will discuss moral empathy more completely in coming chapters, but it helps to shine a light in the context of in- and out-groups in order to help explain the limits of empathy. Morally distancing yourself from others within your own in-groups perpetuates a lack of respect and acceptance; empathy is eroded by moral judgment. In an ideal world the empathy ripples from one organization will overlap with others to form a web of empathic connection and respect that will be a formidable challenge to destructive webs woven by organizations that perpetuate hatred, discrimination, and prejudice.

Empathy for others can also be influenced by your own emotional state. This is sometimes called "projective empathy" because you project your own feelings onto others based on how you feel or how their story leads to egocentric associations of your own. In one recent Austrian and Swiss study, researchers examined regions of the brain that were activated when participants were exposed to specific visual and tactile stimuli. One group was primed with exposure to disgusting images of maggots and handling a slimy substance while another group was exposed to positive images of puppies as they stroked a blanket of soft fleece. The researchers found that those exposed to negative images projected their own negative emotions onto others and believed that the positive stimuli group was less happy than they actually were. Meanwhile, those exposed to the positive images felt the other group was much happier than they actually were. With fMRI imaging of the brain, the researchers could see the neural disruption in specific brain regions (in the prefrontal cortex) that normally correct for what they call "egocentric bias." Whether influenced by positive or negative stimuli, those areas were disrupted.

The bottom line is that even for those who have sufficient gray matter in the areas we are discussing, empathic capacity is malleable and notches up or down based upon a given state of mind. You are continually presented with opportunities to be either less or more empathic, and your neuroanatomy is uniquely constructed to make empathic decisions. Knowing this, however, brings you at least one step closer to being able to compensate for these disruptions.

"Out" of Thin Air

As Elliott's eye color exercise demonstrates so well, it can be easy to thoughtlessly and arbitrarily place people in out-groups and assign them negative attributes, especially when you are the one in authority. When asked how she devised her experiment, Elliott replied, "Well, I didn't design the exercise. I learned it from Adolf Hitler. I picked out a physical characteristic over which people have no control and assigned negative traits to them on the basis of that physical characteristic."

We know how this kind of "out-grouping" goes. Though our better natures try to learn from history, we as humans are wired to constantly create out-groups, sometimes even from within our close in-groups. As we do so, we don't build empathy among ourselves; we destroy it. Only when we can deem all human beings worthy of respect and empathy, overcoming our natural inclinations to place them in out-groups, will civilizations realize peaceful coexistence. I do see promising signs of this reaching across boundaries in times of emergencies and natural disasters.

When people in the US saw the devastation of the tsunami in Japan on their screens, they could find a way to empathize with the mass suffering of the people in the area. The same empathic behaviors were seen after the earthquake in Haiti as images of destruction, injury, and death were conveyed on our screens. Pop stars performed to raise funds; governments and private citizens donated millions of dollars. The same outpouring of support happened on American shores with the devastation of hurricanes Katrina and Harvey.

Screens, the internet, and social media are normally dividers because they erase the empathic keys from our interactions. Take the tragic case of a young boy who was snatched away from a beach at a Disney resort in the jaws of an alligator. The moral judgment leveled against the parents poured out onto Twitter, Facebook, and Snapchat, where posters used selective facts to condemn the parents as unfit. Rather than imagining how it must feel to lose a child in such a horrible way and what the parents must be experiencing, they quickly judged the parents as irresponsible despite reports that the father was sitting right next to his son and struggled frantically to pry him from the gator's teeth. It was so easy to play judge and jury in a comments section without witnessing the consequences of unkind words and uninformed conclusions.

Yet I'm hopeful that the very screens on our TVs, phones, and tablets that often close us off from each other can also sometimes become agents of change. When you turn on the news and watch the pain and suffering of people in places like the slums of our inner cities or far-off places like Syria or Somalia or Rwanda from your own living rooms, perhaps their pain becomes more real, and at least some of us will feel the tug of human connection. Here the empathic keys are at work virtually. Perhaps seeing tragedy up close and on a more personal level will evoke some very powerful feelings as these people cease to be nameless or faceless. (I will discuss the opportunities for and limitations of empathy in the digital world in detail in chapter 8.)

One of the reasons it is so important to get in touch with your own empathic capacity is that it helps you recognize your shared humanity and not get caught up in your own particular subgroups, ethnicity, race, or social class. When we subgroup ourselves, we miss the point that all human beings matter and that we are all connected. Universal care-based morality must ultimately straddle older evolutionary motivational brain mechanisms that favor tribal and in-group preferences. This explains why empathy is not a direct line to morality and can at times be a source of immoral action.

Today we don't live in small tribes separated by miles of forest, desert, or oceans as our ancestors did. We live in a hyperconnected global world. Moral progress may help us expand who we consider to be "in our tribe." And expanding the tribe from family to group to domestic and international communities to humanity is the global challenge we face today. Though we can now interact with people around the planet with ease, we increasingly do so in a way that is devoid of opportunity to use E.M.P.A.T.H.Y. tools.

Some writers have focused entire books on the pitfalls of human empathy, and attack this human trait by emphasizing the tendency of people to favor in-groups with their deepest empathic concerns to the exclusion of broader global suffering. This account seems unduly shortsighted to me. It takes a long time for genetics and epigenetics to work their way into changing the human brain species wide. Through an interplay of cognitive and emotional factors, there is a growing awareness that tribal solutions no longer work in today's interdependent world. Changing the brain takes time, and as tribal solutions lead to more war, devastation, and destruction, world leaders need to consider how a single-minded focus on national interests to the exclusion of their global impacts is no longer a viable option. Rather than declare empathy as a misguided human capacity, a more productive focus would be to teach how to expand our concept of who belongs to the human tribe. Who gets to decide who is in and who is out?

The moral outrage that's been mobilized by the Trump administration's decisions to ban Muslims from the United States, to withdraw from the Paris climate accord, and to denounce our nation's neighbors as "murderers and rapists" is the response of those in the United States who have empathy for out-groups. While the current administration continues to attribute the moral outrage of liberal voters to being "sore losers" because their candidate did not win the election, this myopic explanation fails to appreciate that the outrage is based on recognizing a perilous disregard for fellow human beings and a dangerous morally bankrupt vision of the future. The out-grouping condoned by the White House is poised to turn back years of progress in expanding empathy to include the global human tribe.

We need world leaders who understand that we are all connected. If countries don't find a way to cooperate as a single tribe, our civilization will become increasingly barbaric. In the most vexing paradox, the Trump campaign mobilized disenfranchised and forgotten people who had systematically lost their jobs to newer technologies and, with those jobs, faith in the American Dream. This important sector of society needed recognition and a deep understanding of their culture and jobs that had defined their livelihoods for generations and ways to help to meet their needs in our changing world. However, rather than raise awareness that these workers and citizens needed resources and means to prepare for new types of jobs for the future, they were pitted against other disenfranchised groups, who were blamed for their predicament. What could have been a radical call to break down barriers and make the American Dream possible for many, tragically devolved into an in-group versus out-group mentality that has crushed the hopes and dreams of many who have come to the United States seeking new hope and possibilities, just as every other non–Native American's ancestors did before them.

Empathy is often considered an important interpersonal, dyadic trait. If one thing has become abundantly clear, it is that empathy informs a vital intergenerational, interracial, and international perspective that must be valued, vaulted, and cultivated on a grand scale. Without expanding empathy beyond our in-groups and borders, civilization as we know it will not survive. Empathy training is the key transformative education.

Part II

6

Growing Up with Empathy

When a baby is born, her first experience with empathy usually occurs the first time she is placed into her caregiver's arms. When they gaze lovingly into each other's eyes, a flood of the "cuddle" hormone oxytocin washes over the brains of both caregiver and baby, initiating the neuroendocrine response of parental-child bonding and sowing the early seeds of empathic connection. A focused gaze tells the baby she exists by reflecting to her that someone else is there. When a mother or father figure cradles a baby, studies show that the distance between their eyes is about twelve centimeters. Isn't it remarkable that this happens to be the sharpest focal point for a newborn infant?

Ultimately, becoming a parent is a grand exercise in empathy. When all goes well, the biological, hormonal, and neurotransmitter activity in the brain and body form incredibly strong bonds between parent and child, making empathy possible. This is why oxytocin rises with the birth of a child, not only in the mother but in the father as well. Empathy allows both parents to become exquisitely attuned to their child through shared neural circuits that relay feelings and emotions and shared perspectives.

How Empathy Grows Up

So we start to learn about empathy from our very first breath. Babies seem to understand this. In research studies, when newborns hear other babies crying, they'll often start wailing too. We can't ask them why they are crying, of course. Maybe they're just annoyed by all the noise. And we don't believe babies possess theory of mind—the ability to recognize that others have their own thoughts, beliefs, intentions, and desires—until at least their second birthday. But we suspect that at least part of the reason babies pick up the cry of other infants is that their own pain centers are activated by the cries of others in the nursery through shared neural circuits in the brain's pain matrix. This overlap between self and other is the substance of empathy.

Empathy matures as the brain matures. Jean Piaget, an influential Swiss child development expert in the mid- and late twentieth century, believed that children did not develop perspective taking and therefore could not express true empathy until around eight or nine years old. More recent research suggests empathy blossoms in children much earlier. The current thinking is that by the time a child reaches his first birthday, he is aware that others experience feelings like his own, though he usually doesn't have the maturity to respond appropriately. A child this age may witness someone getting hurt and feeling upset but not necessarily know how to help. In simulated research situations, a young child will coddle his own hand when shown a photo of a mother faking a hand injury. Children this young appear to correctly identify the empathic keys of body language, emotion, and tone of voice and can distinguish their meanings but can't necessarily show a compassionate, helping response.

By age two, two and a half, toddlers begin to recognize another's pain as similar to yet separate from their own. Empathic patterns begin to emerge around that two-year mark that provide an inkling to where a child falls on the empathy continuum. You'll see behaviors ranging from the highly empathic to the more aggressive end of the spectrum from kids who haven't yet developed a capacity to untangle all their feelings. Some children, though not all, have the listening and responsive skills to offer comfort. After I had foot surgery when my daughter was about two years old, she toddled over with a pillow in hand after noticing my foot resting on a wooden chair without the pillow that had been supporting me for weeks. Even at this young age, she understood something wasn't right and tried to help.

A little girl in pre-K may bring a comfort toy to an upset classmate because she knows that a toy cheers *her* up when she feels bad. She figures it will make a sad friend feel better too. There is an age range for empathic capacity, and we should not expect all children at this age to show it. Children who are still sorting out their emotions may feel frustrated or even lash out instead of help as a way of responding to the stress of others.

If a child isn't consistently showing empathic behavior by this point, it's probably normal. Some children will react to an upset classmate by crying too, presumably because they were experiencing similar feelings of separation (or had in the past) and could relate but not respond. Other children might have almost no reaction at all, not because they are devoid of empathy but because they haven't yet developed the tools to express how they feel. Just as when learning to walk and talk, each child develops empathy at an individual rate.

About age eight seems to be a major cognitive development phase for empathy. That's when cognitive abilities such as perspective taking develop and children begin to understand another person's life circumstances more completely. For example, if a classmate's mother has cancer, a child may be able to comprehend the circumstances from his friend's perspective. Even if the child witnesses his friend laughing and having a good time at a party, he may still grasp that life is generally sad and unhappy for his friend because of his mother's illness.

By the tween and teen years, lifelong empathic patterns are more established, and you can see the compassionate person the child will become. Early role models such as parents and caregivers were the ones who imparted the building blocks of empathy, but as tweens move toward young adulthood, peers, teachers, books, TV, the internet, and other influences make their mark on how, why, and when they will feel and express empathy. Once they reach adolescence, most children, assuming they are neurotypical, will be able to understand, use, and respond to all seven empathy keys.

Throughout every stage of development, parents shape a child's ability to give and receive empathy. This, again, brings in the concept of proximal versus distal empathy, which is important to parenting from the very start. Proximal empathy is an immediate reaction, whereas distal empathy is a delayed response. Sometimes proximal empathy is needed, such as when a child falls down and gets hurt. At other times it is one of the ways parents show children misguided empathy because it interferes with what's best for a child in the long run.

I'll give you an example. Let's say your son doesn't finish his homework, and he begs you for a note so he can stay home and finish up his assignments. The proximal empathy you feel is the shared distress that your son hasn't completed his assignment and will now face the consequences. This tempts you to say, "Okay, let's call in sick." Distal empathy allows you to step back and ask yourself what is good for the child in the long run. Is the best thing to get him out of his immediate jam or is it better to let him experience the consequences of his inaction? When we use distal empathy at the right moments, it allows us to bear the temporary discomfort of our children in favor of essential life lessons.

This is a difficult challenge for some parents. But sometimes we need to shift our gaze to the future. When you say no to that thirteen-year-old begging to go to a party because there will surely be drinking involved, you may be saving the twenty-one-year-old she will become from getting so impaired that she makes dangerous choices. The point is that as a good parent it is easy to get pulled into the immediate stress and lose sight of why saying no is a much healthier approach.

These lessons of empathy we teach our children send ripples of implications throughout their lives. Fortunately, if they've had some hiccups along the way, it doesn't have to define their destiny. Recent studies suggest genes account for between 10–35 percent of how we perceive and express empathy on the cognitive and affective continuum. And the way we receive empathic lessons depends on age, gender, and a combination of environmental factors and experiences. Empathic values—how important empathy is to you—can be shifted. Having children of our own is often a turning point for many of us in terms of how much we care about empathy because we wish to set a good example.

That said, the earlier children learn to give and receive empathy the better. That's not to say you can't course correct. It's never too late to guide a child toward greater appreciation of others' feelings. A child with healthy empathic tendencies and strong perspective-taking skills is more likely to get along better with his peers, play nicely in groups, have fewer behavior problems, and be more successful in the future because of well-developed people skills. It sets him up for happy relationships in life. Less empathic children tend to act out aggressively more often, express negative emotions such as anger and depression more frequently, and in general struggle to get along with others. You give a child the best shot at becoming an empath if he experiences empathy early and often. There are, however, some children who experience the feelings of others so intensely and exquisitely that they need no coaching in empathy. Children who become overwhelmed by the distress of others can benefit from self-regulation skills training and decreased exposure. There is such a thing as having too much empathy.

The Child in the Mirror

One way parents teach a child empathy is through mirroring: the automatic reflection of facial expressions, speech patterns, and attitudes of their child. When your kids are little, you provide a spontaneous and joyful response to those early toothless smiles and giggles with your own smiles and giggles. Because most parents relish their children's first attempts to freely interact with the world, they probably mirror them right back with eye contact, body language, and tone of voice. This is not just about a baby's smiles but about her discoveries, her efforts to draw, to build, to learn new things; reflecting your appreciation and delight teaches her that she is special in your eyes.

Austrian-American psychoanalyst Heinz Kohut was the first to recognize how important parental mirroring is for raising a healthy child. As the father of a branch of psychological theory called "self psychology," he understood that children have a more solid sense of self when they see themselves reflected in their parents' eyes, starting at birth and continuing throughout their lives. Interestingly and presciently, he called this the "mirroring" transference, well before mirror mechanisms were discovered in the brain by neuroscientists decades later. Simply put, it means that children witness their own strengths, uniqueness, and specialness reflected in the eyes of their caregivers. In my own practice, I frequently see the painful consequences of repeated failure to mirror, which can result in gaps in the child's sense of self and confidence. Children who rarely experience their success mirrored in a parent's eyes often grow up feeling insecure and ashamed of their own agency. When they feel a sense of pride that's met with neglect or disinterest, they can easily doubt their own feelings and become discouraged and unmotivated to try new things.

To understand the power of mirroring, let's examine the result of what happens when there is no mirror. Picture the emotional experience of the first-grader bursting through the door and shouting, "Daddy, look what I drew today!" The dad, preoccupied on his cell phone or computer, barely turns around. He doesn't so much as glance at the child's paper or remark, "Oh, that's a great picture you drew of our dog!" or otherwise let the child know how proud he is of his creation. There is no eye contact, the tone of voice is flat, and the dad barely listens to the child's excitement. When a child's enthusiasm and efforts are not mirrored back, he may experience a sense of deflation as well as shame; he thinks he has done such great work, but his own parent doesn't appear to think it is worthy of a response.

Children consistently deprived of this loving mirror early in life may struggle to form secure attachments. Eye contact, as you already know, is one of the seven keys to living an interpersonally connected life, and its influence on empathy starts from the moment we enter this world. Mirroring is more than eye contact. A child longs to see his parents reflect his facial expressions, posture, affect, and tone of voice. He needs to be heard and get an appropriate response. When a warm and reassuring mirroring response is lacking, a child can grow up feeling unworthy and insecure and may have trouble forming close and trusting relationships.

That "gleam in a parent's eye" is not only one of the most important signs of a parent showing love; it is also essential for sowing the seeds of empathy in a child. Kohut described this gleam as "psychological oxygen." Children look for that reflection as confirmation that they are valued. When they don't receive this affirmation often enough, they can grow up feeling almost like a stuffed animal without the stuffing. Because they haven't had validation internalized, they are constantly looking for affirmation that they are okay and acceptable from the outside world. When a child is not mirrored, he may give up trying to achieve his goals, or if he becomes a high achiever, his accomplishments may give him little pleasure.

Fortunately, most parents don't have to think about mirroring their children. Just as we don't think about breathing our next breath, mirroring usually occurs quite naturally. Parents who are tuned in to their children will most likely respond to their presence and developmental steps with joy and pride. Yet external pressures that keep parents from attending to their children, such as work stress or financial concerns, might distract them from viewing each child as a unique individual who needs to be seen, heard, and affirmed. Families with a sick or impaired child are especially at risk for under-mirroring healthy siblings who are often at greater risk for developing low self-confidence and an inability to soothe themselves if the foundations of empathy and affirmation have not been set in childhood. Additional support for the healthy children must not be overlooked. Even if they don't seem distressed now, they might be down the road.

That said, "over-mirroring" can also lead to bad behavior and lack of empathy. When a child is complimented too much for mundane accomplishments that should simply be the norm—for example, "That was such a good sneeze" (yes, I have heard a parent say this to a child!)—he comes to expect that he will be acknowledged for literally every achievement no matter how insignificant. We shouldn't be giving out participation awards for prosaic successes. Not that we want our kids to have to fight like gladiators for recognition, but there's got to be a happy medium.

Mirroring must also be age appropriate. As children grow up they still need recognition and attention but how and how much needs to evolve. If they received enough validation as children, a sense of confidence will be internalized. Kohut called this "transmuting internalization." As they get older, they will rely on a confident sense of self and understand that the world isn't going to respond with unconditional praise for every achievement. Constant craving for accolades to celebrate the smallest accomplishments is an exhausting trait to manage in an adult and ultimately leaves the adult feeling inadequate because no amount of praise is ever enough.

I have a growing concern that mirroring has been deemphasized in the electronic age. The gleam in the eye is being displaced by the gleam of a screen. With parents and children spending so much time with their faces staring into a phone, tablet, or TV screen rather than looking at each other, there is less meaningful eye contact and bonding. With fewer opportunities to experience the release of oxytocin that occurs when parents and children meet each other's gaze and experience their mutual love and appreciation, the need for external validation becomes ever greater.

Lack of face-to-face time also begins to extend into friendships, and we are seeing the effect in the rise of bullying, cyberbullying, and trolling. (See chapter 8.) Screens can be a barrier to empathy because they take away opportunities to notice how other people respond and feel. To empathize, you must first make eye contact and notice keys to empathy like posture, facial expressions, and tone of voice. When you don't have this input, it's much harder to follow through with listening and responding appropriately.

Role Models for Empathy

Another way children do—or don't—learn the lessons of empathy is through their role models. Children want to idealize somebody. In the beginning, it's usually Mom and Dad. If you've been idealized as being responsive, caring, and present as a parent, your children are more likely to look for friends and partners later in life who have the same qualities and who will treat them with similar respect. They will also carry forth these behaviors toward others.

Role models are really important in child development at all stages because a child is constantly looking for normative patterns in his life. If the norm at home is that someone pays attention to her and attends to her feelings, this consistent empathic communication is what becomes the norm in her mind. The listening and responding empathy keys become reinforced, and she learns that what she does and says has value. When this is missing, it makes her doubt her worth and generates feelings of insecurity.

Children also have a natural desire to view their parents positively even if the parents don't treat them well. Why? Because kids know they are very small and powerless. Lest you forget, it can sometimes be intimidating walking around in the world when you are just two feet tall and your view is a forest of legs. Children have an intrinsic need to bond with their parents and a natural inclination to show them affection because it makes them feel safe and protected. So, bad or good, kids emulate their parents from an early age.

Parents usually aren't a child's only role models. Perhaps they come to admire a teacher or a babysitter, an aunt or uncle or older cousin, an astronaut, veterinarian, artist, or chef. A little boy I know named Hudson lives across the street from a fire station. By the time he was five, he worshiped the firemen who worked there so much that he was begging for daily visits. His parents were happy to accommodate, and the objects of his admiration were kind enough to let him sit in their trucks and wear their hats. Meanwhile, his police-enamored friend David wore a cop uniform everywhere, and his doctor-obsessed friend Vanessa carried a plastic stethoscope to school. It's wonderful that these kids have such positive role models. Having a hero or someone to look up to makes a child feel special and encourages him to strive for what he thinks is important. And it helps build up a muscle for healthy striving as well as self-esteem.

Having some bad role models is important too because it teaches children what not to do. This assumes they already have a pretty clear experience with good role models so they have a very clear distinction between right and wrong. Of course, if the bad exposure outweighs the good, it becomes a problem. Children constantly subjected to people who don't treat them with respect or take them seriously can grow up thinking their thoughts and feelings are not worth much.

There is also a danger of children internalizing the negative empathic habits of adults. I knew a high school history teacher who bullied his students so badly with an unreasonable workload and pop quizzes that they decided to put their heads on the desk in protest. He threatened to lower their grades by a point each time he called a name if a student didn't respond, starting with the student he knew cared about his grades the most. On the one hand, some of the kids in the class understood that the way he was treating them was unfair and wrong. However, others may have learned that overriding empathic keys in favor of bullying, meanness, and manipulation is an acceptable way of behaving and getting what you want.

Ultimately, children are most likely to internalize the positive qualities in parents and other role models they have subconsciously learned to idealize. They adopt what feels comfortable and familiar. That's why it's so critical to model empathic behaviors. Through this idealization process a child learns to form her "ideal self." Her sense of self will then be unlikely to be too ruffled when, as she grows up, her parents' frailties and mistakes are revealed. By upholding good examples, delivering on promises, and dealing honestly and empathically with a child, we reinforce the types of people she invites into her own life. However, when a child sees a trusted adult acting unkindly or thoughtlessly, it may be too much for her to confront the fact that someone with so much power over her is a bad person. As a psychological defense mechanism, the child may convince herself that other people deserve to be treated unkindly or thoughtlessly, and begin to copy the same sort of behavior. In psychological terms, this defense is called "identification with the aggressor." Either way, you choose how you will help shape who your child ultimately becomes.

Double the Experience

Another very important process in the way children develop empathy is a concept known as twinship. As kids get older, relationships outside the home begin to matter more. Children start to enjoy the company of others even before they learn collaborative and cooperative play. It reinforces a person's sense of self and makes her feel as if she belongs.

The need for twinship is universal. She may be drawn to some of her peers for all sorts of reasons. Sometimes the bond is obvious: they both love *Star Wars*, horses, books, or Legos. Such early kinships help a child branch out from her parents and help her feel as if she is like others and her life experience makes sense. In her "twin," she finds someone who understands her point of view and "gets her." She may outgrow some early relationships and seek new ones based on shared values and experiences. The little girl with whom she took every dance class when they were five may drift away when she becomes interested in soccer and her friend develops a passion for the theater. But the desire for twinship experiences always remains. Twinship builds empathy because it helps a child realize that someone is like her. Her experiences are understandable and sharable. The barrier of shame that a child may carry is reduced to the degree that allows honesty and vulnerability between the child and her "twin." This is such a profound experience because it activates shared neural circuits in both brains to create a sense of safety and belonging. When enough of these similarities map on the brain, a child feels more comfortable exposing her vulnerabilities. Early forays into disclosure can forge extremely powerful bonds of trust that can influence relationships for the rest of her life.

Fitting in and having friends can be all-consuming to some kids. Nobody wants to be a misfit. Every kid wants to be picked for the team or find a social group he fits into. That need for twinship experiences continues through to the teens and into adulthood. Over the years kids will prefer to spend time with kids with whom they share things in common, and it's these shared skills, talents, and passions that reinforce their own interests and selfhood, which in turn creates an environment in which they can thrive and that leads to greater empathic capacity. That's why kids who play sports are often closest to their teammates while the ones who become passionate about theater hang out most with their theater friends.

Twinship can go wrong if, instead of giving the emotional lifelines of acceptance and understanding, it offers defensive and distracting solutions. Instead of mutual support and someone who understands and can soothe him when he's emotionally hurt, a "twin" might introduce him to numbing behaviors such as drugs and alcohol. Or, if he lacks a twin he may try to fill the void with antisocial behaviors in an attempt to cover up loneliness, isolation, and feeling like an outcast. It's as important to expose children to positive opportunities for twin-ship as it is to expose them to positive role models.

If you are a parent to young children, pay attention to the idea of twinship into the teen years. The people your children choose to associate and identify with can have a profound effect on the course of their lives. Problems arise when children don't choose resilient companions, and instead choose peers who encourage them to mask their feelings with drugs and alcohol, look to pornography for sexual excitement rather than caring relationships, and take dangerous risks that could get them hurt or killed.

The Empathy Fork in the Road

Nearly all parents have a naturally born, oxytocin-fueled empathy for their children. But parents become challenged in teaching true empathy in those stressed-out moments when their desire to keep their children emotionally happy in the short term diverges with the actual task of prac-ticing and teaching empathy for its long-term psychological benefits. It's a delicate balance, for sure.

Support for a child must naturally change over time. In the early days of a child's life, physical and emotional needs tend to blend together. The baby cries; Mom or Dad provides nourishment and changes diapers. If he's feeling tired and cranky, a parent rocks him to sleep. Traditionally in the first few weeks of life, parents assume most of the caregiving duties. And indeed, research shows that the support of a parental figure through-out childhood is a prime predictor of a child's capacity for empathy and perspective taking.

This makes sense. A supportive parent is in tune with her baby's needs. She takes the baby's point of view into account as she tries to figure out why he's crying and then remedy the situation accordingly. Parents of both sexes will tell you that they can often tell the difference between a cry that means hunger, one that means a wet diaper, a plea for attention, and so on.

My guess is that nearly all parents have read articles and books about how long to let their child cry in the crib before running in to meet his needs. The sound of your crying infant permeates your consciousness like no siren ever invented. Every fiber of your being reacts. But parents who never tone down the hypervigilant support they give to a newborn and who continue to attend to every need, want, and demand the instant it happens do their child a disservice. Over-attending to developing children can have a lasting negative impact on their security and empathic capacity that could be almost equal to ignoring them.

Children who can cry for a bit before having their every need instantly met develop a capacity for self-soothing through a process known as *optimal frustration*. Overly attentive parents risk raising under-empathic children by cheating them out of the experience of waiting, which can build trust. When a child must wait for a short time—but not too long a time—for relief of her problems, she learns to develop trust that her caretaker will soon be there for her. Parents can become so derailed by their children's screams and tears that they lose all rational decision-making. It's simply not possible to respond immediately every time your child cries unless you never take a shower or go to the restroom or have any other children whose needs are also imperative. Babies can wait a few minutes to have their needs met without being harmed.

I consider the lack of ability to teach a child optimal frustration a form of misguided empathic behavior. It represents a parent's intolerance for a single second of unhappiness in their child's life. Empathic concern is needed when your child skins her knee or has a fight with a friend and you are there to help soothe her pain. These are the very situations our mechanisms for parental empathy are built for. But if she has a major tantrum because you bought the wrong color of paper towels and you find yourself apologizing—that is parental empathy gone off the rails. One mother I worked with found herself taping potato chips together because her daughter grew purple with rage if her chips were broken. If you're taping together snacks to appease a child's anger, I can assure you that what you are teaching your child is far from a healthy sense of empathy. It is pure affective, emotional empathy minus the cognitive, thinking part of empathy and conveys a message that she should not have to tolerate the slightest of life's disappointments.

You are practicing misguided empathy as a parent when you fail to see why always saying yes is not good for your child. Your goal is not to create an endless stream of happy experiences but rather to teach your child both how to enjoy happy moments and how to deal with life's challenges. In the same way that some people naïvely view marriage as a "long date" filled with nothing but roses and romance, some parents think their job is to make sure their children are perpetually amused. There is so much about life that is not pleasant that will teach a child grit, perseverance, and resilience.

Many parents don't understand that optimal frustration helps a child build resilience and trust. It teaches them the idea that "even if I don't get what I want today or this minute, through trust, perseverance, or effort, eventually my needs will be met." A baby who learns this gradually puts herself to sleep and doesn't get overly fussy if her diaper is wet for a few minutes. As a toddler, she doesn't have a meltdown in the middle of Walmart when you say no to her request for a toy. As an adult, she knows she's got to put in the time and the work to get that big promotion.

I work some with couples who are parents with no tolerance for their child's unhappiness. This gets to an aspect of empathy that requires self-regulation skills on the parent's part. One of the pitfalls of empathy is to have these shared neural circuits with your child that are so powerful that his every disappointment leads to your own emotional distress. When your child is crying and you yourself become so emotionally distraught that your prefrontal cortex, where reason resides, has been overridden and your response is purely emotionally reactive, it's time to step back and reassess.

Part of what I hope parents learn from this chapter is that when they find themselves gratifying every whim that the wiser part of them knows isn't right, they can hit the pause button and take time to reflect on whose needs they are responding to. Is it what is best for the child, or to put an end to a disagreement about what the child wants? For their own and their child's sake, they must find ways to learn how to tolerate their child's dissatisfaction. Want to raise an empathic child? Stop practicing misguided empathy. Start early by teaching her how to fall asleep by herself and build trust that you will be there when she really needs you.

The same goes for feeding. I know parents (as I'm sure you do) who prepare a separate dinner for each child in the family. What are children learning by having every food demand responded to with no guidance toward eating a more balanced diet? And how about the inconvenience of preparing a separate meal for each member of the family? Surely some resentment will eventually creep in for the parent who's been turned into a short-order cook. This can play out later in life when young adults feel frustrated, unhappy, and insecure because the rest of the world doesn't immediately jump to accommodate their every desire. This is not what you intended, of course, but because of misguided empathy, it can be the result.

Jane, a small businesswoman I know, told me a story about a young employee of hers named David. David apparently felt he was ready for more responsibility and perhaps a promotion. Rather than speaking with her directly, he had his father call her. She recounts the bizarre conversation with the dad, whom she had never met and who lived hundreds of miles away, telling her how much more his twenty-six-year-old boy was capable of handling as this capable boy sat a few hundred feet down the hall.

That's an extreme example of a parent who hasn't let go of his managerial past. It's also an example of misguided empathy at its worst. A relationship like this will cripple a child to the point that he may not be able to function as an adult. As a kid, David's father likely taught him that everything should go his way and if it didn't, Dad would provide the instant gratification for making it so. Where's the optimal frustration? Where's the idea of working hard, standing on your own two feet, and feeling the accomplishment of earning your own way in the world? A father inserting himself directly with his son's boss to advocate for a promotion is not how most of the world typically works.

I have seen many parents who want to maintain power and control as their children move into adulthood. These are parents who feel the need to emphasize that they know what's best and don't seem capable of validating children when they become adults. You must be supportive, but you must also graciously allow children to make their own mistakes. If you remain autocratic, as if you are forever the expert and your children will always remain children, you may cheat yourself out of the joy of a truly rewarding adult relationship when your children grow up, and they may never see themselves as productive adults.

At some point parents can learn to say, "I warned you about this type of situation, and now I'm going to back off and let life be your teacher." The more you fill the tank in terms of practicing and teaching empathy when they are younger and allowing optimal frustration to teach them about expectation for gratification, the more likely they are going to speak up for themselves as adults. You've helped them build self-confidence and encouraged them to take risks and aspire for what they want to accomplish. If you've helped create an environment from which they can stretch to become their ideal selves, it's more likely your children will choose to stay connected as they grow older and as you grow old. In old age, sometimes the most meaningful relationships are with the children you've raised who witness the whole life cycle and have been allowed to face, enjoy, and adapt to the many vicissitudes of life.

The polar opposite of over-empathizing is, of course, neglect. The impact on academic achievement is profound, with one study revealing that neglected children perform poorly, score lower grades, and receive more suspensions, disciplinary referrals, and grade repetitions than their counterparts. Interestingly, at times moderate neglect can motivate kids to become spectacular achievers. They may try to get attention in the world by doing remarkable things and racking up serial accomplishments. Yet despite all their achievement, they often feel a void that comes from a lack of empathic understanding of who they are. They may be achieving on the outside, but on the inside they are suffering because they never felt mirrored or affirmed. It is very common for adults who were somewhat neglected in childhood to have a burning desire for affirmation and empathy that shows up in their personal relationships, but they may have difficulty showing their more vulnerable sides if their self-worth was inadequately mirrored.

Massive, wholesale neglect is an entirely different story. Children in such homes find it very difficult to attain a sense of self that feels worthy. When a child is raised by a narcissistic or abusive parent, he will rarely want much to do with that parent as an adult. I hear this all the time from adult children in my practice: "They weren't there for me and now I don't want to visit." Many of these grownups feel guilty about not wishing to spend time with a parent. But the cycle can be broken, and by offering empathy, support, and understanding throughout a child's life, parents almost guarantee that their children will want to continue to connect with them as adults.

Some parents believe that offering presents, gifts, fabulous vacations, and other material things will do the trick, but these are no substitute for seeing the children for who they really are. Accepting your children paves the way for a future adult-to-adult relationship. Empathizing with our children inevitably comes back later as mutual empathy. The good news is that even in the face of extreme parental neglect, some really resilient children can find role models who help them become effective in the world. They will learn to emulate and look up to adults who give and receive empathy. This point is critically important and explains how even children who can point to no strong supports within their family of origin can become leaders with strength and integrity because someone else in the world stepped in and saw who they were capable of becoming.

Good Enough Is Probably Good Enough

Parenting is not just about teaching empathy; it's also about testing your own. When a child stretches your empathic limits to the breaking point, it helps to keep in mind that beneath all the difficulty is someone who longs to be loved and understood. The best way to show empathy is by putting to work one of the most underused keys to empathy: listening. Be attentive when your child speaks. You may not agree with anything that comes out of his mouth—and perhaps all that comes out is balderdash.

But let him say his piece. If you simply listen without comment, you gain a window into your child's life and reinforce an open dialogue.

When a child goes through a disagreeable, combative, and secretive phase, this may test a parent's ability to empathize, but it could be a time when he needs his parent's empathy the most. During the teen years, for example, children often seek more independence. Perhaps you recall the turmoil you felt from the confusing cocktail of raging hormones, social pressure, and academic demands you experienced when you were a teen. At this age they may resist the parental mirror. Because of this resistance, many parents put down the mirror at this point. This is a mistake.

You can always offer any child of any age "the gleam" in your eye when it is appropriate. Human beings never outgrow their need for that. As children's skills develop and they build a sense of confidence and competence, they still need their parents' attention, encouragement, and mirrored excitement. However, empathy tends to be the most critical when it is most tested. If your son or daughter transforms into a self-centered, sulky, and disrespectful creature (at least some of the time), try to remember that he or she still needs you. I see a lot of turmoil in families where the parents can't muster the compassion they need to deal with a child who turns sour and begins testing the limits—all age appropriate within reason. This happens most often when parents try to continue in their role as a child's manager instead of a consultant. Parents have to step in when children engage in behaviors that are very risky and dangerous, but they don't have to offer their opinion about or contradict everything the child says or does. Understanding that childhood, especially as children enter the cusp of adulthood, is full of transitions and emotional turmoil, it is best to be a consistent presence and to be there for advice when they need you most.

Parenting is a difficult job. No one in history has ever done it perfectly. You won't either. That's okay. All you can do is your best. Instead of making perfection your goal, you may take comfort in the concept of being a "good enough" parent, with your positive interactions outnumbering the negative ones. Psychologist Barbara Fredrickson's illuminating research has shown that a ratio of positive-to-negative comments of 3:1 predicts a strong relationship with a child, and a ratio of 5:1 positive-to-negative comments predicts an outstanding relationship. If you aim for the realistic standard of 3:1, you will likely be rewarded with more peace during the turbulent years and a mature and loving adult relationship when your children are grown. If you succeed, you will raise someone whose company you enjoy and who will be there to share in all of the remaining phases of your life.

7

The ABCs of Empathy in Education

L incoln High School in Walla Walla, Washington, was considered a "last chance" dumping ground for the failing, troubled, and violent kids from all over the county. In just one school year, Principal Jim Sporleder turned the school's prospects around in dramatic fashion.

Sporleder instructed the teachers and staff to limit punishment whenever possible and to treat the students with kindness and understanding. There was still accountability for poor choices and inappropriate behavior, but now, rather than suspension or detention as a first-line response, the kids were offered help. Those who failed a test, skipped class, or got into trouble were "punished" with study hall, counseling, and supportive services.

The results were incredible. In the first year, expulsions dropped by almost 65 percent, and written reprimands were nearly halved. Suspensions plummeted by nearly 85 percent. By year four, there were no suspensions at all, and expulsions had dropped even further. Test scores, grades, and graduation rates had also begun to trend upward impressively.

Sporleder understood that many Lincoln High students didn't have the luxury of a stable and supportive home life. More than 80 percent of them came from economically disadvantaged backgrounds, and more than a quarter of them had no home at all. Many of them were subjected to violence, substance use disorders, and a fractured social structure on a daily basis. From his research, Sporleder knew that all this chronic and toxic stress took its toll on their developing brains, especially in the areas responsible for executive functions such as reasoning, planning, and prioritizing. Punishing misbehavior only made things worse by piling more trauma on kids who were already at their breaking point.

Grilling and Pimping

Lincoln High, featured in the documentary *Paper Tigers*, is a good example of how when empathy is present in education and learning, it can make a substantive difference. You can try to cram facts and figures into someone's mind, but it requires the full spectrum of empathy for knowledge to truly take root. On the cognitive side, teachers must be able to adopt the students' perspectives and possess an aptitude for theory of mind to be able to understand their thoughts and intentions. On the emotional side, teachers must understand what students face every day and how they feel about what's going on in their lives well before they walk through the school doors each morning. Without empathic concern for your learners, you risk wasting everyone's time, including your own.

My friends in education tell me that it's still common practice for instructors to put students on the spot by attempting to shame them before their peers when they don't know the answers or didn't do their homework. They mock them in the classroom, single them out, and pepper them with questions in rapid fire so they barely have time to sputter out a response. Such "grilling and pimping" techniques, as they are known in the teaching world, are associated with humiliation, embarrassment, and anxiety. Educators who use these methods aren't usually coldhearted. They may genuinely believe that shame is the best motivator. I respectfully disagree, with some research to back me up.

Empirical studies strongly suggest that emotions influence how well a person learns. Students in positive mood states (happy and relaxed) have an easier time focusing on the big picture and tend to do well on tasks that require memory retention. Those in a darker frame of mind (anxious and stressed) are more likely to concentrate on small details and struggle to use their knowledge in new ways. In studies, good moods are associated with superior problem solving and creative thinking, whereas bad moods seem to close the mind and promote inflexible thinking. While a student may long remember the one fact he was humiliated for not knowing in front of his classmates, he will be more likely to forget everything else associated with that lesson and be unable to transfer that knowledge to new situations, only remembering the shame he felt.

I think we can agree that being shouted at or tossed out of class, even if you have it coming, is more likely to put you in an angry mood than being treated with respect will. Worse, negative memories seem to stick like Velcro in the brain, so a bad educational experience will be remembered and relived over again for a long period of time. From a neuroscientific point of view, it makes more sense to offer affirmative corrections. Respectful treatment and encouragement stimulate the brain to produce dopamine and other neurochemicals associated with happiness and satisfaction—thus promoting optimal learning.

Obviously, education can't all be gold stars and pats on the head. Corrective measures have a place in education just as in parenting and society at large. But zero-tolerance policies along with other harsh and punitive approaches for managing student behavior stifle the learning environment and embed cynicism into the system. They may resolve behavioral problems in the short term, but they foster fear and contempt in the student-teacher relationship in the long run. When students aren't given the opportunity to practice constructive behavior, you reinforce the less desirable conduct. One Australian study found that students who were given multiple suspensions were nearly five times more likely to engage in antisocial or criminal activity.

Leveraging the Social Brain

Of course, for empathic teaching to be effective it must go well beyond reward and punishment responses. Perspective taking—the ability to see the world from the student's point of view—is critical for learning. We know that children's brains are not simply miniature versions of adult brains. Adolescent gray matter is still developing until it reaches full maturity at around age twenty-five, according to current neuroscientific thinking. This means that throughout the years of formal education, a child's brain is in constant flux, shaping, molding, and adapting to new stimuli. Rather than growing larger, it forms stronger connectivity between regions that underlie a person's basic learning abilities. The brain develops more slowly in regions that govern emotions and executive functions such as reasoning, decision-making, and self-control.

Social and relational areas of the brain are active at all ages, but in the young and evolving brain these areas are particularly busy. By the time a child is in middle school, the importance of the peer group soars above all else, and adults are often viewed as boring, know-nothing figures. Studies show that when at rest, most kids are thinking about social relationships. Their minds are naturally engaged with the drama of who is friends with whom, what people are saying about so-and-so, how their friends perceive them, and whether they will be included or excluded by peers.

This emotion-laden developmental stage is well documented and widely acknowledged by parents—and by researchers and teachers. For example, a team at UCLA looked at a collection of studies that compared rote memorization techniques to socially motivated learning techniques. One of the studies they cite placed participants in fMRI brain scanners, presented them with a few paragraphs describing concepts for new TV shows, and then asked them to pitch a pilot using these story ideas to hypothetical bosses. By observing which parts of the brain lit up before and during the pitches, the scientists were able to identify high activity in a neural region located in the brain's social center they refer to as the "mentalizing network."

Mentalizing is synonymous with theory of mind, or the ability to imagine the thoughts, feelings, intentions, and desires of others. What is really remarkable about the study's results is that the information itself—the TV pilot description—was not personally relevant to the participants. It was just some information they were given. However, as the scanned students' brains showed, they processed the story lines in an area where they could retrieve it easily and accurately, most likely because they were aware they had to offer a clear explanation to another person. These are the same brain regions identified with cognitive empathic skills. In studies in which subjects are asked to memorize facts for a test, they appear to store the information in a completely different region of the brain than that devoted to rote memorization.

Yet even though we know that younger brains are socially motivated, traditional classic classroom learning has usually focused on a different part of the brain, the area that houses memorization. To me that suggests a missed opportunity to present subject matter in a relational context that would allow students to absorb information into their already primed empathic brains. According to National Center for Education Statistics, the typical American student will participate in nearly twenty-thousand hours of classroom education by the age of eighteen. In some countries it's even more. While educators worldwide have made an institutional bet that children's education should feature rote, fact-based learning as its centerpiece, research shows that children retain only a small fraction of what they learn in the classroom. There's no question that we need to pave new roads in education.

There are some more inspired educational approaches that do take advantage of social dominance in the brain. One of them is called Project Based Learning, or PBL for short. It started gaining prominence in the latter half of the twentieth century, though the ideas behind it, "learn by doing," date back to Aristotle and Socrates. Its early proponents included Italian educator Maria Montessori; Jean Piaget, the celebrated developmental psychologist; and John Dewey, the twentieth-century voice of the educational theory and (for those of you old enough to remember) the inventor of the Dewey decimal system that was used to categorize library books before computers.

PBL is predicated on the concept that people, especially children, learn by asking questions, reflecting on ideas, and interacting with others. At the crux of PBL is the notion that you can solve real-world puzzles through both problem-solving exercises and group projects. Students learn together through collaboration, questioning, and creating. They go beyond repetition, memorization, and regurgitation of facts to develop critical thinking and communication skills that help them face ongoing challenges in school and beyond. Studies show that PBL and similar education styles increase subject retention and improve students' attitudes toward learning. They seem to better prepare students for deeper learning, higher-level thinking skills, and intra- and interpersonal skills. And you can't talk about practicing interpersonal skills without recognizing the integral roles that empathy and shared mind intelligence play in this kind of learning.

I'm happy to say that adult education is picking up on the experiential learning model too. I myself have been fortunate enough to attend experience-based courses designed by Elizabeth Armstrong, director of the Harvard Macy Institute, including courses on physician leadership in education and leading medical innovations. The influential and late dean of Harvard Medical School, Dr. Daniel Tosteson, hired Armstrong, an education expert, decades ago to help revamp the school's curriculum into a case-based learning approach. They believed that traditional teaching methods of ingestion and repetition of facts robbed students of the mental skills needed to solve actual patient problems. Their goal was to change the foundation of medical education with problem-based learning and a more self-directed approach by understanding that lifelong learning skills were essential to the practice of medicine and superior patient care. This novel approach guided many other medical institutions and endures at the heart of medical education today.

When I spoke to Armstrong recently, she told me that she firmly believes that primarily learning by rote memorization needs to go the way of the dinosaur. "In this century, I feel it's more important for people to learn to explore rather than rely on classifications and memorization. They need to be motivated to ask questions and solve problems," she says. "Memorization and regurgitation of vast amounts of information do not always create the best, most emotionally attuned students. The future of medical practice will more heavily utilize artificial intelligence and big data. We will need our practitioners to learn how to mine that information."

Instead of teaching a series of protocols and procedures, as many classes do, Armstrong encourages students to place an emphasis on real patient cases, work collaboratively in groups, and continually expand their knowledge. I loved the case studies because they allowed students to apply what they already knew to real-life situations in ways I hadn't thought of before. They required students to imagine a patient as a whole person and real live human being, including their social and emotional challenges, rather than simply a collection of cells and maladies. It allowed me to see that when students view a patient as a fellow human being, it naturally leads to greater empathy and understanding.

E.M.P.A.T.H.Y. in the Classroom

When empathy is missing from teaching, there is often a tendency to place value exclusively on performance and measurable metrics with no real consideration for why teachers are getting the results they are seeing. Focusing exclusively on intellectual output without reflecting on emotional factors that contribute to learning robs us of the chance to really inspire students or understand, why we are leaving some of them behind. In my practice we call this the difference between the "chief complaint" and the "chief concern." The chief complaint might be that a child is getting poor grades. The chief concern is the reason that led to her poor performance. Put in the context of the E.M.P.A.T.H.Y. keys, this translates to "H": hearing the whole person.

Perhaps one of the best examples I know that takes this concept into practice is the Epiphany School where my friend Caroline Abernethy and her daughter Frannie Abernethy Armstrong work. The Epiphany School is a middle school located in a poor community just outside Boston serving children in grades 5 through 8. Founded in 1997, its goal is to ensure economically and socially disadvantaged kids live up to their full potential.

Early on, the school figured out that if they wanted the kids to learn, they'd have to feed them three meals a day. This may not seem like a typical conclusion for an educational institution focused on academic results, but when Caroline and Frannie visited the children's homes, they saw that many families didn't have enough money to put food on the table, let alone nutritious, healthy meals. They didn't need a study to tell them that students who sit in a classroom with rumbling tummies are at a disadvantage. The school now opens its doors early enough to offer a healthy breakfast and then keeps the kids in their infant-to-kindergarten program and middle school all day, serving them lunch and dinner as well.

From a purely academic standpoint, this whole-child focus has been a success. Epiphany students typically start at least one grade level below average, but by eighth grade they score two to three grade levels above average. While a mere 8.3 percent of students from the lowest economic quartile graduate from college nationally, more than 60 percent of Epiphany alumni earn a college diploma. Most impressive is the fact that Epiphany's college grads have come back to teach, so the investment the school has made in education is already beginning to pay cyclical dividends.

Frannie draws a straight line from feeding hungry children to expressing empathy and the school's success.

"We don't think it is showing empathy if a student doesn't do his homework and we say, 'That's okay,'" she reasons. "We find out *why* he didn't do his homework. If he didn't do it because there was no food in the house and he was hungry, that's the problem we go after—and that's showing empathy for a child's education."

I agree. This gets right to the point of why it's so important to "hear the whole person" in education rather than treat each student as another empty vessel that must be filled with knowledge. Schools don't teach math, English, and science; they teach *children*. Epiphany's approach takes a child's home life into account and then provides the structure that most of us take for granted. It goes beyond feeding them breakfast. A parent or caregiver who inspires a student to excel is another built-in advantage that many children don't have. The school also adds time in the day for students to do their homework on the assumption there might not be someone at home to provide the structure to get it done.

Just down the street from the Epiphany School in Dorchester, Massachusetts, the kitchen of a new nonprofit grocery chain called Daily Table that sells low-cost, healthy foods offers another form of empathic education. Founder Doug Rauch, former president of Trader Joe's, observes, "One of the missing ingredients in most approaches to providing food to the economically challenged is the lack of dignified choices that provide a sense of agency in providing for one's own family, and that includes learning how to prepare healthy foods."

Food insecurity is a problem affecting one in six Americans, with 17 million children not getting the food they need. Doug also understood the vital health benefits of healthy eating. This is part of a new movement known as "upstream medicine," where the focus is on preventing disease rather than treating it.

Fostering healthy eating habits that decrease the likelihood of diabetes, obesity, hypertension, and other health problems that disproportionally affect the poor, Doug's teaching team cares as much about their customers learning *how* to cook the food as what they buy in the store. One customer proudly exclaimed, "Since I've been shopping here I've lost seventy-five pounds, and I'm off my diabetes medication!"

Moving directly into the classroom experience itself, we see that the rest of the E.M.P.A.T.H.Y. keys also contribute to a stimulating learning environment, albeit in a more straightforward way. A good teacher uses the keys to make the material they teach exciting and interesting. Even the most progressive curriculum will fall flat if those keys are missing. An unempathic teacher is much more self-focused. He spends most of his time dispensing knowledge. An empathic teacher delivers his knowledge through the lens of the learner, paying attention to the learner's state of mind and emotions.

The best teachers, no matter what they teach or to whom, make eye contact with students and are keen observers of facial expressions, posture, and body language. They know that when they see a classroom full of knitted brows and squinted eyes, the students are probably confused. And if the chairs are supporting slumped bodies and blank faces, they've lost the class to boredom and indifference.

From the students' point of view, a teacher who drones on without varied inflection is the oral equivalent of watching paint dry. Studies show that students decide whether someone is a good teacher in just fifteen seconds based on tone of voice alone. A teacher who is paying attention will know how to energize her affect or change the tack of the lesson to make it more relevant. I once had a teacher who knew kids weren't exactly overjoyed to be in math class, so he kept things interesting by plucking examples from our everyday life, like finding the square root of the number of flowers in a student's garden or using our names in place of variables. All these years later I still remember how to balance equations!

If you are passionate and really care that students are there to learn, I consider that an expression of empathic concern and a true gift to your students. Full engagement from teachers is more likely to inspire full engagement from students. When I teach or give a talk, I take it as a personal challenge to keep my students engaged and participating. In my smaller, more intimate seminars, I make a point of noticing each student's eye color, which helps me hold a gaze with them just a little bit longer. I refer to each of them by name as much as possible. I'm constantly scanning the room, assessing facial expressions and body language to ensure I'm holding the attention of my class. I also allot time for some discussion so I'm not just hearing the sound of my own voice. I welcome the chance to listen by giving students a chance to express their opinions and ask questions.

The Future of Education

As educators wake up to the value of experiential methodologies, there is also a movement in the opposite direction toward digital learning. This is ironic since online classes seem to remove the human relationship and erase the empathic keys between students and teachers.

Massive open online courses, or MOOCS as they are typically called, are provided by organizations like Coursera, edX, or Canvas Network. This form of education started taking off right after the turn of the twenty-first century, and currently more than seven hundred universities from around the world, including prestigious institutions such as Harvard, Oxford, and Princeton, have launched free or low-cost online classes. Already nearly 60 million students have taken a course online, with some classes attracting hundreds and thousands of students.

Open access classes have the potential to democratize learning. They hold out promise and opportunity for millions of people who wouldn't otherwise have the chance to learn subject matter from some of the top professors in the world. For someone who is highly motivated and self-driven, online courses can help launch a new career and change lives.

But here's the problem. The majority of students have a tendency not to finish the courses they start online. Although millions of students signed up for classes through Coursera, the company and its university partners have awarded a meager 280,000 certificates of completion. In general, the rate of completion in MOOCS is about 15 percent. Harvard X and MITx report a completion rate of only 5.5 percent.

How can this be? Especially as all sorts of experts predict digital learning will soon replace face-to-face learning.

Unsurprisingly, surveys suggest that people prefer in-person training. Some students have limited computer literacy and have difficulty navigating the courses, or they don't know what to do when faced with technical problems. Others have trouble managing their time or staying self-motivated. But the biggest complaint? People miss teacher interaction. They find in-person classes a far more rewarding experience when they can ask questions or perhaps hear a few words of encouragement directly from the teacher and their fellow students. With all seven E.M.P.A.T.H.Y. keys missing, the experience seems to boil down to staring at a screen that doesn't talk back.

Yet I'm hopeful about the prospects of MOOCS, and I don't dismiss them as inferior. In the first place, there are some advantages to offering a self-paced learning option. It allows learners to spend as much time as they need on the curriculum, without any shame or embarrassment. In the second place, I think there are some easy ways to add some of the personal elements back into digital teaching. My own company, Empathetics, offers part of our curriculum online. And yes, we are teaching empathy!

Many online education companies have wisely taken a step back to consider how they can introduce a human element into the MOOC experience. They've come up with "blended" solutions that combine the best of online and real live human interactions. At Empathetics, our online courses are rich in video material, and we also offer learning communities live workshops to deepen the material and customize learning for specific audiences. Some platforms have added conference calls, video chats, and discussion boards. In the absence of direct access to professors, students can talk to each other in online discussion rooms.

I spoke with a woman recently who took an online writing course where the instructor created a chat room and held video conference calls for his more than twenty thousand enrollees. During one call, he chose her essay to read aloud and praised it as one of the best examples of writing he'd seen in years. This student felt proud and acknowledged. She considers this approval a huge gift in her education and says it gave her the confidence to launch what is now a prolific writing career. Even though he read only a single essay, he did something for the other students as well. He showed them that he was actually listening and that they were more than just a faceless, nameless mass of students. I can't prove this, but I suspect acknowledging the work of one student may have motivated more than a few to try harder in the hopes of gaining recognition for their own work.

In our Empathetics courses we take a similar approach, but we go even further. We have a team of experts who go on-site to "train the trainers" at other hospitals and clinics so that the e-learning aspects of our courses can be precisely tailored and customized to the needs of the learners, whether they are surgeons, primary care physicians, emergency room nurses, or frontline staff. Some of our material remains universal and offered online, while some of it can only be taught when teachers and students look each other in the eye and meet emotionally. This blended approach seems to be ideal, and I think for digital learning to succeed over time, it's the way it has to go.

Graduating Kids with Empathy: The ABCs

So far, we've been talking about creating an empathic learning environment. But what about creating empathic students?

Students treated with empathy will naturally be more inclined toward demonstrating empathy and compassion themselves. They have a better chance of developing a strong sense of social and emotional intelligence if they are taught by people who also possess these traits. Considering that by age five, kids are spending six to seven hours or more a day at school, their educational experience will have a great influence on their empathic tendencies. School ranks up right alongside parents and peers for teaching the lessons of both cognitive and emotional empathy. The ABCs of empathy you learned about in chapter 1 teach that students need to learn how to (A) acknowledge their own emotions and those of others, (B) learn to take deep breaths when emotionally triggered, and (C) develop curiosity when they don't understand another person's responses to gain more understanding and a chance to resolve differences.

The vast majority of people I meet who are happy in their careers had a teacher who awakened them to some inner potential or a realization that they were really good at something. Many of us had teachers who helped us on the journey to become who we wanted to become. What about you? Did you find one or more of your teachers to have empathy for you? Did he or she make the effort to connect with you? We remember these teachers because they cared. They cared not just about our grades for the course they were teaching, but many of the good ones cared about our whole lives. They helped us see the big picture, our potential, and that we had promise. Take a moment and reflect on what you are doing in your life, and try to find the teacher who may have set you on this path or helped you discover what you are meant to be doing with your life. That's the power of empathic teaching—there's almost nothing more important than this to make our lives hum with purpose and meaning.

I like this example from a Denville, New Jersey classroom, where the concepts of empathy were taught in very explicit terms: In this instance, the teacher presented middle-schoolers with a digital simulation game that assigned each player a character name and a backstory of either a migrant trying to cross the border into the US or a border patrol agent who was trying to stop illegal migration. Migrants stocked up on supplies and planned their route through a treacherous Arizona desert, often led by shifty guides who sometimes robbed them or left them stranded. If someone in their group became sick or injured, they had to make tough decisions: Should they carry them along or leave them behind? Meanwhile, the border patrol players tracked undocumented migrants not only to prevent them from crossing, but also to provide first aid and to collect the remains of the dead.

On the migrant side, this simulation forced students to think about what it is like to be part of a traditional out-group desperate to start anew. Based on real-life situations, migrants were only trying to survive and make their way to a better life. On the other hand, the students also understood the border patrol's point of view. Their goal was to protect their country from illegal immigration but also to offer aid and support to the very people they were trying to turn away. These are themes that test the empathy and understanding of many adults.

When students are asked to take both points of view—that is, to share the mind of the immigrant who wants a chance at a better life and also consider the border patrol's dilemma of allowing more people in the country than they believe can be adequately cared for—creative solutions to this crisis emerge. The danger of all-or-nothing thinking is that it can lead to both the easiest and the most problematic solutions. Such thinking is devoid of nuance, subtlety, and incremental solutions that address humanistic concerns while also ensuring that countries do not become overwhelmed. Asking students to grapple with complex dilemmas like this affords them opportunities to integrate several perspectives. When they grow up, we hope they remember these lessons to help make thoughtful and just decisions. Planting the seeds of empathy in early childhood education helps them become adults who understand human emotion, basic fairness, and justice.

I've seen empathy added into adult education as well. My friend Aviad Haramati, known to his friends as "Adi," leads the Center for Innovation and Leadership in Education (CENTILE) at Georgetown

University School of Medicine, which focuses on developing faculty educators. Adi has added mind-body physiology into the medical student curriculum, including tools for self-care such as mindful meditation and yoga—very progressive ideas in medical training. This program demonstrates a great opportunity to teach medical students to become more aware of their emotions and how they may reduce bias in interpretations, perceptions, and actions through reflective exercises and simulated situations. In addition to concerns about trainees' well-being, emotions may have a significant impact on clinicians' ability to perform at a high level. CENTILE has raised international awareness of this program by highlighting it in the conferences it has convened.

The courses I took at the Harvard Macy Institute also created instant communities. One of Director Elizabeth Armstrong's strokes of genius was to realize that medical educators need a sense of belonging. Having a lifelong peer group fosters collaboration and innovation. It provides a sense of support and belonging that was frankly missing from the day-to-day lives and overall careers of the educators she was teaching. Making life better for the teachers in turn made life better for the medical students and, ultimately, the patients they will care for. Armstrong explained that the instructors had to be taught how to teach and also receive affirmation to feel fulfilled. She recognized that excellent teaching needed to be recognized with awards and acknowledgment, to inspire and empower physician educators to prioritize excellent teaching as an integral goal of their chosen professions.

Empathy can also be designed into a curriculum in more subtle ways. While you may not remember all the details from your favorite stories, you likely do recall the overarching themes because of how the characters and their experiences touched your heart. Maybe, as a tyke, it was Dr. Seuss's Sneetches longing for stars on their bellies. Or when you were a middle-schooler, it was Harry Potter's ache for his lost family. Or as you entered high school, it was the fated love of Romeo and Juliet.

In many stories, you don't always know a character's mind, thought for thought, moment to moment, situation to situation. Because of this, you rely on your imagination to fill in the gaps to help grasp her intentions and motivations. When you truly connect with a character, it creates a psychological awareness you subconsciously carry into your own life. It shakes up your expectations and forces you to confront prejudices and stereotypes, moving you toward a better understanding of others: here is someone who may not think like you, but you can understand her thoughts and feelings. Now in your own life, when you encounter an unfamiliar or complicated individual, you may have an easier time relating to him because the novel's character has helped you practice the skills of empathy. We will explore the research supporting this in chapter 9, where we look at empathy's relationship to the arts and literature, including the findings of an excellent study on genres of literature.

In my work to enhance empathy in medical students, I've heard comments along the lines of "These are the skills people need to learn in kindergarten—why do we need to teach them now?" My answer is that many students did not learn empathy in kindergarten. On a happy note, the tide is starting to turn.

Curricula such as "Open Circle," where children are taught to express their own feelings and listen to the feelings of others, are now available in many elementary schools in the US. Programs like this teach kids that feelings matter, and that when expressed and listened to, hurt feelings are better understood and gradually they start to feel better. One grandmother whose grandchild went through an Open Circle program shared this with me: "I was at the sink doing the dishes when my five-year-old granddaughter was talking. She gently took my hand and said, 'Grandma, my teacher says that when people are talking you're supposed to look them in the eye like this . . . (and she guided me down to her eye level) and that helps you listen better.' She learned this in Open Circle."

This grandmother says her conversations with her granddaughter have taken a whole new turn. Now they listen to each other with their ears, their eyes, and also with their hearts. I believe it is never too late to learn these skills. And I wonder: What would our world be like if everyone learned to listen and respond to feelings in kindergarten?

Early educational opportunities to help others in need through service volunteering also appear to ignite empathic capacities in children. Cradles to Crayons is a nonprofit organization whose mission is to provide children living in homeless or low-income situations with clothing and essential items they need to thrive. Founder Lynn Margherio observes that families who introduce their children to volunteer work give their kids an opportunity to think about other children their own age who are in need. Children in affluent communities often have no exposure to those who live in poverty. Margherio shared this example: "A ten-year-old boy on the autism spectrum volunteered to help clean and sort shoes. On his way home, this boy, who is quite nonverbal, said to his mom, 'That was powerful.' His mom was taken aback—she didn't know he understood the word 'powerful.' But it was clear he did. When he got home, he organized all of his own shoes that he could donate. In that pile was a pair of brand new Nikes. He had begged for them, and when his mom asked if he was sure about donating them, he insisted that another boy have the chance to wear them. Cradles to Crayons sees empathy in action by young kids every day, because their parents give them a chance to flex that empathy muscle."

8

Texts, Screens, and Digital Empathy

Several years ago, the vicious online harassment of *Saturday Night Live* star Leslie Jones became a national story. Racist and misogynistic comments began flooding the African American comedian's social media feeds soon after she announced her starring role in an all-female remake of the movie *Ghostbusters*. The malicious attack culminated in Jones's website being hacked, her passport and nude pictures being leaked online, and the hackers posting an image comparing her to a gorilla.

The architects of the assault, including extreme right-wing internet troll Milo Yiannopoulos and his website Breitbart News, claimed in several articles that Jones was asking for it. She was active on social media, and as a famous person, she should have assumed she was fair game. Also, free speech. The tweet war raged on for days until Yiannopoulos and his army of digital hecklers were finally banned from Twitter for life.

Shallow Empathy

Trolling is the starkest example of how our digital screens are sending us sliding down a slippery slope to a loss of empathy. However, internet trolls are not the only ones who fail to see real humans behind their social media avatars and handles. It's often just "normal" people who leave careless, mean, or snide comments on Facebook. Our quick-hit culture makes it all too easy to send out a blast without considering the unintended effects.

As Emmy Award–winning journalist Frank Sesno puts it, "Digital communication, especially social media, oversimplifies and anonymizes everything, accentuating the exclamation points rather than question marks. It squeezes out complexity which makes it a perfect platform to hurl insults."

Sesno, a former CNN anchor who now directs the School of Media and Public Affairs at George Washington University, points out that funneling a large part of our communication through social media has had the surprising effect of segregating us rather than bringing us together. Thanks to creations such as Facebook groups, text chains, and Twitter lists, it is much easier to create information bubbles and closed communities. "For the first time in history anyone can reach thousands of others all at once," he says. "It accelerates discourse while at the same time puts it through a strainer to filter out anything we don't want to hear."

Adding to the breakdown in empathic communication, people now consume their information differently than they used to, preferring shorter and more frequent bursts of data rather than absorbing knowledge in longer stretches. We know, for example, that college students read less today than students of the past. The rapid dipping in and out of social media platforms, texts, and comment sections conditions the human brain for shorter, quicker interactions. Using quick hits for information gathering leads to a more simplistic and shallow understanding of subjects compared to the past. The accelerated pace at which we attempt to process huge volumes of material leads to quicker leaps of judgment.

Thinking back to the E.M.P.A.T.H.Y. tools from chapter 4—eye contact, muscles of facial expressions, body language, tone of voice, and knowing the emotions of others—these important cues vanish when we converse through our devices. Without the empathic keys to guide us, we are robbed of the opportunity to process the emotional context of our interactions. Without realizing it, you probably have become a less empathic communicator. If you've ever unfriended someone on Facebook or "ghosted" a relationship by failing to respond to repeated reaching out, you've been shielded from the emotional reactions of the person on the other end of the transaction.

Stop for a moment and consider why big business deals are almost always done face to face rather than by text or email. In theory, you could wrap up the entire transaction by email. But as I mentioned earlier in the book, when millions and billions of dollars are at stake, business partners still want to look each other in the eye so each can assess the other person's honesty, integrity, and genuineness through facial expressions, tone of voice, and body language before they sign on the dotted line. Empathic cues are essential to understanding a business partner's desires and intentions. Any time a person on the other side of the negotiating table averts her gaze or crosses her arms, she's leaving emotional breadcrumbs for you to follow. It could be a sign that she's not on board with something, she's holding back some key bit of data, or perhaps she's not being completely honest with you.

So why, then, are so many people comfortable dating purely by text? Are affairs of the heart any less important than matters of money? There's a strong disconnection here. I have witnessed people who date exclusively through text, and when the texts dry up, they know the relationship is over. We are missing so much human information by having our emotions and intentions reduced to letters on a keyboard.

Digital media is a far more ambiguous way to have a conversation. We still get a whiff of the affect, but we don't know if the emotion we infer from a text or a tweet is accurate. With the face, voice tone, and body absent, we're forced to pay more attention to details like delays in response. When talking on the phone, you at least have verbal clues such as pauses and silences to go on, and you can ask for clarification when you hear one. But if someone ignores a text or you don't get enough likes on a Facebook post, you leap to your own conclusions. It is very confusing when you can't see behind the curtain to ascertain what the other person is thinking. Is she busy? Did his iPhone fall into a puddle? Was my last text offensive? Will I ever hear from her again?

All of these uncertainties can be spinning around in your mind just because someone didn't answer a text or post right away, leaving you with a sense of insecurity. Meanwhile, the person on the other end of the communication may have no idea her delayed response is causing so much emotional distress because there is a parallel inability to consider what you might be feeling as you wait for a reply. There is no opportunity to provide an empathic response because there's no recognition that one is needed. This can stir up a tremendous amount of uncertainty about other people's emotions and wreak havoc on relationships.

The steady stream of perfectly dressed and coiffed friends at beaches, ski slopes, parties, and vacations who run through our social media feeds also contributes to growing insecurity. It suggests that life for everyone else is seamless and effortless, making your own (real) life pale in comparison. As a friend of mine recently observed, "Everyone seems to post the photos of the vacation *they wished they had* rather than the real trip they took, the one with missed planes, rained-out tours, and arguments." This cropped, Photoshopped, and Instagram-filtered view into the lives of others can leave us with a feeling that our real lives are somehow inadequate and we should strive to live up to the same parade of perfection.

The Changing Brain

The information superhighway is changing our brains and how we relate to one another. With conversations now zipping along at warp speed, there is little time to reflect or consider how they land before firing back responses. Little by little, this sort of shallow interaction chips away at our empathic capacities. I don't mean to minimize the many advantages of technology. It allows me to FaceTime my kids when they're halfway around the world and schedule meetings in a heartbeat. However, we are spending an extraordinary amount of time on our screens. The Kaiser Family Foundation reports that eight- to eighteen-year-olds spend an average of 11.5 hours a day using technology. Older American adults spend 5 hours a day on digital devices and an additional 4.5 hours watching TV. The average mobile phone owner checks her phone once every 6.5 minutes—more than 150 times a day.

All that screen time appears to be altering the way the brain works, starting with the brain's reward systems. Phones and other digital devices deliver a collective addiction to dopamine, creating a virtual sense of social connection that hits the brain with every text and social media "like," "comment," and "share." The flood of neurochemicals creates cravings for these bursts of attention and makes us constantly attend to our phones to experience the next "hit." Several studies have noted that the mere sound of an incoming notification releases more dopamine than reading the actual content of the message. As the human brain becomes more accustomed to rapid and short bursts of information, there is speculation that attention spans will be increasingly challenged and shortened.

When life is constantly punctuated by the pings of text and messaging signals, we fail to be fully present with others. Face-to-face interactions begin to fade as screen-to-screen conversation becomes the norm. A recent *Time* magazine survey on "digital natives"—people born into the internet era—found that 54 percent of them agreed with the statement "I prefer texting people rather than talking to them," compared with 28 percent of those born before the internet ruled the world. In fact, the mere physical presence of a digital device creates communication problems. In one series of experiments, University of Essex psychologists found that having a mobile phone on a table between two people chatting was highly distracting and disrupted the flow of their conversations. Other objects such as books and notebooks didn't diminish the subjects' feelings of closeness and connectedness the same way a phone did.

Studies find that people in their teens and twenties already struggle with understanding the emotions of others. When shown facial expressions, they are challenged to identify the different emotions represented. Young people are still developing the capacity for empathy and the ability to understand another person's emotional point of view. The teenage brain is already primed to be at least somewhat unempathic because the teen years are typically self-focused years. Spending so much time staring at a screen and so little time looking at real faces may interfere with the development of basic empathy skills, such as maintaining eye contact or noticing subtle changes in facial expressions that can range from confusion to anger to disgust all during one conversation.

Middle-aged and older digital "immigrants" are also not immune to digital down-regulation of empathy. Though empathy can be learned, it can also be unlearned. By logging inordinate amounts of screen time daily, we may be desensitizing ourselves to the nonverbal cues of empathy and creating our own empathy deficits. When our brains become rewired to dissociate from human experience, we lose a part of our humanity, undermining the ability to create a real connection with people in our lives. Everyone loses out when this happens.

Because gazing into a screen removes inputs such as eye contact, posture, affect, tone of voice, reflective listening, and just about every other component of nonverbal communication from the equation, we lose all the important emotional cues. Without them we are left with words on a screen and no way to parse emotional subtleties. It is hard to listen empathically, and we don't witness the reaction of the person with whom we are communicating. This creates a growing sense of detachment, desensitization, and emotional indifference that increases the likelihood of misunderstandings and feelings of isolation, loneliness, and powerlessness.

I don't think it's an accident that the rise of the mindfulness movement has paralleled the rise of electronic communication. Mindfulness seems to be, at least in part, a response to the emotional dysregulation that comes from a lack of experiencing empathic understanding. Taking a yoga class, meditating, or going for a walk can serve as a way to manage the anxiety of the confusing emotions that come from our increasingly flat style of relating to one another on devices.

We know that for people to feel empathy toward one another, they can't be in a constant state of emotional distress. They can't be open to what others are experiencing when they are expending all their efforts managing their own stress hormone levels and fight-or-flight responses, so they need techniques such as diaphragmatic breathing and mindful awareness to identify when they are experiencing an emotion, to name it, and to decide how to react, rather than allow knee-jerk responses that they will later regret.

What Drives Keyboard Trolls?

High-profile trolling incidents like the Leslie Jones example often make the headlines. But as we all know, any one of us is vulnerable to online harassment. Cyberbullying has reached epidemic proportions. Nearly half of all internet users report being the target of online mistreatment of some kind, according to a recent Refinery29 survey. When you separate users age eighteen to twenty-nine, that figure rises to nearly 70 percent. Dosomething.org reports that nearly 43 percent of kids younger than eighteen have been bullied online, with one in four saying they've experienced more than one episode.

Bullies, well known to have little empathy, have existed since the beginning of time. The internet simply allows them to slink about with ease and anonymity. And social media makes it possible to weaponize unkindness. Keyboard trolls can spread their nasty opinions like bullets onto Twitter, Facebook, Instagram, Snapchat, YouTube, reddit, Tumblr, Barstool, and dozens of other social media platforms. Haters broadcast their hate on any piece of digital real estate they can log on to.

We know that the vast majority of internet trolls are men, and many of them are under the age of thirty. Often young men who cyberbully may not yet have fully developed the capacity to understand the consequences of their actions. I'm not excusing their behavior, but neuroscience has confirmed that the brain is not fully developed until well into the mid-twenties, especially in males. Teenagers are also prone to peer pressure and emotion contagion in general. They often lack the sophistication to understand what may be driving their aggression toward others. There are teens who wouldn't think of leveling such cruelty on another person by themselves, but if condoned or egged on by a bully through emotion contagion, they may join the gang because it has become a norm. Unfortunately, these traits can persist long after the teenage years have faded.

Interviews with internet trolls are shocking in that they reveal these online agitators don't tend to view their victims as real people. Even though their harassment can ruin lives, and in extreme cases, drive their target to suicide, web bullies don't seem to care; bullying makes them feel empowered instead of helpless. They tend to be antisocial by nature and often lack the real-world social and emotional skills to resolve interpersonal conflicts—online or off. In a recent study, Canadian researchers who cross-referenced online personality tests with trolling behavior discovered that trolls tend to score off the charts for the "Dark Tetrad," a term that was coined to describe four overlapping personality traits including narcissism, psychopathy, sadism, and a manipulative deceptiveness known as Machiavellianism.

With no social cues to process, a keyboard troll cannot witness the fearful looks, tears, or defensive postures that might deter him. If the victim does manage to express the pain and suffering the attack causes, the troll can simply block the feedback. The more removed he becomes from his victim, the more he can dehumanize her and the easier it is for him to justify his bullying. He may come to believe that the object of his ire is not deserving of kindness or respect, and in extreme cases, he can convince himself that mistreating or even destroying her is actually the right thing to do.

We know that victims of online harassment often feel depressed, anxious, and defeated as a result of the abusive experience. Trolls appear to pay a psychological price too. If we think about these feelings as a mirror of what the cyberbully feels internally, we may get a glimpse of a person who feels powerless, anxious, and depressed and who knows no other outlet than to provoke such feelings in others. Rather than act as an outlet for pent-up frustration, trolling, while temporarily generating feelings of power, seems to be self-defeating, resulting in increased depression, loneliness, and isolation.

Shame often beats within the heart of the internet bully. (You feel guilt when you know you've done something wrong whereas shame comes from feeling that there is something wrong with you.) Shame is often the consequential emotion that arises from mistreatment by others, such as neglect, abandonment, constant exposure to ridicule, or physical, emotional, or sexual abuse. People who live on the margins and believe they will never find their own in-group are more prone to feel shame and become bullies. Some find their own precarious offline social standing and potential exclusion emotionally intolerable and engage in internet antics to maintain a connection with a perceived in-group. We ignore this pain at our own peril. Left unchecked, it can be leveled toward others with dire consequences.

Lindy West, a well-known comedian and writer, took a brave and uncommon approach by unwittingly turning the tables on the more desperate and lonely aspects of troll psychology. She decided to write an article about the pain she felt after a particularly pernicious online attack. In a long post for *The Guardian*'s website, West described how hurtful it was to have a troll stalk her through cyberspace, making disparaging remarks about everything from her writing to her appearance.

To her surprise, the troll wrote her a letter of apology, explaining he never considered the real person he'd been assailing until he read her piece. When they eventually spoke by telephone, he confessed that his own feelings of inadequacy and lack of self-esteem had driven him to be so vicious toward her. West came to pity the man. They ultimately met and shared an understanding of each other's humanity beyond their internet avatars.

"I didn't mean to forgive him, but I did," she writes.

This shows a rare glimmer of empathy on both sides of the trolling equation. For West's troll, hurling barbs on social media was an exercise in throwing darts at a dartboard. You don't stop to consider whether the dartboard feels pain; you're just trying to hit the bull's eye. Perhaps he was acting out of loneliness and pent-up rage, but when West bared her soul in an act of self-empathy, it made him realize his digital darts were landing sharply on a real person.

Given the extremely antisocial nature of the troll mentality, I'm not sure West's story is a typical, generalizable example. Usually I think it's best not to feed the troll, as the saying goes. Though trolls tend to cover their tracks and make it difficult to trace their real identities, there are anti-cyberbullying laws in many states. If trolls become too threatening or dangerous, they can be reported to the authorities. Perhaps responding with an emoji police car may jolt his prefrontal cortex and reasoning capabilities into considering the consequences. Another approach could be to take advantage of a trait research has found to be intolerable among bullies: boredom. When a cyberbully's craving for a response is frustrated, it may motivate him to move on. Because we cannot count on most trolls to respond like the one who tormented West, the better part of valor may be to ignore the behavior.

A Picture Is Worth a Thousand Emotions

We need new ways to interpret emotion in the age of sound bites. Enter the hieroglyphics of yellow smiles, smirks, and frowns.

The use of emojis in digital communication to depict emotional empathy developed surprisingly quickly after text messaging began to take off. At the start of the text revolution, people used emoticons to represent basic feelings and intentions. This is when you type a colon, then a dash, then a parenthesis to represent a smiley face. Then in 1999, Shigetaka Kurita, a Japanese economist, created the first emoji as part of a team that set out to revolutionize Japan's means of communication. The traditional way people in Japan speak to one another in person and through handwritten letters is traditionally lengthy, full of praise and respect, and laden with good will. Kurita realized that keyboard messages stripped people of the ability to express themselves in ways they were accustomed to, leading to miscommunication and widespread communication breakdowns.

It's precisely because humans rely on the seven keys of empathy that, without evidence of eye contact and facial expressions, postures, or tone of voice and murmurs, we soon find ourselves lost. Without emojis to intuit emotional context, we risked a style of communication that was devoid of empathy. Emojis function as analogs to tone of voice and body language. Of the 3.2 billion people in the world who now have regular internet access, studies show that 92 percent regularly use emojis. Regardless of native tongue, emojis appear to provide universal clues to emotion and intent.

It's fortunate we have emojis to guide us through the potential emotional minefields that digital communication has created. Perhaps we'd be lost without them. We can't communicate without them, but do they go far enough? Are they still creating ambiguity when someone needs you to relate? When you look at most people's text chains, emails, and social media posts, they're full of smiley faces and looks of surprise. The repertoire quickly moves beyond facial expressions to thumbs-up, hearts, and "like" buttons that symbolize even greater nuance of thought and feeling. Now we have everything from unicorns to hashtags to short moving clips known as gifs to help us reintroduce some of the intended emotions back into digital messaging.

There aren't enough data at this point in time to be certain, but we can surmise that seeing a bright yellow smiley face probably activates neural circuits for happiness and likely gets your brain to light up in a similar way as when you see an actual happy face in front of you. But emojis aren't a substitute for true empathy. Is a sad face really the appropriate response to a breakup? A post about a death in the family? While they do seem to convey some of the emotional intent and provide some clarity of meaning, emojis are not perfect analogs to emotions.

I see, for example, a confusing array of reactions to things like social media posts. Why did five people click the heart button underneath the cat video on YouTube but one person clicked the angry face? Is it rude to leave a thumbs-up on a Facebook post if everyone else leaves a heart? And do you invite trouble if pressing the like button on a tweet risks violating your workplace's social media policy?

Emojis may not yet go far enough. Perhaps we need another level of emotional emojis to trigger true empathy: something that says, "I need to talk" or asks, "Can you talk now?" The problem with the way we use emojis now is that they convey a feeling but they are not very accurate about what the feeling might mean, nor do they say anything about a person's emotional needs. I fear that people are still seeking an emotional response with these little pictographs, but the emotional risk of exposing this need may be too great. If you send a picture of a frustrated face, the receiver may understand you are frustrated but might not be able to pick up that you are so frustrated you are about to cry. There is no way to distinguish exactly what response you are looking for. I also worry that in today's digital world, taking the risk of expressing not just your emotion but also your emotional need might feel like too much of an imposition.

Human communication using facial expressions has been challenged since the advent of the telephone. With the shift to digital messaging, new technologies such as Bitmoji—personalized avatars that allow you to portray yourself the way you want the world to see you—are emerging to add facial emotional expression to refine communication. The line between you and your digital self is quickly disappearing.

Some new technology is already experimenting with facial recognition software that maps the face to generate personalized emojis. Some have developed the capability to customize animated messages that use your voice and reflect your facial expressions in real time. Such advances in technology reveal the fact that people who communicate via text and email are continuing to seek more precise ways of communicating and responding to feelings. Because empathy and compassion rely so heavily on the seven keys of empathy, ever more sophisticated software will continue to develop until greater empathic accuracy is possible.

One has to wonder how much time, effort, and money will be spent trying to imitate what human beings are so uniquely poised to do: perceive and respond to the emotional needs of one another. It will be a sad day indeed if these humanizing traits are someday expected to be fully relegated to machines. While advances will continue to be made, do you really want your doctor or nurse, teacher or lawyer to be a robot? Hopefully machines will always be there to assist with communication but will not replace the heart and soul of what it means to be human. In our society's ongoing thirst for new technology, I hope we never forget the comfort of the human touch, the warmth of a hug, or the knowing glance from your friend that lets you know she saw what happened from your perspective. We all need to know we are not alone in this world and that we are lovable—and that's something machines will not be replacing any time soon.

9

Empathy, Art, and Literature

The night before Alan Alda started to work on *M*A*S*H*, a show about a medical unit on the front lines of the Korean War and one of the longest-running television comedies in US history, he had a face-to-face meeting with the show's creators.

"I wanted to make sure they weren't going to treat it like a dimwitted comedy," the actor recalls. "Where the war was taking place on stage and these were just hijinks at the front, I hoped—I didn't just hope, I wanted to get their agreement—that we were going to show the war for what it was. That it was a place where people got hurt. I remember thinking here we have surgeons—so if you don't show us doing their work, it is not true to the lives that real people lived."

When I asked Alda why this was so important to him, he told me that trivializing war makes it easier to start the next one. "If it not only seems like a place where you can be glorious and show how brave you are but you actually show that it is a fun place to be, then you've taken away all of the sense that you should think twice before joining up in a war."

What Alda is saying, if I may attempt to translate the words of this brilliant multiple Emmy award–winning actor, is that he wanted to inspire empathy and that empathy can play a key role in changing hearts and minds. *M*A*S*H* was indeed based on real physicians, nurses, and soldiers who served in the Korean War. He knew that to make light of their life experiences would do a disservice to both the inspirations for the characters and the show's audience. Witty writing and great acting aside, one of the biggest reasons this sitcom about war was so powerful and beloved was because viewers were able to relate to what they saw on the screen and imagine themselves in the government-issue boots of these brave men and women.

Alda goes on to say, "Viewing a piece of artwork or a moving performance is like hitting the refresh button on how you see the world. I think theater arts or novels where there are rich characters and a rich authentic emotional world refresh me emotionally for the rest of the day. And even the next day I feel better about things. Because we've been in the company of people who were coping with strong emotions. We are humanized by one another. Like when people are crying or laughing together in a theater, it is such an extraordinary experience."

So let's talk about art and how it can help us understand, feel, and express empathy—and perform that reset on how we see the world. And when I say art, I'm not talking only about Italian films, German operas, and French paintings that hang in museums. Artists, and consumers of art, come from all walks of life and every socioeconomic stratum. Shakespeare may seem high-minded by today's standards, but remember—he originally wrote for the common masses. Exactly what art is and means depends upon who you are. Some of us love sculpture and theater and jazz. Others may love modern dance or graffiti art and comic books. When art is at its best, no matter where it comes from or who the audience is, there is nothing more powerful to move society toward a more empathic stance.

The Science of Empathy Through Art

Empathy and the arts have a long-shared history. In fact, it was the aesthetician Robert Vischer in the late nineteenth century who first used the German word "Einfühlung" to describe how observers of artworks project their own feelings onto the creation of the artist, allowing them to appreciate and experience the beauty and emotions that the aesthetic experience elicited. The philosopher of aesthetics Theodore

Lipps extended this concept to interpersonal understanding and used the term as similar to the older notion of sympathy. German philosopher, psychologist, and sociologist Wilhelm Dilthey then broadened the use of the term to describe the process by which one person comes to know how another person thinks and feels, which we have already defined as theory of mind. Edward Titchener, a British-American philosopher, ultimately coined the English term "empathy" by translating it from the original German word. In doing so, his intention was to convey the human capacity for introspection and ability to enter the emotional state of others that went beyond "sympathy," which today means feeling bad *for* someone else's suffering. The "em" prefix to the word empathy referred to entering *into* another's suffering by understanding her thoughts and feeling her pain *as if it were the observer's own*, thus feeling *with* another.

With the arts we revert to the origins of empathy—in Einfühlung—as it relates to the viewer's feeling emotionally impacted and moved by the art. We often value art by how well it evokes emotions. These aren't necessarily emotions that were felt by the artist, but woven into a work by either craft or circumstance to evince a visceral feeling in us. Unlike empathy as we see it in daily life (I watch someone get hurt and feel her pain), there is a process for the artist in creating the emotion. Unless captured in a photo of a moment—such as a child being carried out of the rubble of his home in Syria or the iconic photo of Carl Yastrzemski willing a home run ball to stay fair—the artist knows what emotion he wants to impart and then hopes to convey that to the viewer. Sometimes we feel that emotion, and sometimes we feel something similar or maybe quite different.

There is often another layer that adds complexity to the message. In the case of the theater, multiple people—the playwright, the director, the actors, the audience, and even the theater critic—join forces, and that can change the message because of the different perspectives each one brings to the work of art. With an image, the artistry that evokes the emotion may be a shadow in a doorway or the way the subject holds himself. For a song, it's a line or the pathos in the singer's voice that implies soulfulness. In drama, it is a phrase that may be written and rewritten and rehearsed and performed with skill. However, art is incomplete without the perceptual and emotional involvement of the viewer. As Alois Riegl of the Vienna School of Art History at the turn of the twentieth century noted, the viewer collaborates with the artist of a painting by interpreting what he sees on the canvas in personal terms, thereby adding meaning to the picture. He called this phenomenon the "beholder's share."

Art is so closely tied to our empathic capacities because it is an exercise in perception and response, similar to a person-to-person interaction. In all forms of art, the beholder blends his experience with what he sees and hears in communication with the artist. Viewing visual imagery such as a painting, for example, relies on eye contact with the work of art, which in and of itself may be enough to evoke an empathic response. When the viewer opens his eyes to seeing what is on the canvas, he finds a window into both the subject's and the artist's inner world. Neurologically speaking, this is very similar to the way the brain processes a human face through eye contact.

The arts draw people together in public and private spheres to share human stories and experiences. I recall standing in front of the Great Buddha in Kamakura, Japan—a moment that changed my life. Built in 1252, this sculpture towers over forty feet above the Japanese seascape where a sacred temple once stood. The peace and tranquility emanating from the Buddha's face stopped me with the power of an ocean wave delivered as softly as a feather. The force of this peaceful feeling seemed to affect every person in the public square. I had a similar, though opposite, experience the first time I viewed Picasso's *Guernica*, his political rebuke of the Nazi bombing of the Basque town of Guernica during the Spanish Civil War. Through brush strokes, shapes, and shades of neutral colors, he was able to portray the tragedy of war and the suffering it inflicts. It stirred so much disturbance and compassion within me that it's part of the reason I became a doctor.

Have you had a similar experience? If so, you've had a very human response to art that, neurologically speaking, dates back to cave paintings and the beginning of our species. Being human comes with an urge to express or respond to art in some form. Living without this expression, the way people serving time in prison do, can be an impoverished and alienating existence. Art is a great unifier, transporting us from a very self-focused point of view to an understanding that there are broader ways to experience and perceive the world.

I had the privilege and pleasure of speaking with Eric Kandel, the neuroscientist at Columbia University who received the joint Nobel Prize in 2000 in Physiology or Medicine for discoveries concerning signal transduction in the nervous system. He describes beautifully the phenomenon of connecting to art on a visceral level in his book *The Age of Insight*:

"Our response to art stems from an irrepressible urge to re-create in our own brains the creative process—cognitive, emotional, and empathic—through which the artist produced the work. . . . This creative urge of the artist and of the beholder presumably explains why essentially every group of human beings in every age in every place throughout the world has created images, despite the fact that art is not a physical necessity for survival.

"Art is an inherently pleasurable and instructive attempt by the artist and the beholder to communicate and share with each other the creative process that characterizes every human brain—a process that leads to the Aha! moment, the sudden recognition that we have seen into another person's mind, and that allows us to see the truth underlying both the beauty and the ugliness depicted by the artists."

When I spoke to Kandel recently, I found it interesting to hear his views on the interaction between art and the viewer of art.

"As a scientist I've taken a reductionist approach to learning. I discovered the molecular biology of learning occurred through modulation of neurotransmitter release. I've always been impressed by what we learn from a reductionist's point of view. The work of Mark Rothko, the abstract expressionist, in his painting of vivid and bright stripes of color—they are so powerful because at first they look like one color, until you see that each stripe is superimposed on a series of others. The one stripe is made up of many others and your perception varies. The more you look the more you see," he says.

In the ambiguity of art, the beholder brings his share to the experience. Through the changes in the brain transformed by the art we witness, we have an invitation to see the world as more layered, more nuanced, and more connected. Art may indeed be the greatest connector for our divided world. It is the essence of empathy.

How Art Builds Empathy

Making art is an act of sharing. It is by definition an invitation to the rest of us to participate in the artist's experience and draw our own conclusions. This shared experience transports the resting brain, a surprisingly active state known as the default mode network, into a less self-focused and more curious state of mind. It opens up the right hemisphere of the brain, which is less involved in task performance and where imagination and creativity are born, enabling us to process whatever the artist is trying to evoke or whatever we project onto the piece of art.

Bridging a link between the creator and the viewer forges a connection to the joy, fear, pain, or any other emotion we universally share. An emotionally moving piece of art can make you *feel* something *before you think* something. It grabs you with a gesture, a facial expression, a movement, a color, or a word. Think about the Van Gogh painting *Starry Night*. Critics say the artist's swirls of paint, texture, and color evoke a turbulent quest to overcome his mental illness. The village is painted with dark colors, but the brightly lit windows create a sense of comfort. Maybe you felt those things without ever reading an art history book.

Imagination is the first step in building empathy: How can I develop empathy for you if I can't imagine what it's like to be you? The arts provide the domain where imagination can take root and flourish. The power of art lies in its ability to stimulate both cognitive (thinking) and affective (feeling) empathy. When we observe a work of art, we bring to it all of our memories, perspective, and experiences and project them on to what we see or read. Through this interplay of the artist's craft and our individual experiences, we stimulate the emotional centers of the brain. The degree to which we are moved is an indication of the artist's ability to expand our senses. It takes us outside the self and offers a different perspective. In some cases, it lifts us from our own mood or state of mind. At other times, it helps us temporarily perceive someone else's pain, sadness, joy, surprise, or anger.

I met Diane Paulus when I was her camp counselor at Interlochen Music Camp in Michigan. Already as a ten-year-old, she made an indelible impression on me with her dynamic core that sparked openness and creativity in everyone around her. Now she is the Tony Award–winning artistic director of the American Repertory Theater at Harvard University. She offered this wonderful explanation of how a truly transformative work of art always takes the audience's point of view into account and how that translates into feelings of empathy.

"What are we hoping to communicate, provoke, and transform?" she asks. "I have a great belief in audience desire for a profound learning experience. This drives me as an artist. Our mission at the American Repertory Theater is to expand the boundaries of theater. There is a human need for ritual, moving in time and space together in a group, a human need for diversion, to go from a place and be diverted from everyday life, taken on a journey, and a need for spectacle, to see ourselves in the presence of something larger."

Paulus goes on to say that the idea is to move from the heart to the mind.

"For the audience, we're getting to a deeper level of the possibility of empathy because as an audience they are not so able, so quick to say, 'That's not me,' 'I don't like that,' and 'I don't recognize that and I'm walking away.' It's not about information—we have more than we can possibly use, and after a while we become numb to it. It is about motivating compassion for that person's story. I think of it as sort of an empathy on steroids and empathy through history." It is precisely because of this important role of the arts in society that support for the National Endowment for the Arts is so critically important. The arts lift us from our own experience to that of our fellow sisters and brothers.

Alda has a similar explanation. He says he thinks of art as a kind of shared humanity.

"Nothing stimulates more empathy than shared suffering," he says. "For me it's the communication that happens between actors and the audience that is the essence, I have come to believe, of what happens between two people trying to communicate."

We find art being used as an effective bridge to empathy in some unexpected places. My friend New York artist Melissa Kraft recalls that medical students at Columbia University were required to take a visual arts seminar in medical school, not to learn about the art itself but to study the faces and bodies of those portrayed and to imagine their stories, their problems, and their lives. The idea, of course, was to inspire empathy in the students. It was a popular seminar despite being "required," and was so pertinent to what will be required of future doctors.

The practice of integrating the arts in medical education has become a priority at Harvard Medical School and many other medical schools around the country.

In 2011 several faculty members at Harvard Medical School formed the Arts and Humanities Initiative to sponsor cultural events. While many medical students and physicians were engaged in writing, playing music, and other extracurricular artistic pursuits, they believed the benefits of these activities belonged front and center in their medical careers. Suzanne Koven, a founding member of the Arts and Humanities Initiative and a Writer in Residence at Massachusetts General Hospital, explains, "Mindfully looking at a painting or closely reading a poem can improve our ability to observe, interpret, and communicate and increase our capacity for empathy—all of which makes us better clinicians. Personally, I know that what I learned reading novels as an English major in college has helped me more as a clinician than studying biochemistry and physics did." Integrating the arts is possibly a way to humanize almost any industry, and could be a gateway to enhancing empathy.

It comes down to this: art can move an empathic idea from the emotional into the cognitive. When art evokes a strong enough emotion, we want to share that experience, often inspiring words and actions. What's really interesting is that art, almost by definition, is a shared experience. When we go to a museum, theater, or concert, we often go in a group and talk about what we see, hear, and feel. Sometimes we just stand together in silence and let the shared feelings crackle through the air like electricity. A song that you listen to on your drive alone to work or a photo you see while surfing the web is a culturally shared experience of a type that has been known to start local, national, and even global conversations.

The Evidence for Art Inspiring Empathy

Scientific research, though currently sparse, is beginning to prove this connection between empathy and art. In 2013, for example, researchers at The New School in New York City examined whether reading literary fiction builds a capacity to understand what others are thinking and feeling. In a series of five groundbreaking studies, they asked groups of people to either refrain from reading or to read excerpts from different types of material ranging in genre from popular fiction, to nonfiction, to literary fiction. After they finished reading, the subjects were tested on their ability to infer other people's thoughts and emotions. The participants took the "reading the mind in the eyes" test, in which they were asked to select which of four emotion terms most closely match the expression of a person in a photograph. Those who were more deeply read in literary fiction scored higher when inferring others' feelings, a faculty, as I've explained in earlier chapters, known as theory of mind.

Reading literary fiction led to higher scores on theory of mind testing than popular fiction, the researchers found. They concluded that this was so because the richness and depth of the literary characters taught readers to predict and interpret their motivations and mental states. Action and adventure genre stories did this to a far lesser extent. Those who read pop fiction such as Danielle Steel's *The Sins of the Mother*, or nothing at all, did not raise their empathy scores from baseline. But those who read Louise Erdrich's *The Round House*, the tale of a Native American boy's coming of age in the wake of a brutal, racist attack on his mother, improved their test results markedly. This is not to say that literary fiction is necessarily better than all other types of writing but only to point out that the way a story is told can have an influence on how we perceive the social interactions of its characters. In its subtle way, literary fiction teaches you that not everyone thinks the way you do.

The results of these studies comport with my own observations from teaching. As these studies show, pop fiction tends to focus more on action and excitement versus complex emotional journeys. The characters' emotions in pop fiction are often painted in broad strokes and to a large extent they're predictable. This tends to play into the reader's confirmation bias of how people will react in certain situations. By contrast, literary fiction goes deeper into the minds of its characters and the complexity of their relationships. When using literature or poetry written by William Carlos Williams, Abraham Verghese, Perri Klass, or Rafael Campo in courses for medical students, we're privy to their characters' inner dialogues and pushed to think about what their intentions and motivations might be, allowing students to confront prejudice and stereotypes and often upending the view of someone from outside their own in-groups.

The New School experiments seem to suggest that this psychological enlightenment can carry over into real-world thinking. Related studies at the State University of New York at Buffalo expanded this idea by demonstrating that people who read the Harry Potter books were more likely to self-identify as wizards and people who read the Twilight series were more likely to self-identify as vampires.

Wizardry and vampires don't truly exist (as far as I know), but the researchers found that readers suspended this disbelief long enough to speculate that belonging to one of these fictional communities—out-groups to the rest of us—may offer similar emotional bonds that people get from affiliations with real-life in-groups. They provide the opportunity for social connection and the satisfaction of becoming a part of something larger. Indeed, brain scan explorations reveal that the part of the brain we use to understand narrative stories overlaps with the part of the brain used when exercising theory of mind, one of the foundations of cognitive empathy.

As I mentioned earlier, empirical research into how art inspires emotions and builds empathy is still in early phases. Kandel is conducting his own empirical experiments on art and empathy at Columbia University, where he and his team are examining responses to figurative, transitional, and abstract art. In figurative art, we see realistic renderings of people and places and things—a face looks like a face. Abstract art uses shapes, color, and textures to evoke an image that calls a face to mind, but needs the imagination, such as Picasso and Braque's cubist portraits. Transitional art is somewhere in between. Think of the gauzy and muted shapes of impressionist paintings. There is no exact likeness, but you can see the images. Kandel notes in his book that our brain devotes more neurons to reading the details of faces than to any other object.

Psychologist Paul Ekman provided emotional facial expression images for my research group's empathy training research at Massachusetts General Hospital. We hypothesized that because reading facial expressions accurately is so critical to our empathic capacities, we needed to add face training to our empathy training curriculum. Our studies showed that doctors exposed to face training (in addition to the other interventions in our courses) received higher empathy scores by patients rating them than those who were not exposed to the empathy training intervention. Our research confirms the important influence that accurate detection of facial expressions has on eliciting empathy from caregivers. Kandel's fascination with facial expression in the Viennese art of the 1900s is largely kindled by the nuanced and subtle facial expressions that belie more psychological and emotional workings in the subjects. Kandel is looking at the different psychological responses to these different types of imagery. Through neuroimaging studies, the Columbia team hopes to examine what happens in the brain when someone is moved by a piece of art and how this relates to their emotional responses in real life. It's a new frontier that I am confident will yield some fascinating results and give us a clearer road map for how we can incorporate different types of artistic endeavors into empathy training for individuals and communities.

Another exciting way art can inspire empathy is through virtual reality (VR). I met film and theater actor and writer Jane Gauntlett in France at the Cannes Festival of Creativity, where we presented together on the science and art of empathy. Jane wrote and produced *In My Shoes* using virtual reality technology. She suffered a severe brain injury after being attacked on her bicycle. Through a miraculous recovery that still left her with debilitating seizures, Jane realized there was a disconnection between what her neurologists felt was "a good outcome" and how she was feeling. Although she was almost seizure free, her mind wasn't functioning at her creative level while on anti-seizure medications. So motivated was Jane to communicate her experience to her doctors that she wrote and produced a virtual reality experience through VR goggles that allowed others to experience what it is like to have a seizure. The In My Shoes Project is a collection of audio/audiovisual experiences. I donned the goggles when we were together in France—eager to experience this firsthand. What I felt was so realistic that I had to remove the goggles three-quarters of the way into the VR experience because I felt symptoms of nausea and disorientation. Jane succeeded in translating her experience to her doctors and now shares it with medical students throughout England and internationally. This is how we build empathy.

The Chicken or the Egg

Psychological experts often ask whether exposure to literature and the arts can make you a more empathic person, or whether it is the other way around: Are art lovers simply more sensitive souls, predisposed to seeking out art to experience a shot of empathy? For example, while The New School literary studies are intriguing at face value, several other teams have failed to replicate their results, suggesting that reading literature does not necessarily enhance empathic capacities. However, their claims of the literature studies are supported by evidence that the same brain networks involved in perspective taking and theory of mind are strongly activated when subjects are reading literary works. And while it's possible that this boost in cognitive empathy only existed for the length of the studies, it is equally possible that literary fiction pumps up the neural underpinnings of empathy to lasting benefit.

It's possible that exposure to art nurtures the capacity for perspective taking. At the same time, I would suggest that people who are primed for empathy probably seek out the sort of art that helps them fine-tune their natural abilities. The existence of neurons that act as tiny neural reflectors for action representations in addition to other shared neural circuits seems to suggest we are born with the capacity for empathy. I believe the arts are among the best ways to activate those neuron systems and to get them firing. Does that mean art lovers are always the most sensitive people in the room? Perhaps not, though they are more likely to have a better understanding than most of what others experience.

In fact, some intriguing research at Cambridge University suggests that empathic people are drawn to certain types of art. The researchers analyzed the personality traits and art genre preferences of over three thousand individuals to reveal a remarkably clear pattern. People who score on personality tests for intensity, edginess, and hedonism seem to largely prefer intense and edgy genres such as punk and metal music, horror movies, and erotic fiction. Those who score high on thrill-seeking personality traits seem to have a preference for action, adventure, and sci-fi. Those with more cerebral personality traits prefer art that relates to current events, nonfiction, and education. People who demonstrated highly empathic character showed entertainment preferences for the two remaining categories: communal and aesthetic. Communal personality traits focus on people and relationships and a preference for talk shows, dramas, romances, and pop music. Aesthetic personality traits focus on culture and intellect with a preference for classical music and art, history, and movies with subtitles.

It's interesting that such diverse genres of entertainment appeal to empathic people. I think it speaks to the dual nature of empathy. In the first place, empathic individuals take a natural interest in other people and in relationships. Secondly, they have an interest in experiences that are outside their own. In that same study, the researchers noted that highly empathic people also seemed to have an aversion to entertainment depicting extreme violence or horror. Perhaps they have a low tolerance for seeing others in so much physical and psychological pain.

Taking Art's Lessons into the Real World

As we look around the world today, we see less empathy than we would like. We've shifted into largely digital communication with ever increasing use of email and social media, which strips away the nonverbal cues represented in the seven keys to E.M.P.A.T.H.Y. As we have seen, it's easy to be rude when you leave an anonymous comment at the bottom of an article or on Twitter. You never see evidence of the devastation and hurt your words have caused. Though we see war and devastation on a daily basis on our screens, it's become so overwhelming that many of us feel numb to it and immune to feeling much for its victims.

I believe the arts can act as an antidote to this estrangement. It helps change our thinking about social out-groups by providing a firsthand experience that brings us closer to understanding others as individuals and fellow human beings. By entering the thoughts and feelings of others in a way that is becoming increasingly rare in the modern world, we find commonalities that make it harder to brush them off as deviant or unworthy of respect. Why do we need art? It gives us the sense that we're all connected in some way. Many of the world's problems occur because we don't understand each other. Art helps us understand. And the more we understand and can slip into one another's skin, the better.

Many works of art ask us to become more humane. Think of the movie *Schindler's List*, which so poignantly told the story of Jews in Nazi Germany. Then there is the *The Killing Fields*, which brought us the horror and devastation of Cambodia from the point of view of a Cambodian man—a point of view we've rarely considered in the West. Movies, series, and books like *The Band Played On*, *The Normal Heart*, and *Dallas Buyer's Club* humanized the AIDS crisis, which was all too real for the gay and lesbian community, a traditional out-group in this society.

I'm sure you can call up many more examples from paintings, sculpture, TV, movies, music, theater, and literature that touched your heart and enriched your understanding of an individual or culture in a way you had never considered. I recently saw a documentary movie called *I am Jane Doe* about sex trafficking children using a website called Backpage, available on Google. The horrific stories of this "legal" website drove home the fact that due to a loophole in the law, using the internet to sell children for sex is not currently a criminal offense. Director Mary Mazzio, an American award-winning documentary filmmaker and attorney, has stepped up to the challenge to change this status. Because of this movie, senators in Washington are listening to Mary and the producers of this film, and in April 2018 Backpage creators were indicted on prostitution and money laundering charges, and the website was shut down by the US government.

The power of art underscores the need not only for the global and cultural touchstones works of art create, but for local efforts as well. Things like community art programs, art programs in prisons, high school plays, and even neighborhood book clubs spread the messages of art at the grassroots level. This is so essential to maintaining civility, kindness, and caring in our world. It's the very essence of empathy.

I also believe that you can take the lessons of art out of the theater, off the canvas, and outside the page and apply them in other ways. No one has a better example of this than Alan Alda.

Understanding the difference between truth and fiction and Alda's love of science led him to dedicate twelve years of his professional life to host the PBS documentary series *Scientific American Frontiers*. This series of documentaries showcased scientists who had made amazing discoveries, and Alda quickly learned that scientists needed communication skills to translate their work into language everyday people could understand. He appreciated that for the average person to grasp what a scientist has discovered, researchers had to learn to effectively share their discoveries, communicating what is real and essential.

One of the most vexing problems of our time is that we've become so polarized about science. We have rising earth temperatures, rising tides, devastating hurricanes and floods, and death tolls in the millions, but empathy is lacking on both sides of the climate discussion divide. What appears to be incontrovertible evidence to one side is a "hoax" to others. How do we understand each side's perspective to move forward to protect humanity?

Alda teamed up with Howard Schneider, dean of the journalism school at Stony Brook University, to create the Alan Alda Center for Communicating Science, a program dedicated to teaching the skills of communication so readily used by actors to scientists, who rarely have those skills. Alda says that the communication that happens between two actors is the essence of what he has come to believe is what should happen between any two people trying to communicate.

"I did the science show because I loved science and I wanted to learn more about it from the scientists themselves. And then once we were doing it, I began to realize I could be helpful through what I knew as an actor to get their science out so everybody watching would be able to follow it. Once I did that, I realized it could be taught. You can improve people's ability to connect.

"There may be a feeling that we're betraying our tribe if we are looking at things from another tribe's point of view," observes Alda. That's the point about tribal nature: empathy is very embedded in this because we have the greatest empathy for people who are like us. We were tribal people at one point, and we were constantly defending ourselves from others. "That gets back to signs and symbols and words that denote certain things that are used by one group of people, and seem to define the identity of the people who use them. And other terms are used by other groups, and they may have been perceived as attacking the other tribe just by using those terms. We want science to be communicated in a way that's clear and vivid but not dumbed down," he says.

Alda set out to find a way to talk about science and, in doing so, realized that to talk about things like poverty, health care, and global warming, you had to be sure not to attack someone else's values or even necessarily their long-held, embedded opinions. One example was helping people in Florida understand the importance of dealing with climate change, a term that is so taboo in many communities it is actually banned from official use.

Some places use the term "inconvenient flooding," Alda explains. "This is a new term, but it's also true." In having this conversation, Alda and the scientists were in no way trying to trick or talk down to anyone. They realized that they had to get to the facts without insisting on what it was called. Florida residents can readily see that there is more flooding on their shores than ever before and it is indeed inconvenient. In this way they were able to find a starting point, a way to underscore the urgency of the problems without being pedantic or insisting upon total agreement.

This was an exercise in empathy—to have a shared mind experience that the problem is real, and can we agree to call it different names if it leads to a solution? In my conversation with Alda, it was clear that his topmost priority was communicating in a way that reached the audience in a meaningful way and did not fall into traps that divide people, but rather brought them together with shared concerns. Artists like Alan Alda and Diane Paulus follow their calling to find novel and creative ways to move people, create shared experiences that lead us to new perspectives and possibilities, and tap into the essence of what makes our experiences human and sharable.

E.M.P.A.T.H.Y. and the Arts

Art opens up the right side of the brain, responsible for imagination and creativity. Experiencing the arts shifts us from self-preoccupation and transports us into another experience, whether it's one that the artist is trying to evoke in us or that we project onto it. The seven keys of empathy are integral to how we process art and how we take the emotions it evokes into the rest of our lives. It's worth a quick overview of how each of them contributes and builds upon our capacity for an empathic response.

Viewing art is a form of making eye contact with the artist's image, as I've already mentioned. Thanks to evolution, most humans have a knack for interpreting messages sent through the eyes. Whether we are conscious of it or not, art can remind us of this. The eyes tell you as much about a character as costume, makeup, accent, movements, or even words. Think of Johnny Depp as the character Edward Scissorhands. You focused on his round-eyed, sad, and lonely gaze as much as his hedge-sculpting appendages. Or Rooney Mara in *The Girl with the Dragon Tattoo*, who does a fine job of capturing the hardness of her character, Lisbeth Salander, in her cold, unrelenting stare. Shakespeare's Hamlet describes his father's gaze as "an eye like Mars, to threaten and command."

This is very related to our ability to understand and perceive the human face. The more we look and the more we are curious about what emotions are being expressed, the more we're going to see what is coming through from that person's inner life. The late brilliant Irish poet and philosopher John O'Donohue described the human face as a road map of emotion. O'Donohue also observed that "One of the deepest longings of the human soul is the longing to be seen." In our conversation, Kandel reminded me that the brain devotes more space to reading the details of the face than anything else. Our neural circuits reflect the emotions we see in the work of art as our own. Alda also believes in the importance of reading faces in art, something he thinks may have roots in his childhood.

"I was looking at the adults like an anthropologist would. Some of this came from the fact that my mother was schizophrenic and paranoid. I had to observe her very carefully to know what was reality and what was just her reality. When I was around four years old, I was with my mother, and we went to a party. She was looking out of one of those windows that is level with the sidewalk, and she had been standing there a while, and she turned toward me. I saw what I would describe now as a distracted look of a depressed person. I remember paying attention to that expression on her face and trying to figure out what was happening to her, what she was going through."

As Alda points out, accurately reading facial expressions can have a bearing on how someone will behave toward you and how you should behave in kind. Some therapists use movies, TV, and art to teach this skill to people who have trouble reading facial expressions, such as those with autism. Actually, this can be a valuable exercise for anyone.

As for the empathic key of posture, it is often used as a device that asks the viewer to feel an empathic connection to the subject. One of the most famous examples of this is Auguste Rodin's *The Thinker*. Here sits a bronze cast of a man in repose, lost in thought. He will not be motivated into action any time soon. Whenever I look at *The Thinker*, I feel contemplative. In contrast, when I look at Picasso's famous *Mother and Child* from his Blue Period, I am filled with a sense of depression, suffering, and despair that emanates from the mother as she cradles her child, attempting to protect it from unseen dangers. Can you recall how a particular work of art made you feel? Think about the body language of famous movie characters, in paintings, or even how they are described on the page. As in life, posture provides clues to someone's inner life. Noticing it can arouse feelings of compassion and curiosity about the subject.

Next, naming the affect we experience from a work of art moves us from emotional empathy to the cognitive. We have a saying in neuroscience: "If you can name it, you can tame it." The whole aim of art is to move people emotionally. You've probably grown misty-eyed as you stood before a painting, listened to a song, read a book, or watched a TV show. You can translate these feelings into life by noticing, recognizing, and naming the feelings you feel while experiencing art. This helps you move from the affective to the cognitive, elevating your ability to feel and express empathy for others.

Alda, even though funny and quick-witted, has a gentle tone of voice that made Hawkeye a universally beloved figure. Think about the powerful effect of tone of voice when you remember the bone-chilling tone of Hannibal Lecter in the psychological thriller *The Silence of the Lambs*. Contrast this with the melodious voices of Joni Mitchell, James Taylor, and Bob Dylan, and again with Green Day or Adele. In an entirely different genre, think about the effects of a Bach cantata, the Gregorian chant, or the singing of a cantor or the voice of an imam. Tones of quiet understanding, of receiving someone's vulnerable story, of celebrating another's victory are generous acts of listening. Matching your own tone with another is a powerful form of empathy.

Alda told me a story about performing in a play called *QED* about nuclear physicist Richard Feynman, in which Alda played Feynman. "I remember the part where he was talking about sitting in Times Square and thinking if the atomic bomb hit here, how far out would the destruction go? And during that section of the play—in California—there was silence. But in New York City the silence was utter. It was even deeper. Because it was three weeks after 9/11. Afterward, we all said we heard that silence. The director said *nobody was breathing.* They didn't just stop fidgeting; they stopped breathing. And to get a communal response like that affects everyone in the room. Sometimes collaborating in an utter silence is more telling than laughter or applause."

This is such a poignant example of what art can teach us about really listening. The entire audience caught the same emotion and held on to it. For most of us, truly listening is an underdeveloped skill. Experiences like this, which movies and theater can do so well, remind us how important it is to really hear what's being said—and pay attention to silences. Often the most important communication is what is not being said.

And finally, how do you respond to a work of art? Everyone who views a piece of art brings his or her own worldview and experience along. At the same time, all artists contribute their own unique perspective. I think the power of great art seems to be in allowing artist and observer to share a vision by providing a bridge between individuals and the wider world. In a way, it's a kind of time travel that transports you in time and space to someone else's point of view or perspective. There is a collaboration between artists and their viewers that transforms sculptures, paintings, music, the written word, and performing arts into an emotional experience that is shaped by both sides of the transaction. Where are you moved in your body, and how are you moved? What has this work inspired in you? Your own emotional and lived bodily experience of art is something you can become more attuned to. Once you make a practice of noticing how your body responds to art, you may be able to conjure up that feeling days, months, or even years after you've been stirred by an artist's communication. Try sharing that with someone who may need a story to bolster his mood. You may be part of the grand ripple effect that art can put into play.

This is the mother lode of how the arts strengthen the ability to flex our empathic muscles. Our response is to reflect on how we have been moved by a story or piece of music to transport us to a different mood or change our perspective. It can uplift us and move us from just functioning and doing to appreciating the textures and nuances and shapes and colors of our lives, helping us tap into creativity and joy. When a piece of art truly means something to us, we are not simply moved to a different emotion; we can be moved to consider a different perspective or action, and a shared emotional experience that unifies our humanity with those who are both like and unlike ourselves.

10

Leadership and the Politics of Empathy

Axelle Bagot was living in Boston at the time of the 2015 Paris terror attacks on the Bataclan nightclub and other locations around Paris. As a French student studying abroad at Harvard's John F. Kennedy School of Government, she was devastated to hear the news that 129 of her countrymen had been killed in the assaults. That evening she went to the Boston Common, a traditional gathering place for students and other Bostonians, hoping to hear some words of clarity and comfort from a French government official. She was stunned that after a moment of silence he left the stage without offering any words of comfort. "One thousand people standing together, looking at a man who didn't manage to voice the solemnity of this moment, who didn't acknowledge our pain, or who didn't know how to do it and decided not to try," she recalls. "In these horrific moments, I believe that leaders must be able to give a crowd the words it expects to hear, to help people heal. He could have read the names of the one hundred and twenty-nine who died, a meaningful poem or a quote, but he said nothing.

"After he left the stage, as we were feeling abandoned and disappointed, a man on my left started singing "La Marseillaise," our national anthem, that united the crowd through song and reminded us of strength when we come together. Sometimes music and the arts bring us together when there are no words coming from leaders."

When Bagot told me her story, it occurred to me that she had pinpointed precisely what is needed from a leader in times of crisis: the ability to identify emotions, to empathize, and to understand the power of healing and restoration of confidence. When tragedy or hardship strikes, a successful leader knows how to unify the aggrieved and keep hope alive. Even in good times, an effective leader understands that leadership is not about rank, authority, power, or privilege. True leadership—whether you command a country, an army, or an organization—hinges entirely on the success and well-being of the entire group.

The Neural Substance of Empathic Leadership

Leadership is about emotions. We often cite intelligence, instincts, and expertise when describing someone we consider to be a great leader, but great leaders are exquisitely attuned to others' emotions and are experts at regulating their own. CEOs and executives are often lauded for their fierce tenacity and decisive actions, politicians for their hard-line thinking, entrepreneurs for their innovative, competitive natures. But these qualities are only a part of the story of leadership. Neurobiology seems to predispose us to a preference for leaders who above all else express empathy and compassion. These have a clearly positive effect on neurological functioning, psychological well-being, physical health, and personal relationships. Richard Boyatzis, professor at Case Western Reserve's Weatherhead School of Management, emphasizes that "lack of empathic concern in organizations results in multiple disasters, including losing touch with the hearts and minds of your staff, your customers, your suppliers, and community. It goes hand in hand with lack of moral concern, resulting in decreased activation of the brain's default mode network, the part of the brain that's active when a person is thinking about others, remembering the past, and planning for the future." The truly great leaders among us have a combination of keen emotional attunement made possible through shared neural circuitry and quick, decisive, and creative minds that find opportunities and figure out how to execute a plan—which may explain why great leaders are hard to find.

Daniel Goleman has described how empathic leadership can change the brain chemistry of both leader and followers by creating an interconnectedness of thoughts and feelings. Goleman calls this "social intelligence," and on a chemical level, the neurotransmitters endorphins, dopamine, serotonin, and oxytocin promote social bonding and inspire us to trust others through openness and cooperation. On a neural level, shared brain circuits reflect the thoughts and emotions of a leader and prompt followers to literally mimic those same thoughts and emotions.

Two additional but less familiar types of neurons are important to social connectedness: spindle cells and oscillators. Spindle cells were first described by anatomist Constantin von Economo and are sometimes referred to as Economo cells. These supersized neurons act as a sort of empathic autobahn; their long, thin branches extend into other neurons, revving up the transmission of thoughts and feelings in the brain. Spindle neurons are found in the anterior cingulate cortex and insula but only in humans, great apes, and other highly social creatures such as elephants, dogs, whales, and dolphins. They are active when people experience social emotions including empathy, love, trust, guilt, and humor and when they self-monitor emotions. As Goleman explains it, spindle cells are important to empathic leadership because they activate our "social guidance system," which helps us make "thin-slice" judgments that, within a fraction of a second, create a rapport and resonance between leaders and followers.

Oscillators, located in the central nervous system, choreograph physical movement between individuals and within groups. You see their synchronized rhythms at work with skating partners who have been together for a long time and, on a more everyday level, couples who have been married for decades. Imaging studies show that the right brain hemispheres of two musicians playing in harmony are more closely coordinated than are the left and right sides of their individual brains. Interesting studies by David DeSteno at Northeastern University also show that by simply tapping fingers in synchrony, subjects experience greater trust and compassion for one another. In leadership, oscillators establish a literal physical connection among groups and between leaders and followers and may account for the contagious nature of leadership. Most workers know all too well what the emotional climate at work will be based on the mood of their leaders, which is conveyed the moment they enter a room by the presence or lack of the empathy keys we've been discussing throughout the book: eye contact, facial expressions, postures, tone of voice, affect, and the physiological responses these evoke. A leader's emotions transmit throughout an organization like a virus. Even unsuspecting bystanders are affected by the contagion.

This highly specialized neural circuitry, along with other related systems within the brain and body, creates a socially aware, shared mind intelligence. And arising from all this chemistry and biology comes a strong sense of both thoughtful and emotional empathy that allows a good leader to take an excursion into the minds of her followers. Empathic leaders create emotional bonds with their groups, teams, and constituents and foster a culture of trust and collaboration. They are competent at understanding and addressing their needs, appreciating and drawing on people's talents, and recognizing others' perspectives in problem solving and including them in making decisions together.

Conversely, when leaders lead purely from their heads without much heart, they may get the job done in the short term, but they rarely succeed in the long term because they stir up fear, anxiety, and animosity in their teams and workforce. Biochemically speaking, anxiety, fear, and stress cause spikes in levels of flight-or-fight hormones such as cortisol and adrenaline and other hormones that increase the risk of anxiety disorders and depression, in addition to obesity and heart disease. Far from being effective, leaders who cannot convey empathy can take an enormous psychological and even physical toll on their followers. Studies suggest that autocratic leaders who are all stick and no carrot reduce productivity, stifle creativity, and dampen motivation.

At the physiological level, humans achieve equilibrium, or homeostasis, with internal systems that coordinate and maintain the stability of temperature, blood pressure, heart and respiration rate, and other factors. This requires a balance between the input of two parts of the autonomic nervous system that operate in the body much like the gas and brake pedals in your car. The sympathetic nervous system acts as the accelerator to raise heart and respiration rate, blood pressure, blood flow to the muscles, emotional facial expressions, and voice tone while the parasympathetic nervous system acts as the brakes to slow down those same processes. The control centers in the brain for these mechanisms, or nuclei, are located in the midbrain, in an area called the pons.

A finely tuned physiological pedal-and-brake system helps leaders lead. If they sense unrest, dissatisfaction, turmoil, or fear, they do not ignore it. However, great leaders project a calm demeanor and steady voice tone, and maintain the keys of empathy even in a crisis. Pilot Chesley "Sully" Sullenberger is an iconic example of portraying self-regulation during an avian storm. Sully, as you may remember, is the hero of the "Miracle on the Hudson" who safely landed a US Airways Airbus on the Hudson River when a flock of Canada geese caused both engines to lose power. In an astounding display of heroism and composure, the calm and steady voice of Captain Sullenberger announced the plans to the passengers and crew and landed the plane on the river.

Sully's obviously well-regulated and controlled parasympathetic nervous system saved the day by enabling him to stay calm and focused, using the single word "unable" when air traffic control directed him to turn left to return the plane to the runway. He did not yell, curse, or become emotionally dysregulated. His focus on the task and skill inspired trust without alarming passengers, and he saved the lives of all 155 people on board.

Empathy, Attachment Theory, and Leadership

Many leaders fail to appreciate the extent to which employees project their own attachment patterns from their childhoods onto their bosses. Each one of us carries within us every age we have been, and early experiences can get triggered without our conscious bidding. Like the familiar Russian *matryoshka* nesting dolls, the younger and smaller versions live inside of us even though the largest is the only one that's visible. We become older and hopefully more mature with age, but under stress those young versions of ourselves are revealed and can override our more mature defenses. Leaders should understand that when people are feeling vulnerable, these younger parts may surface, and fully grown adults may temporarily behave more like children because they experience an authority figure as more intimidating than he or she actually is. Kindness and fairness can restore these relationship glitches.

Children are exquisitely attuned to the moods of their parents early in life because of their complete dependence on them. Similarly, workers tend to project their perceptions of early authority figures onto their bosses and leaders, and attribute great significance to their moods and behaviors. At a subconscious level, employees often play out their own needs for attachment, acceptance, appreciation, and worthiness with their leaders. Consistency, predictability, and empathy lead to secure attachments in family life and stimulate the bonding hormones of warmth and trust. When leaders demonstrate these same traits, their followers feel those same emotions.

The tendency to catastrophize and exaggerate threats in a workplace often has roots in an early childhood where a lack of control and fear of abandonment may have been pervasive. John Bowlby's theory of attachment posited that a strong emotional and physical connection to at least one primary caregiver is essential for healthy personal development. Eighty percent of abused children have been identified with disorganized attachments, which accounts for unpredictable responses under stress. While it's not appropriate to treat workers like children, remembering that all people have differing needs for support and encouragement when they are feeling insecure should motivate leaders to minimize threats and use other tactics besides fear and intimidation to motivate their teams. Especially when letting someone go to find a new opportunity, organizations can conduct layoffs in a way that preserves respect and conveys hope that there will be a better match for the worker's talents or skills in the future.

The Empathy Index

Though hard data is scarce, the Global Empathy Index, often described as "the corporate Fitbit for measuring empathy," suggests that empathy can boost corporate profits. In its 2015 survey, the top 10 businesses among 160 in the index generated 50 percent more net income per employee than the bottom 10. The index analyzes such factors as how well companies treat workers and communicate with customers.

My empathy research team recently published an investigation on a purported "warmth/competence tradeoff" that challenges a long-held belief that there is an inverse relationship between perceived warmth and competence. Previous evidence suggested that nicer people are often judged as less competent. But in fact, unempathic leaders have trouble maintaining the confidence, respect, and trust of followers. Conversely, people skills are increasingly recognized as important for what we consider proficient behavior. Our recent study, conducted at Massachusetts General Hospital, showed that study participants rated doctors who displayed nonverbal empathic behaviors not only as warmer, as would be expected, but also as more competent. Previous fears that showing a more human side would make a doctor appear as though they didn't know as much as they should appear to be unfounded. Our results suggest that people skills and emotional intelligence factor into the perception of competence. A leader who is oblivious to the emotions of his followers is likely to encounter obstacles in working together to reach common aims. Otherwise, who is the leader leading? As pastor and motivational speaker John Maxwell says, "If you are leading and no one is following, then you are just going for a walk."

Empathic leaders excel at managing relationships. Trusting relationships with and among groups enhance people's ability to receive and process information and to find solutions. They are the strong social glue that creates bonds and holds groups together, making them better able to connect and understand one another's interests and perspectives. They establish safe environments in which people can express hopes and fears and generally avoid punitive and judgmental criticism as a management style. However, empathic leaders do not twist themselves into a pretzel to please everyone. My friend Emma has a boss she doesn't necessarily like as a person but describes as a terrific leader. "I see her vision, and I know I have her full support. I wouldn't necessarily want to have lunch with her, but I'd follow her into a burning building." Empathy essentially allows a leader to read the emotions and minds of his people to gain perspective so they can find the best way forward with greater vision. Because it is "contagious," empathy contributes to better negotiation, collaboration, and conflict resolution. Leadership positions also require clear boundaries. Greater understanding of others will help leaders broaden their perspectives and see the human side, which doesn't preclude holding others accountable. By maintaining their roles, leaders will be respected and consulted, even in times of hardship and crisis.

Missing and Misguided Empathy in the 2016 US Presidential Election

Some in power understand how to crowdsource mood very well. They understand how to read the emotional temperature of their followers. Daniel Kuhn, a reporter from the American University School of Public Affairs, describes the mood at a pre-election Donald Trump rally like this: "Really, a Trump mega-rally is part rock concert, part WWE match. The mood inside is electric. You walk in, and people are excited . . ." The reporter goes on to illustrate how Trump absorbs the charged-up atmosphere of the crowd and feeds it right back to them with repetitive lines like "Make America great again," "Build that wall," and "Very soon we're gonna start saying Merry Christmas again." Those in the room know his one-liners and are delighted to join in.

Is this an example of leadership? An example of empathic leadership? Is it even an example of empathy? This leadership style is built on what neuroscientists call "emotion contagion." Emotion contagion is what happens when someone yells, "Fire!" in a movie theater. Intense emotions are picked up instantaneously in the brain by the thalamus, a router that signals the amygdala, the brain's emotion center, to trigger rapid changes in facial expressions and to send other signals that rally people's emotions to synchronize. Emotion contagion is necessary to send the alarm when escaping from a fire, but it is also used to rev up crowds and cause mayhem. That's a good segue to talk about how empathy can sometimes be used and abused in political leadership.

Empathy is the glue that binds our humanity. It's how we know what is important and deeply felt by our fellow human beings. When used to broaden care and stewardship of our communities, empathy serves as a guide to governance. When misused by means of coercion or manipulation, or prioritizing one group above others, it can lead to polarization, denigration of groups considered "other," and a fractured society. A misuse of empathy leads to raising false hopes that the emotion contagion generated by a leader means the leader really cares.

Our political leaders hold the keys to how society is governed. In our interconnected world, leaders' decisions and actions do not only affect their own countries; they have ripple effects throughout the globe. Those who exploit their positions of power for self-aggrandizement, personal splendor, and wealth, and who dominate populations with tactics of fear and hate, degrade societies. It is not entirely clear whether individuals with low neural empathic capacity are drawn to become such leaders or whether power reduces empathic capacity. I suspect the two operate at once in leaders who dominate others. Empathizing with people beyond a country's borders, and regarding humans as belonging to the human race regardless of skin color, religion, or creed, would reflect the pinnacle of human empathy. Much progress has been made by human rights and civil liberties organizations and by those who uphold democratic values that "all men are created equal," but tremendous setbacks continue to occur.

The use—or manipulation—of empathy in political leadership has led to some of the most destructive and divisive horrors in history. As we have witnessed many times, from Napoleon to Hitler, empathy can be used disingenuously. We have seen leaders who use the shadow side of empathy, the ability to know what people want to hear and then give it to them, even if it hurts them. Such leaders make promises to rally a subset of people who feel marginalized, even when doing so flies in the face of democratic doctrines and principles.

We need only look at the degree of polarization in the US after the 2016 election to see how empathy can run amok. And before I continue this discussion, let me stop here and say that I am not condemning or condoning the voters of either party. I am only viewing the presidential election through the lens of empathy to make some greater points about its use in leadership—both the ways it was misused and the ways it was entirely lacking.

Let's start with how a disenfranchised, forgotten segment of our society led to a groundswell of support for Donald Trump. One of the triumphs of the 2016 election was to make visible the names and faces of these overlooked members who are part of us. Ironically, prior to the election, Trump showed little regard for the plight of unemployed, financially challenged, poor white citizens. Despite his anti-immigration, pro–American worker rhetoric, reports reveal that Trump frequently hired illegal immigrants to build his empire. His "Make America great again" slogan belied the fact that many of the products sold by his family are manufactured offshore. And despite his reputation as an elitist billionaire with an unfortunate habit of underpaying or stiffing the very demographic he was trying to convince and win the votes of, he was able to convince many of those who felt marginalized and left behind that he felt their pain. This is possible by accessing the affective neurocircuitry of people who feel high degrees of anger and pain by mirroring their experience in the moment. When that is done effectively, cognitive processes in the prefrontal cortex that enable rational comparisons between what was said on the campaign trail and how reports describe his actual practices are superseded by emotion.

Trump's "America first" slogan may seem relatable, but it lacks genuine empathy. He imbued it with the idea that America was no longer great, despite the lowest unemployment rate and highest economic stability that the nation had seen in decades, even before he announced his candidacy. In doing so, he recognized a specific segment of the population—middle- to lower-income whites—whose voices have not been heard by establishment politicians, and who are crushed with debt and a loss of the American Dream. This appearance of empathy led to a throng of ardent followers who needed to hear a message of hope. They turned a blind eye to his practices of cheating workers, fat shaming beauty pageant winners, and grabbing female genitalia because the pseudo-empathy he showed for their plight was what they so desperately wanted to hear.

Trump tied his message of jobs for the unemployed to other messages that disrespected, demonized, and vilified other members of our society—and flew in the face of our democracy. Instead of unifying those in need who had similar aspirations for a better life through hard work and hope, his rhetoric trampled on the promise of the American Dream for other groups such as immigrants, people of color, women, Muslims, and the LGBTQ community. While he mimed empathy for lower-income, forgotten white citizens, Trump managed to unleash vitriolic hostility toward people considered "other" and out-grouped in our society. In effect, he showed the exact opposite of empathy; he showed disdain, disrespect, and contempt for huge segments of vulnerable people in American society.

Trump whipped up open enmity and disparagement of Mexicans, Muslims, immigrants, and women to name a few of his chosen outgroups. This led candidate Hillary Clinton to utter some of the most shockingly unempathic words of the campaign by referring to his supporters as "a basket of deplorables." By judging Trump's followers to be as "deplorable" as the political platform he was creating—and using elitist phrasing to do it—she distanced herself from millions of Americans. She failed to understand that lack of empathy toward them by the political establishment was a significant reason so many people were drawn to him in the first place.

Clinton's "deplorables" comment had a catastrophic impact. She may have been focused on the democratic values she assumed were the foremost priorities for most Americans, but she didn't fully appreciate the human hierarchy of needs, well described by American psychologist Abraham Maslow in 1943. She therefore was unable to explore a shared mind experience with these voters' pain, instead judging them by assuming they all shared the same values as her opponent.

Maslow postulated a theory that psychological health is predicated on fulfilling innate human needs in priority order. Most people are first focused on survival requirements such as food, shelter, and safety before they move up the ladder to more reflective and philosophical concerns such as racial and gender equality, free speech, and democracy. The lowest rung on the hierarchy of needs is physiological, followed by safety, love/belonging, esteem, and, at the highest point, self-actualization. A living example of this comes from a survey conducted by Transparency International, which asked Bulgarians immediately before an important election if they would sell their right to vote. More than 10 percent admitted that they would, and for as little as $20; in the US nearly 70 percent of respondents who said they would readily sell their ballot for cash listed poverty as the principle reason. Similar surveys have been carried out all over the world with similar results, demonstrating how people prioritize immediate needs over future needs to the point that they are willing to sell a highly prized privilege for a relatively paltry sum.

Clinton seemed unable to relate to the deep insecurity and fear that was epidemic in the rust belt, the heartland, and the Bible Belt of America. As Maslow's hierarchy dictates, most people need the assurance of a paycheck (aka their survival) before they worry about civil rights, the plight of immigrants, or the environment. Consequently, and most unfortunately, the shared and lauded American values of democracy that she espoused became ridiculed as elitist. Common ground disappeared so quickly that the gap between the "deplorables" and the "snowflakes" grew as wide and deep as the Grand Canyon.

Meanwhile, Trump implicitly understood the thinking of traditional American workers. He took advantage of their fear with his sham-empathy by focusing his message on an "us versus them" rhetoric. By tapping into ancestral, tribal thinking, Trump shored up his base by appealing to the fear centers of the brain, which create defenses, barriers, and isolation. Former Obama speech writer Sarada Peri, in an essay she penned for *New York* magazine, summarizes this well.

". . . while so appalling to much of the country, [the us-versus-them rhetoric] appeals to the small group of people he has identified as 'us.' They're not interested in hearing that he also cares about others. They want him all to themselves."

Peri goes on to point out that most of the greatest leaders in history, from Washington to Lincoln to Theodore Roosevelt, have taken the opposite tack to Trump's. "They deliberately chose to transcend our baser instincts and, instead, appeal to our shared humanity," she writes. And, as she additionally notes, Trump is no ordinary politician. As a result, he does not face the normal empathy trade-offs, at least not yet. He speaks to his diehard following alone, and they believe they are finally being heard.

By exploiting the class divide created by a swiftly changing economy and terror attacks by foreign nationals, he energized a class of people whose voices about economic hardship had long been ignored; he craftily married these concerns to hatred of immigrants, suspicions of people beyond our nation's borders, and tolerance of white supremacist and neo-Nazi groups and supercharged the fear centers in the midbrains of his supporters, making empathy for other disadvantaged groups a zero-sum game. These are not the values of middle America, but with ersatz empathy and false promises, he hooked the disenfranchised into believing he was a leader who could promise economic security, and we now know, at a great cost to humanism.

Because so many people *are* in dire straits, Trump's misuse of empathy and his pitch to America worked. When they look into the future, it seems no better. In a 2016 exit poll, 15 percent of voters listed a candidate "who cares about me" as a very important trait. Clinton led Trump by 23 points on this quality. But among the nearly 40 percent of the electorate who said "bringing about change" was the most important trait for a candidate, Trump led the way by a whopping 68 points. Could it be that Americans weren't fooled into thinking Trump actually cared about them? Perhaps they just wanted change more, and Clinton's lack of empathy for this group made change an even greater priority.

Former CNN anchor Frank Sesno thinks that Trump was able to exploit the information bubbles created by social media to spread his messages more effectively than Clinton. Sesno, known for his expertise in asking the right questions, explained in his book, *Ask More*, that Trump understood how people have consolidated to communities of like-minded people online. "He knew where to find them and how to talk to them through perspective taking, the more calculating facet of empathy, whereas Clinton was trying to speak to the entire nation at once with the same message," he points out.

Interestingly, the perception about how you operate as a candidate versus an elected leader doesn't always jibe. As president, Trump's delayed response in condemning the white supremacists and neo-Nazis who stormed Charlottesville, Virginia, injuring hundreds and killing a peaceful protester, spoke volumes to the majority of Americans, including many of his supporters. At first, he stayed silent about the tragic events. When he finally did respond, his statement was that "jobs are the answer to racism." Once again Trump chose to blur the lines between tolerance of bigotry and economic security.

Similarly, his need to use empathy "cue cards" when speaking to survivors of the Parkland, Florida, school shooting conveyed his lack of confidence in his ability to comfort the aggrieved parents and students at the time of one of our nation's most egregious losses. His shifting stance on raising the age of people who can purchase deadly assault weapons also spoke volumes about whose concerns were foremost in his mind.

Empathy is deeply, profoundly lacking here, and some worry that the price could be our precious freedom and democracy. Furthermore, he continued to make the case that those who are against his principles are merely "sore losers" because Clinton lost the election. This mischaracterization of Democrats diminishes and devalues the degree of alarm provoked by his denial of climate change, intolerance of immigration, and disregard for equal rights, and highlights a disrespect for humankind as a community of people.

I've heard people present as Exhibit A that he is capable of expressing empathy because, love him or hate him, one thing everyone admits about Trump is that he has extremely close ties to his blood relatives and their spouses. Having never examined him nor spoken to him personally, my guess is that he can feel something for people he regards as an extension of himself, which defines his immediate family. A primer of Trump's teachings for his children appeared in a series of articles in the July 31, 2017, issue of *People* with the cover story titled "The Trump Family Secrets and Lies: Donald Trump taught his children to fight dirty and win, no matter what the cost. How the ruthless family culture has shaped Don Jr., his siblings—and the Presidency." Can we infer that those teachings reflect his form of empathy?

Trump has little empathic capacity for people he doesn't know, including his loyal base or even his inner political circle, but his ability to use weakness to his advantage has enabled him to make himself their champion. As a candidate at a time when people were hungering for change, his ability to exploit the suffering of poor white society created loyalty and allegiance. But in situations such as the Charlottesville riot, many Americans were hoping for an empathizer-in-chief to bring a divided country together. No such luck.

Trump, of course, is not the only political leader who has failed the empathy test. History is littered with examples. In America's recent past, George W. Bush was widely viewed as detached for the way he responded to Hurricane Katrina, an aloof and uncaring reputation that clung to him for the rest of his presidency. Barack Obama, too, was often criticized for failing to make supportive statements whenever a member of law enforcement was killed in the line of duty. And I've already mentioned Hillary Clinton's apparent lack of empathy for voters who felt left behind by American prosperity.

Fortunately, we do have some real examples of empathy in politics. Sometimes our leaders get it right. As much heat as George W. Bush takes for his tepid and off-key Katrina response, the majority of Americans would agree he was there for the country right after the September 11 terror attacks on Washington, DC, Pennsylvania, and New York City. He visited crash sites and spoke directly to the American people, making sure to stress that most American Muslims are loyal, decent citizens. It was the right thing to do. What good has ever come out of blaming and othering an entire race for the bad actions of a few?

In a similar vein, Senator John McCain famously defended Barack Obama, his opponent in the 2008 election. A woman came up to McCain at a rally and spoke into the microphone, "I can't trust Obama. I have read about him, and he's not, he's not—he's an Arab." McCain immediately began shaking his head. He gently took the microphone away from the woman and replied, "No ma'am. He's a decent family man, a citizen that I just happen to have disagreements with on fundamental issues, and that's what this campaign is all about."

McCain defended Obama further: "He is a decent person and a person that you do not have to be scared of. If I didn't think I'd be one heck of a better president, I wouldn't be running, and that's the point.

I admire Senator Obama and his accomplishments; I will respect him. I want everyone to be respectful, and let's make sure we are. Because that's the way politics should be conducted in America."

Here McCain demonstrated truly admirable leadership because he was able to express his values without demonizing the other side. By making such an emphatic statement defending Barack Obama's character, McCain demonstrated what true empathy is: respecting a person regardless of political differences, and judging a person by signs of character, including honesty, genuineness, actions consistent with rhetoric, and respect for humanity. He could have taken the bait and demonized his opponent for his political views, but instead he spoke what he knew to be true about his personhood.

E.M.P.A.T.H.Y. in Leadership

When writing about empathy, some authors have focused on the pitfalls of human empathy and belittle this human trait by accentuating the tendency of people to favor in-groups with our deepest empathic concerns to the exclusion of broader global suffering. This point of view seems unduly shortsighted. It takes a long time for genetics and epigenetics to work their way into changing the human brain on a population scale. Through an interplay of cognitive and emotional factors, there is a growing awareness that tribal solutions no longer work in today's interdependent world. The brain takes time to evolve, and as outdated tribal solutions lead to more war, devastation, and destruction, world leaders will need to consider that a singular focus on specific national interests to the exclusion of their global impacts is no longer a viable option. Rather than declare empathy as a misguided human capacity, a more productive focus would be on how to expand the concept of who belongs to the human tribe. Who gets to decide who is in and who is out?

One way to break down the barriers and walls between people is to implement the E.M.P.A.T.H.Y. keys within groups rather than just one-to-one interactions. Body language and other nonverbal cues are good sources of information that signal what the group is feeling. Few smiles, slouching postures, and a demonstrably reduced energy level provide subtle yet unmistakable clues about a lack of connection to others. I once went to a conference attended by more than ten thousand people where the entire convention center was bathed in a dull energy and indifference. When I stopped to consider where this feeling was coming from, I noticed how many people with empty facial expressions and slumped shoulders were walking through the hallways. This conference took place only a few months after the 9/11 terrorist attacks, and the conference had forged ahead with its prescribed agenda, ignoring the national devastation and how it made people feel. It was a complete flop.

Portraying genuine strength and power requires a bidirectional approach employing empathic accuracy, which allows the audience to inform the leader how to best deliver the message. Effective leaders understand that the ability to perceive shared emotions is a foundation of their empathic response; they use visual and verbal cues to interpret a group's state of mind. They need to be able to label the crowd's emotions and adjust the message accordingly through their own verbal and non-verbal cues while maintaining integrity, honesty, and trustworthiness.

Eye gaze between leaders and followers can be an especially powerful force. Subjects in fMRI studies who are shown angry faces with averted gazes and fearful faces with direct eye contact elicit very strong responses in the amygdala, the emotional center of the brain. This response is normal because threats activate defensiveness and early memories of powerlessness and fear. This is why the gaze of a leader can be so powerful.

The psychology of using eye contact within a group is just as important as it is during a one-on-one encounter, but with a different implementation. Those who are effective speaking into a lens can gaze directly into the camera as if it were another person's eyes while avoiding the non-blinking ten-yard stare that comes across as insecure and ineffective. With a live audience, it's useful to scan the room and make brief eye contact here and there with the audience. Even this fleeting direct gaze at a few people creates a sense of connection with everyone in the room because it conveys the notion that the leader sees not just the group, but each individual as well.

Tone of voice, as you may recall, conveys an estimated 38 percent of the emotional content of what a person communicates. Tone is often more important than the actual words we say and can determine empathic communication, and this is not diminished when speaking to a large audience or through a screen. In his research on effective leadership, Richard Boyatzis has identified that leaders who maintain a calm tone of voice, even when delivering very bad news, can remain effective and respected. Tone of voice is affected by the two nervous system controls. One operates during the fight-or-flight response with raised or shaking voice, unmasking fear and anxiety, and the other is a calm, cool, rational voice in the face of danger. The most effective leaders are able to maintain their cool in the midst of a storm by focusing on what they can control and conveying that they are handling the situation rather than feeling derailed by it.

Hearing the whole person enables leaders to maximize engagement and employee satisfaction. Studies have shown that especially when companies are forced to downsize and lay off workers, conveyed empathy and compassion contribute to employee loyalty both to the organization and the leader, even among those who are let go. But if downsizing is done callously, that company will have a very hard time regaining those valuable employees in the future when things improve. Shared neural circuits appear to have a long memory.

When using your empathic capacities, you engage not only in active listening, but also in compassionate, responsive listening. Whenever possible, empathic leaders focus on the shared mind connection as much as the points they wish to get across. They are nonjudgmental, even when the feelings of others are in direct conflict with their own. They acknowledge but don't necessarily allow emotions to control the outcome of events. Spending time as an emotional observer cultivates sensitivity.

While business leaders may believe that the bottom line is their most pressing concern, it's actually the engagement and vitality of the workforce that determine their success. Empathic leaders understand the purpose that drives people forward. Leaders who place themselves in the shoes of their workers attend to what matters most to their employees: life balance, support, flexibility, goals, and a culture of respect and inclusion. Salary and wages matter much less than most organizations realize.

Leaders with tough and curt attitudes may believe they are projecting authority. Surveys of business leaders find that almost 40 percent worry about being too nice, and more than half think they need to flex the muscle of their authority to stay on top. This fear may be more top of mind with women, who are more predisposed to empathic concern but don't see this trait so often in some male colleagues. Yet employee surveys say the opposite. They find that leaders are better regarded when they behave with respect and civility. Rather than demonstrating power, strong-arm tactics appear to undermine performance and confidence. In business, people who work for tough, uncaring bosses often say that it saps their motivation and makes them feel less committed to their work. Nearly a third would switch jobs for equal pay if they could work for a company they perceived as more compassionate. We also know that high levels of unrelenting stress lead to a greater number of psychological and physical health problems, which in turn can lead to higher rates of absenteeism, burnout, and lost productivity.

In the end, if you want to be an effective leader, empathy is well worth cultivating. Though it seems like a soft skill, empathy can be learned by intentional training, and it achieves concrete results. Empathic leadership can be a powerful influence in making the world a better place by uniting hearts and minds and bringing separate factions together. A leader with insight understands that the story that plays in her head is not necessarily the same story everyone else has. When a leader uses the E.M.P.A.T.H.Y. keys effectively, his response comes across as sincere empathic concern, whether appealing to a group of 10, 10,000 or 10 million.

11

Digging Deep for Empathy

I t's a fact of life that sometimes you have to search deep inside yourself to feel something for another human being. Empathy is informed by biology, upbringing, society, personal beliefs, and experience, which means everyone has unique reasons for the softening or hardening of their hearts. It's just as important to step back and evaluate why you feel little empathy in some circumstances as why it comes so easily in others.

We've already discussed that most people find it very difficult to stir up empathic concern for someone they consider part of an out-group. Most of us simply don't experience the same tug of emotion when hearing about the struggles of a foreigner who lives in a faraway place as we do for someone in trouble who is closer to home or who looks like us or lives a life similar to ours. I would argue that indifference, ignorance, and unfamiliarity drive a large part of our tepid empathic responses to such groups, though there are some prejudiced and racist individuals who try to justify their lack of empathy toward such groups and proudly proclaim their justification to anyone who will listen.

The groups I'm talking about in this chapter are not the ones toward whom many feel a passive indifference. These are the individuals many people don't open their hearts to under any circumstances. We stigmatize them while rarely stopping to consider the pain this causes them.

Some of the people in these groups may include a person sitting right next to us or even someone who shares our DNA. Sometimes they are so cast out by the majority of society that we don't even notice they exist even when we walk right past them.

Give Me Your Tired, Your Poor . . .

Social neuroscience offers a window into the reasons why homelessness has become invisible to most of us. To feel empathy, you must first recognize another as a fellow human being, with thoughts, feelings, and emotions similar to your own. When someone has certain off-putting qualities such as filth or a bad odor, they can be denied their humanity by others who then fail to experience warmth or an urge to help. In social-scientific terms, it's known as dehumanization.

Consider the movie *The Dinner*, where two families come together after their teenage sons set fire to a homeless woman who was asleep and blocking their access to an ATM. The boys jeer and torture her as if she is an object before she is killed. Their families are not united in their reactions. One family defines it as murder, while the other finds a way to justify this heinous act by suggesting the woman was nothing more than an inconvenience with no right to be in front of their son's ATM terminal. The vehemence with which one family defends the actions of their teenage son is bone chilling—and it is done by solely defending his perspective.

Studies have pinpointed the neurological processes that desensitize us in this way to the suffering of "extreme out-groups" like the homeless and the indigent. In experiments in which scientists expose subjects to photographs of homeless people, scans show that the parts of the brain that are activated are the ones associated with disgust. These are the same areas that light up when you encounter sour milk or a nest of cockroaches. At the same time, the parts of the brain in the prefrontal cortex that are necessary for social processing aren't as active.

The staggering number of women who have been dehumanized by powerful leaders as sex objects and whose vulnerability has been preyed upon as a rite of passage in the entertainment industry and other professions indicates that dehumanizing others is ubiquitous and does not only affect extreme out-groups. The #MeToo and #BlackLivesMatter movements have given a voice to groups that have long been silenced by fear and shame. The courage of those who are out-grouped because of gender and race to speak up has begun to crumble walls of silence that once protected those who treat others as objects and has opened the floodgates for empathy and new ethical and legal standards to be set forth. There is hope that these movements could change the narrative of how peoeple are treated in the twenty-first century.

Studies also suggest that when persons are "out-grouped" to excess, they are perceived as so vastly apart from society that they cease to evoke any emotional response at all to their suffering. We stop viewing their poverty as ugly and begin viewing the persons themselves as ugly. We subconsciously trick ourselves into believing that they don't experience the same complex emotions, such as discomfort, sadness, and depression, that the rest of us do. Again, less than human.

Not everyone turns a blind eye to those in real need. Just look at the many programs set up to help homeless people. Many caring people work for organizations that help those on the streets. However, in recent years, tolerance and understanding for homelessness has seemed to be fading, even as this tragic problem has grown exponentially. Some experts have suggested that when a problem like this becomes so overwhelming, people begin to feel compassion fatigue, and they cease to process it on an individual or global scale. On some level, society has begun to treat the tragedy of homelessness less as a social ill and more as a criminal act. In many cities, there are laws against sleeping in public, loitering, and panhandling. If the cities were providing sufficient shelters for our homeless, that would be one thing, but where they are not, such laws remove empathy from the equation by denying homeless people basic human needs like a place to sleep, eat, or go to the bathroom.

Yet despite this evidence to the contrary, the majority of people say it's important to address the homelessness crisis. A recent survey by the group Public Agenda found that more than 70 percent of New Yorkers feel that as long as homelessness exists, we are not living up to our values as a country. Nearly 90 percent think tax dollars that help the homeless are well spent and that one way to help them would be to provide housing, a solution that has proven highly effective, notably in Seattle, Utah, and Finland. Other beneficial approaches include job training, addiction rehab, and basic mental health services. The Community Day Center in Waltham, Massachusetts, and others around the country provide shelter, counseling, and telephones to help homeless people come together, find jobs, and contact employers and receive calls back. These are tangible ways everyday citizens can help with the problem of homelessness that expand on the cash or cup of coffee given on the street to get at the root cause. Such programs also help the homeless get the physical and psychiatric care they need.

Interestingly, some of the concern for homelessness seems to be driven by people who can imagine themselves in the place of someone who has no shoes; more than 35 percent of New Yorkers surveyed by Public Agenda fear becoming homeless themselves, and 30 percent have had a loved one on the streets. I once asked a homeless woman how she came to be homeless. She told me, "It's a long story, and I never thought it could happen to me. My husband left me, I wasn't working, I couldn't pay the mortgage, and my house was repossessed. Before I knew it, I was sleeping in my car, and it didn't take long before I had to sell it to get by." I think a lot of people worry that if one domino in their life falls, it's a slippery slope to their own long story.

As I've said before, it's hard to withhold empathy when you get to know someone. If seeing people on the street or watching stories about refugee camps or knowing there are victims of bullying, violence, or hate in your community is something that has been tugging at the edges of your comfort zone, why not pull the thread? Start by volunteering once a month at a local homeless shelter or food delivery service. By getting involved, you may get to know firsthand someone who finds himself desperate to find a way forward.

The Mentally Ill

Having a close relationship with a chronically mentally ill person is a tough road with many twists and turns. The troubles are compounded by a societal tendency to stigmatize mental illness and add a shroud of shame and guilt to those afflicted. In my practice, the way families start out dealing with a mental illness tends to fall into three camps. One camp tries to grin and bear it, hoping tolerance will help improve the situation. Spending time with the person is stressful for everyone, but the family member is grudgingly invited to family dinners over and over again, each time with the hope that things will be better than the last, while doing nothing to name or address the problem that everyone knows exists. We call this "*relentless* hope." The second camp cuts the person off as much as possible or perhaps entirely. Families that make this decision may view it as "tough love." The third camp is in denial. The family becomes frozen and powerless in the face of a loved one who exhibits emotional dysregulation. They suffer in silence and pretend there isn't a problem because they can't bear to face the devastating reality that their loved one can't get better on her own. The very idea of confronting an angry, sad, manic, or otherwise out of control relative frightens them. It's easier to bury their heads in the sand. In some families all three strategies are tried, and fail.

Each of these three approaches seems to be taking a stand for "empathy," when in reality not one of them is an empathic solution. They all display blindness to the realities of mental illness. The one constant in these situations is that someone afflicted with mental illness will inevitably repeat the same cycles of behavior again and again until the underlying condition is finally addressed. Like cancer, a broken leg, or any other medical condition, treating or curing mental illness requires medical and psychological evaluations and therapy.

And if the person's own family can't handle their mental illness, the world at large most often is even less understanding. There are still a lot of people who believe that mental illness is all in the mind. They believe that those who are living with a mental illness should stop feeling sorry for themselves and just act normally. Mental illness is often conflated with bad character, a flawed nature, or a manipulative personality. Despite a growing societal awareness that the inability to control moods, anger, rage, or impulsiveness is a disorder that requires treatment, the stigma against psychological conditions is still so tragically ingrained in our society that encountering someone who has mental issues often creates a sense of fear and revulsion.

Entire volumes are written on the topic of the bias against mentally ill individuals, especially those with mental illnesses such as schizophrenia and bipolar disorder. Often it is challenging to gain a basic understanding of many mental conditions, and even harder to obtain a definitive diagnosis; therefore, those who suffer often don't find their way to mental health professionals until late in life. And in a cruel contradiction, it can be very challenging to understand someone's erratic behavior before it is defined with a medical label, and at the same time a label can create more stigma. I've had many family members tell me a burden has been lifted once they receive a diagnosis that offers a logical explanation for their loved one's atypical behavior. That's why the most empathic solution for any mentally ill person is to get professional help as soon and as often as needed. Understanding that the person with mental illness requires aid, not judgment, is critical.

Some people with a mental illness can be taught to recognize the signs of their emotional dysregulation. They can employ perspective-taking techniques to rein themselves in. However, not everyone has the ability to hit the pause button. With various conditions, there's an impairment in reading social cues, an inability to foresee consequences, and a lack of ability to self-regulate once emotionally triggered. It's very hard to have empathy for someone who just yelled at you, demeaned you, or defamed your character. Yet it is quite possible that the person who "lost it" is losing it on a regular basis and really needs help regulating his emotions.

I find the least effective time to talk about getting help for a person who is dysregulated is in the heat of the moment. Nothing productive happens when someone is in "the red zone," that awful psychological state that is all emotion and no rational thought. Neurologically the red zone is the result of the amygdala, the brain's threat alert system that's activated in just 50 milliseconds (the "fast road"), whereas the "slow road," the thinking, reasoning, planning part of the brain, the prefrontal cortex, takes a relatively slow 500 milliseconds to rev up. Neurotypical people would never think of yelling at their bosses the way they might at their children, spouse, or sibling. This is because the prefrontal cortex weighs in and helps hit the pause button before behaving in a way that will ensure getting fired. But someone whose system's balance is off may fly off the handle at anyone for any reason or no reason at all. Such behavior creates societal barriers to empathizing with those with mental illness.

Societies have always struggled with understanding and caring for the mentally ill. Unlike cures for physical illnesses such as tuberculosis or pneumonia, cures for some mental illnesses have remained elusive for centuries. In the past, mental illnesses have been conflated with frightening phenomena such as demonic possession and witchcraft. Because the manifestations of mental illnesses can be so scary and difficult to understand, the easier route has been avoidance, distancing, judgment, and stigma.

Before the Community Mental Health Act of 1963, persons with severe mental illnesses were locked up in state hospitals and kept out of sight. When those systems were challenged in the name of community psychiatry, patients were released from institutions and then had to fend for themselves and find care among scarce community resources. This presented a tremendous challenge to cities and societies that were ill equipped to understand and care for those with mental illness.

You also may ask yourself as you read this, *Isn't it up to an individual to take responsibility for his or her own life?* Sure. But some folks never get the help they need because they have convinced themselves and others that nothing is wrong, or they don't have the resources to get help themselves. Tragically, decades may go by before there is enough self-compassion from within to admit their lives are not working and that they need help. In some cases, family members collude with the struggling person to pretend that everything is okay. When this happens, sadly, there is not much that can be done until the impairment becomes so obvious that no one can ignore it. Sometimes friends and relatives outside the immediate family are able to offer help and support because ingrained patterns and triggers embedded in family systems may run too deep.

Substance Use Disorders

Our empathy is further challenged when it comes to addiction. One in seven Americans will face a substance use disorder problem at some point in their lives. We know from the epidemic opioid crisis currently sweeping through the country that substance use disorders cut a wide swath across our society, touching millions of people, with no regard for education, class, race, employment, or socioeconomic status. Each day there are 175 deaths from drug overdoses alone, according to the President's Commission on Combatting Drug Addiction and the Opioid Crisis.

With such an unthinkable number of people from all walks of life afflicted, why is empathy for those with substance use disorders so low? They are among the most misunderstood and reviled groups in society. The very terms used to describe those with substance use disorders have contributed to the stigma that surrounds them. Words such as "addict," "abuser," and "abuse" imply a willful desire to use substances and become addicted, which increases stigma and decreases the quality of care. Most people don't feel sorry for those with substance use disorders, either because they've done something illegal or because people believe they can stop using if they really want to. Like those with mental illness—and the two often go hand in hand—substance use disorder is seen as a weakness, something that happens to those bereft of willpower, character, and morals. But current research strongly suggests this is not the case.

New findings in neuroscientific studies have redefined addiction from a condition of flawed character to a model of biology and disease. We now know that the brains of people who become addicted are different from those who do not. It appears that brain reward centers in an area called the nucleus accumbens are so powerfully activated when exposed to opioids, alcohol, or other addictive substances or activities that the prefrontal cortex is outmuscled by the reward centers of the brain, over-powering reason, resolutions, willpower, and promises. This explains organizational psychologist and author Gerard Egan's observation that "An addict is willing to give up everything for one thing, instead of giving up that one thing so they can have everything." It makes no logical sense that individuals with substance use disorder would choose over and over to ingest what they know is bad for them, unless they are powerless to give up the temporary relief or "bliss" they experience from substances.

Interestingly, part of what makes people with substance use disorder so unsympathetic is that they themselves can lose sight of empathy. They can become so consumed by their addiction that they no longer take into account the thoughts and feelings of other people, including the ones they love. The truth is they do still care, but the empathic centers of their brain have been hijacked by addiction. Research shows that those with substance use disorders do seem to present a clinical lack of empathy. Studies by the State University of New York at Buffalo and others identify a psychological syndrome known as alexithymia, an inability to identify one's own feelings, in almost 40 percent of those with alcohol use disorder compared to just 7 percent of the general population. It isn't clear whether individuals start out feeling less empathy or the addiction creates an empathy deficit. I suspect it is the latter. There is no doubt that substance use disorder neurologically impairs the empathy centers of the brain. As drugs or alcohol become more important in their lives, individuals become emotionally invested in seeking out the relief from their physical and emotional states or the high. As they struggle to manage the symptoms of cravings and withdrawal, it becomes an all-consuming, emotionally and neurologically draining task.

However, this is a good time to remember the difference between sympathy and empathy for those afflicted with substance use disorder. Sympathy sadly acknowledges the addict's situation while empathy understands what the person is thinking and feeling. It is much harder to feel and express empathy versus sympathy toward those afflicted because empathy forces you to genuinely listen and relate. This is not to say that empathy is permissive. It simply concedes to everyone, including the person with the disorder, that you appreciate how difficult it is to give up something you physiologically and psychologically crave. An old recovery saying captures this best: The person is never the problem. The problem is the problem.

With that said, we've all heard horror stories about an uncle who flew into a rage at the Fourth of July barbecue because his hamburger was overcooked, or the bridesmaid who showed up intoxicated, fell, and knocked over the wedding cake. We may understand the biology of addiction on an intellectual level, but accounts like this still elicit outrage and confirmation that the individual's behavior is totally outrageous, inappropriate, selfish, and self-centered. Let me tell you the story of the Johnson family, and perhaps I can convince you otherwise.

The Johnsons' only child, Sarah, was a great kid, an excellent student, varsity basketball player, popular, and attending a prestigious college. She started drinking in her freshman year and that escalated into a full-blown drinking problem after graduation. One day, Sarah's boyfriend called her parents, tearfully explaining why he couldn't stay in a relationship with her any longer: she was addicted to alcohol.

After consultation with some professionals, the Johnson family decided to enter the family program at Hazelden, part of the Hazelden Betty Ford Foundation, which is structured to help families support their relatives as they integrate their lives back into the world. The way the program works is that families with an afflicted member are placed in groups, not with their loved one but with others struggling with substance use disorder from the program.

In the Johnsons' group sessions, the tears and anguish flowed, laced with frustration and resentment. The families expressed incomprehension and anger about the many chances they had given to their sons and daughters, husbands and wives. They felt betrayed and dismayed that their loved ones were willing to throw their lives away.

Then they listened. But because they were not related to the families in the room, the Johnsons had an easier time suspending judgment and letting go of their emotions. They heard Jane, the same age as Sarah, talk about how ashamed and embarrassed she felt for lying to her parents and abusing their trust. She described how terrified she was to stop using drugs for fear of losing all her friends. Jane admitted she couldn't see a path forward after finishing her stay at Hazelden because she couldn't imagine a life without her two most reliable companions, drugs and alcohol. Through Jane's voice, the Johnsons were able to hear their daughter's side of the story, a story she was never able to tell them herself.

Sarah's mother and father finally understood addiction from her perspective. They began to understand how powerless she felt over the strong chemical pull of alcohol. In spite of all the reading and research they'd done in the past, they'd always believed it was a matter of will-power and a willingness to change. Now they understood the grip that addictive substances like alcohol had on their daughter's worldview and the lack of confidence she had in her ability to live a clean life.

The Johnson family told me that they were all forever changed by this experience. They used to believe Sarah could have done better if only she'd tried hard enough. Now, with this durable sense of under-standing and compassion, the parents learned they were not responsible for Sarah's substance use disorder. Nor were they responsible for her recovery. What I especially liked hearing about the Johnsons' expe-rience was that Hazelden employed the crucial empathic practice of *perspective taking*. By having family members sit with an unrelated person in similar straits and hear her story, families are able to take a more objective and less emotional perspective. They were able to employ more cognitive empathy and less emotional distress that had been triggered by their helpless feelings in the past.

Now that nearly everyone knows someone with substance use dis-order, it may be possible to shift from judgment to understanding. When you consider an addictive state of mind a medical condition rather than a moral flaw, it's easier to respond with cognitive empathy, knowing the difference between understanding the problem and being supportive of the person's recovery versus enabling their destructive behaviors by feeling pity and supporting the addictive behaviors.

LGBTQ

I vividly recall a day as a second-grader back in the 1960s when I vis-ited the drugstore with my mother. The new clerk behind the counter looked like a man, but he wore a blond wig and a heavy application of makeup. I remember being confused that his deep voice didn't coincide with his feminine accessories, but when I asked my mother, "Why does the lady look like that?" she simply stared straight ahead, squeezed my hand, and refrained from responding. It was enough to convey her discomfort but provided no answers.

This is the first encounter I can remember with someone from the LGBTQ community, which as you may already know is short for lesbian, gay, bisexual, transgender, and queer. Homosexual, bisexual, and transgender persons are now a more visible and vocal minority than they were when I was a child. By some estimates, approximately 4.1 percent of Americans identify as gay or lesbian, with a much smaller percentage of the population identifying as transgender; reports vary from 0.3–0.6 percent. (Though even the miniscule 0.6 percent who identify as transgender still translates to 1.4 million individuals.)

Despite their growing profile in everyday life and culture, people who are LGBTQ evoke more ire and distinct antipathy than just about any other segment of society I can think of. It's an attitude that is deeply ingrained. In 1890, philosopher William James theorized that the revulsion people feel for those who have had sexual contact with the same sex is innate, especially in men, but might be overcome by training. Others have speculated that the bias against gays actually arises from a kind of ancient survival instinct designed to save us from "others who weren't like us." Still others cite evolutionary biology and the fact that same-sex couples cannot reproduce with one another.

Some religious groups regard atypical sexual orientation as sinful. Some secular groups believe LGBTQ individuals suffer from a disease or disorder. Others believe that gay individuals are deviant, lustful aberrations of the laws of nature. Predictably, studies and surveys find that people with the most homophobic attitudes have had little personal contact with someone who is gay and tend to live in areas where bias is the norm. Men demonstrate a stronger predisposition for intolerance to gays; and in general, people express more negative attitudes toward homosexuals of their own sex than of the opposite sex.

Whatever the reasoning, a pervasive prejudice persists against the LGBTQ community, which fosters intense discrimination, bullying, and hate crimes. Some states have sought to criminalize sexual orientation through marriage, employment, and bathroom laws. Other countries punish homosexuality with imprisonment and death.

Even if you don't agree with people living as homosexual, bisexual, or transgender, I want to urge you to stop for a moment and consider having a more empathic response. I recently attended a medical risk conference where a speaker talked about the importance of understanding LGBTQ patients because their health issues are easily overlooked when doctors don't know and don't ask about sexual orientation and gender identity. The speaker, a nurse named Susan, told the most inspiring and courageous story about her own need to know, understand, and empathize with this population better, based on her own experience with her child.

Susan's teenager, Emile, came home on the first semester break from college and announced, to the shock of both parents, that since early childhood she had felt like a boy living in a girl's body. Susan didn't know what to think. As she listened and tried not to judge, she couldn't help feeling a whirl of confusion, dismay, and dread. She'd never confronted her biases and fears about transgender people, and now here she was faced with them in her own family. Like the Johnsons, here is a parent who initially felt she had failed her child over circumstances beyond her control.

Susan decided to educate herself about transgender identity. She learned that most children know at a very early age, usually during grade school, that their bodies don't reflect their true gender identity; they somehow know that there is a mismatch between physical appearance (phenotype) and gender identity. The more she read, the more she learned that being transgender is not in fact a disease or a disorder.

Susan also made an intentional decision to use the keys of E.M.P.A.T.H.Y., moving far beyond gathering factual and clinical information. She carefully perceived her teen's nonverbal cues—his eye gaze, tone of voice, and emotions during their conversations. She recognized her own reactions and then put them aside to listen fully to the emotions expressed before her. She used perspective taking to see the situation and world from her child's eyes, allowing her to understand how hard it was to live in a body that felt foreign. Her emotional empathy resonated with her child's. She was able to move out of her own shoes and to experience to a significant degree what it would be like to be her child. She embraced the shared mind experience and then moved into the role of supportive and loving parent.

Ultimately Susan realized she needed to grieve for the loss of her daughter and preserve her relationship with her child, no matter what gender. Her empathic abilities enabled her to move outside of her own wishes to be open to the needs of her child. What was so incredible about this account was that it was clear that it wasn't easy for Susan, but empathy and love made it possible. As she spoke to a packed auditorium, people were so moved by her words that they leaned forward in their chairs. You could have heard a pin drop. She gave us a genuine example of how perspective taking and empathy led to maintaining her cherished relationship with her own child.

Susan's story shows how important it is to maintain empathy for people, for their humanity, and for their differences. I admired Susan's courage in sharing her story with an audience of medical risk professionals who could have judged her, dismissed her, and denounced her but instead gave her a standing ovation. Empathy must extend to all of humanity if we are to live in a humane society. This heroic act of putting aside her own wishes and dreams for a future she had envisioned and opening herself up to the future that was right for Emile has bound their relationship into an extraordinarily close and loving one. Such stories serve to inspire society to see the possibilities of connection when we see the world through the eyes of another.

Autism and Empathy

People on the autism spectrum (AS) are often hard to empathize with because they don't respond in expected ways. It's easy to judge someone with autism as "other" if you don't understand the many challenges they face. Those on the AS have deficits of their own in expressing empathy, which appears to be linked to an inability to take the perspective of others and abnormalities in social and emotional communication. They also show displays of obsessional features from a young age. These atypical social responses, such as lack of eye contact and inappropriate facial expressions, make them difficult to relate to, and as a result they are often out-grouped and isolated from childhood.

We've learned that empathy is a mirrored phenomenon: when you receive it, it's magnified in you. But people with autism don't typically respond to emotions with the standard facial expressions. If you're a fan of the CBS television series *The Big Bang Theory*, you know that Sheldon, a character who is on the spectrum, constantly asks for clarification on displays of emotion—and then misunderstands or dismisses the explanations he's given. He comes across as cold and unfeeling. And, though his antisocial displays lead to trouble, misunderstandings, and hurt feelings, Sheldon is lucky. He's found a group of friends, and even a girlfriend, who are willing to overlook his social deficits and inability to appropriately process social cues. Unfortunately, I think many people on the spectrum aren't so lucky.

Autism appears to affect about one in seventy children and is on the rise. The diagnosis encompasses a wide range of limitations in social functioning, from severe difficulties in relating to others to milder forms. Autism researcher Simon Baron-Cohen (the uncle of the famous comedian Sacha Baron-Cohen) has extensively studied the decreased neural activity in brain regions associated with empathy among those with autism. He's found that people with autism have difficulty interpreting emotional facial expressions in others and have a limited ability for perspective taking. The lack of ability of those with this disorder to appreciate what others are going through or to have insight into their own reactions can result in misunderstandings and judgments of character. These, in turn, can lead to social disconnections rather than empathy for their challenges. Even in higher-functioning autistic adults, who may be exceptionally intelligent and capable in some areas, lack of social awareness and accurate emotion detection can lead to tremendous difficulties in maintaining interpersonal relationships.

Just as with every other out-group, autistic individuals require more understanding and patience than many others. Though it's sometimes hard, perhaps we can remember to have an appreciation for the biological gaps in some individuals' brain development and try to imagine what it would be like if you or your son or daughter had this disorder. You would want others to give them the benefit of the doubt and exercise patience. And most importantly, when someone displays atypical behavior, we'd like to think that most of us would think twice before judging or dismissing them.

Find Your E.M.P.A.T.H.Y.

When empathy is the most difficult, that's the time you most need to evaluate what blocks you from accessing it and ask yourself whether you are showing respect, a word that literally means to "look again." When we are respectful, we take another look after our first impression and try to view others without judgment. I know it isn't always easy. I'm hoping the keys to E.M.P.A.T.H.Y. can help you identify your empathy roadblocks so you can work through them or come to terms with them when empathy is not possible.

Have you ever looked into the eyes of a homeless person and been jolted by the sense of bewilderment and distress she must be feeling? Or the eyes of a drug-addled loved one and seen the depths of their pain and despair? Be motivated to notice. Also, be more understanding: people with autism and individuals from other cultures may not be able to hold eye gaze the way you'd expect. Keeping this in mind can help explain behavior and lead to greater understanding.

Interpreting facial expressions provides a lot of information about intent. Hateful or disturbing behavior may actually be a cry for help. The better you know someone, the easier it is to interpret the subtle nuances in how she uses her eyes, mouth, and other facial muscles. The more you practice, the more your recognition skills will improve. Some people tell me they're pretty good at deciphering the emotions of people they see on TV when the sound is turned off. I think they could be on to something. Think about a character in a play, show, or movie who is less than perfect, yet the actor is able to portray him as sympathetic. Much of this is conveyed through the actor's facial expressions.

Posture offers additional observational clues you can add to what's displayed in the eyes and face. Very few people in anguish stand up straight with their shoulders thrown back. A person's posture is often a telling clue about their emotions. If your friend is slouching in his chair, has his head down, and looks as though he is physically collapsing rather than upright and energetic, consider that he may be dejected, disappointed, or even depressed.

For some of the groups I've discussed in this chapter, affect is compromised. People with autism, for instance, don't always have the same emotional affect as everyone else in the same situation. Or if someone is impaired by alcohol or drugs, they may not respond in a typical manner. In such cases you can't always rely on mirroring or your own innate instincts. You can understand affect better in someone you know well despite their challenges with expressing emotions, but even this can be difficult under pressure. Educate yourself as to why some people react differently than expected so you can adjust your expectations accordingly and avoid passing judgment. In some situations, the best you can do is make sure your own emotions are clear in expression, manner, and actions.

Ninety percent of what we communicate is communicated nonverbally, and 38 percent of nonverbal communication is through tone of voice. When listening carefully, you may actually hear more by listening to the tone rather than the words. When a person with a substance use disorder uses threatening and intense words, perhaps making excuses or trying to cover up the truth, the desperation you hear is most likely the truest communication. The words and manipulation will put you off, but recognizing the need for help and refusing to enable the addiction could help set them on a path to recovery.

There is no greater compliment or gift than to give someone your full attention. Hearing means *hearing the whole person*. Not only the words they are saying but the context in which they are telling you their story. Put down your device, take out your earbuds, get off the phone. Make it your goal to ask questions and listen to the responses. If you know a situation will be challenging beforehand, set aside time when you won't be distracted with other things. Make fully listening a tribute to your relationship with the other person, the way Susan did when Emile shared his story of his true identity with her.

Finally, "your response," the "Y" in the E.M.P.A.T.H.Y. acronym, is not about the words that you will speak next. Pay attention to how your body is responding to a conversation. If you notice yourself tightening up, your stomach knotting up, or your heart pounding, try to take some deep breaths and name your emotion. If you feel anxious, say, "I need to think about this for a moment." If you're angry, you may try saying, "I'm having a strong reaction to what you're saying right now, and I need some time to think about a thoughtful response." If you feel calm and good when speaking with someone else, that's most likely how they find you, because most feelings are mutual. However, if you are with someone who has an impairment in expressing their own emotions, you may notice your response and make the choice to give that person the benefit of the doubt and hear him out. That is putting empathic listening into practice, and you may notice that your initial tense physical sensations may just give way to a more peaceful bodily state and greater connection.

Feeling for the Monsters among Us

Truly evil acts don't elicit much empathy. They inspire fear, disgust, and anger. These are the acts of murderers, child molesters, the Nazis, and the dictators among us. I cannot say these people don't deserve any empathic curiosity into what motivates their behavior. But I will say they challenge the depths of our empathic capacity.

Take, for example, individuals who themselves appear to lack empathy for others. They may manipulate others to follow them, and when the results of their actions are fully exposed, it is very difficult to conjure up any positive emotions for them. They raise a host of vexing questions: What makes people behave this way? If we knew more about their backgrounds and the lives they have lived, would we find that they had suffered similar cruelty? And would being victims themselves of physical violence, hate, or psychological manipulation excuse their behavior and make it any more forgivable? Or is there something fundamentally flawed in these people due to neurological deficits? Does this missing emotional chip excuse them from their monstrous acts?

Neuroscience researchers have shown that the neural mechanisms for empathy appear to be damaged in people who display psychopathy. Neuroscientist and Irving B. Harris Distinguished Service Professor

Jean Decety at the University of Chicago has done extensive research that suggests psychopaths are devoid of empathy and that the brains of psychopaths are indeed different from typical brains. They often do not register fear in the faces of their victims and remain unmoved by wails or cries of distress. They have none of the shared neural circuits or empathic capacity for the suffering of others. Psychopaths harm others with apparent ease and no conflicts of conscience. The extent to which these deficits are nature or nurture is not entirely clear.

The signs of antisocial personality elucidated by Simon Baron-Cohen's work point to traits that are common in psychopathic and sociopathic groups. These traits include deceitfulness, impulsivity, aggression, reckless disregard for the safety of others, irresponsibility, failure to conform to social norms of lawfulness, and lack of remorse. To see such traits on full display, we need look no further back than the Charlottesville protest, where a white nationalist extremist full of hate willfully plowed his car into a crowd of protesters, killing a young woman who was peacefully demonstrating. People like this who have hatred for others and who are devoid of empathy pose a serious threat to the workings of our society.

World history is marred by figures who have shown the most extreme hatred and hostility to minority groups, resulting in the deaths of hundreds of millions of people. The tactics they use are to dehumanize and demonize out-groups to the extent that killing them becomes justified. How do we begin to understand the minds of a Hitler, Stalin, Lenin, Mao Zedong, Osama bin Laden, or the leaders of genocides in Rwanda, Armenia, Yugoslavia and the mass killings in Syria? What empathic feelings can we spare for psychopathic mass murderers like Ted Bundy and John Wayne Gacy? We know that psychopathic individuals lack the crucial substrate for empathy. What is behind the acts of terrorists? Members of neo-Nazi groups and the KKK? Animal abusers? Are such people monsters? Are they aberrations of nature? What do we owe them emotionally? Who can say that there are people who do violent things and deserve no empathy?

As you can see, perhaps there are more questions than answers. One thing is certain: there are people for whom having empathy is much,

much more difficult. But we must be careful. Empathy is a slippery slope. If we decide that there are certain individuals or groups for whom feeling empathy is not an option, where is the bright red line? Does it begin to extend further and further until empathy becomes the exception rather than the rule? Even in the most difficult cases, understanding before casting judgment is essential. However, understanding does not preclude accountability. Consequences are based on actions and behaviors, no matter how well we may understand why people do terrible things or are on the far outs. However, understanding what leads to violent attitudes, tendencies, and actions is imperative if we are to find constructive and positive ways forward as a society.

12

Self-Empathy

I magine you have a close friend who's going through a rough patch. Wouldn't you rush to her aid, offering love, support, and understanding and be unlikely to judge her? As a true friend, you'd be there with a kind word, a listening ear, and a comforting tone of voice rather than piling on shame or blame. Why do so many of us refuse to offer the same sort of kindness to ourselves? Self-criticism seems to be an automatic response for the smallest mistakes we make, and a rush to judgment for the slightest misstep. We pride ourselves on kindness and compassion toward others, yet when it comes to the person we see in the mirror each day, we regard empathic concern as a sign of weakness.

It's time to give ourselves a break.

In this chapter, we will focus on self-empathy. *Self*-empathy, you say? Isn't empathy something we're supposed to feel for *others*? Isn't it a contradiction in terms? If we return to the seven keys of empathy, we realize that we rarely apply these cues to assess our own feelings—*putting an "eye" and "I" and "Y" into empathy.*

Most of us don't make a regular practice of analyzing our own facial expressions and postures or putting a name to our own feelings when we are upset, but maybe we should. Giving yourself permission to have a good cry can also provide an emotional catharsis. Studies performed by A. J. J. M. Vingerhoets, a Dutch expert on crying, found that 90 minutes after watching a tearjerker of a movie, people who have a good cry are in a better mood than before they watched the film. As Vingerhoets explains it, weeping may be an effective way to recover from a strong emotion. And because crying and sad expressions connect more deeply to our own true feelings, they help us feel empathy and compassion for others as well.

We also know that putting a name to an affect or the emotion of others, such as "he looks happy" or "she looks sad," helps us experience greater empathy for them. It turns out that the same is true of naming our own emotions. When overcome with an emotion such as anger, fear, or disgust, giving it a name helps with self-regulation by recognizing it as a temporary situation that does not define you forever. In effect, it allows the prefrontal cortex, the part of the brain involved in appraising an emotion, to gain a little distance from the feeling.

Perhaps the most important key of all to self-empathy is the "Y" for your response. It's no accident that we associate so many emotional expressions with the body. Our bodies are the instruments that signal our emotions. The heart races with terror when you're scared, the pupils dilate when you are in love, and the stomach fills with butterflies when you are nervous. Tuning in to the bodily responses teaches us to recognize and respect the ones that require self-care. It's an important skill for managing our own health, emotions, and relationships.

It may seem strange at first to realize that "your response" refers not only to your response to *others*, but also to your own response to *your own* experiences. One way to think about this is the difference between "I" and "me." "I" is the observing part of ourselves that observes "me" in action. For example, "*I* realized that his comments really hurt *me*." This observation does not define my whole self as being hurt, but observes that someone's comments hurt the feelings of a subject—me. The "I" is the observer of what happens to "me." We need to tune in to learn more about our own emotions, and your response is the key to knowing your own feelings.

Understanding Self-Empathy

One reason we resist practicing self-empathy is that we mistake it for self-pity. We view it as a soft and fuzzy euphemism for self-indulgence. The difference is that self-indulgence can become a destructive force that allows you to give in to anything that makes you feel good despite its unhealthy effects, such as excessive use of food, drugs, or alcohol to numb feelings. Self-empathy requires greater self-awareness, discipline, and sensitivity to self-suffering and also a commitment to finding helpful solutions. Self-empathy is the acknowledgment that, like all human beings, you deserve understanding and compassion. To truly practice self-empathy to its fullest, you must be willing to use it even when you trip over your own feet and make mistakes that leave you feeling embarrassed or wishing you had stayed home. It is an exercise in humility that requires acknowledging that you are human and fallible, and that mistakes are part of the broad human experience.

When you have empathy and compassion for yourself, it allows you to compare your own experience to everyone else's and acknowledge that whatever your troubles or concerns are, they have been experienced by others and are worthy of compassion. In a way, it's the ultimate form of perspective taking because you slip into your very own shoes and look at yourself from a compassionate point of view. In the same way that understanding how others think and feel tends to prevent you from judging them too severely, extending that same courtesy in your own direction prevents you from wading too far into a pool of self-judgment. This doesn't mean you are superior or more deserving than anyone else or that your mistakes should go unchallenged. Self-empathy does not relieve you of accountability or a need to apologize if you've let others down. It merely means that you, just like everyone else, deserve empathic concern, love, and care even when you make mistakes. When you learn to become more compassionate with yourself, you learn to treat others with similar kindness. Once again, it is the empathy loop in action.

In today's world, self-empathy is an underrated psychological proficiency. When things go wrong, we're inclined to withhold those psychic hugs from ourselves because we don't want to lower our standards or because we equate doing so with egoism, permissiveness, or laziness. Yet the opposite is true. Studies show that people with self-empathic tendencies are less likely than self-critics to lounge around on the couch all day. On personality tests, self-empathy is strongly correlated with positive traits such as motivation, resilience, creative thinking, life satisfaction, and empathy toward other people. Conversely, the faultfinders among us tend to score higher for personality attributes such as hostility, anxiety, and depression and lower in qualities such as life satisfaction and outwardly empathic behaviors. In other words, the way we treat ourselves is often the way we treat others.

Empathy has traditionally been considered a characteristic that allows us to understand and share the emotional experiences of other people. We view it as an essential ingredient for good interpersonal relationships but not necessarily something we turn inward on ourselves. Let's shift that thinking. The kindness and understanding you express for yourself are the empathic equivalent to an oxygen mask on a plane. Before you can offer empathy and compassion for others, you need to "pull down the mask" and inhale the oxygen yourself.

Compassion researcher Kristin Neff has recently done some trailblazing work on the concept of self-compassion, breaking it down into three main components: self-kindness, shared humanity, and mindfulness.

Self-kindness refers to the practice of being understanding and forgiving toward oneself, including in times of failure or pain. Being gentle with yourself is an essential aspect of self-empathy because it prevents you from judging who you are too severely. Far from creating a self-centered view of the world, a self-forgiving attitude is one of the best defenses against narcissism. You can move on from mistakes without allowing them to pile up and bury your confidence and self-esteem under a mountain of doubt.

A sense of shared humanity means you perceive your own experiences as part of the larger human tapestry rather than as separate and isolating. Shared humanity feeds self-empathy by reminding us that we are not alone, even in our failings. As Alexander Pope once wrote, "To err is human . . ." But let's not forget the second part of that quote: "to forgive, divine." By recognizing the fact that suffering and personal inadequacy are natural parts of the common human experience, you can forgive yourself and move on.

Mindfulness, which has become something of a buzzword of late, is the ability to identify your thoughts and feelings without reacting to them or judging them. Appraising the contents of your mind from a third-person point of view affords you the self-awareness to understand the difference between the actual self and the thoughts and feelings that the self is having. It's like taking a seat in the balcony to watch a drama starring your thoughts and feelings as they play out on a stage. Becoming an observer of the drama rather than an actor allows you the freedom to consider different beliefs and attitudes about what is happening in your life.

Of the three components of self-empathy, mindfulness has been the most extensively studied and is best understood. The reason it has received such an enormous amount of attention is that mindfulness has been theoretically and experimentally associated with psychological well-being. Mindfulness has been shown to help us self-regulate our emotions more effectively. Also, studies link regular mindfulness activity with heightened levels of focus, awareness, and nonjudgmental acceptance of moment-to-moment experience. By priming the brain to take greater control over attention, it helps us focus on what is important, fine-tuning our ability to switch attention onto something else when necessary. We know that when people feel centered and can live their lives with equanimity, the way they approach the world is very different from when they are distracted and emotionally dysregulated.

Neuroimaging studies find that the brains of people who routinely perform some sort of mindful meditation operate differently from those who don't. Buddhist monks who practice daily meditation have cortical thickening between the cognitive and emotional centers of the brain, rendering them less reactive to emotional stimuli. These same sorts of brain changes have been demonstrated in novice meditators in as few as eight weeks. There are also some interesting data from studies where the brain is hooked up to an EEG monitor that translates its electrical activity into "waves." People who meditate show more persistent alpha wave activity, associated with a restful metabolic rate; for example, lower heart rate, slower breathing, and so on. Additionally, they've been shown to have a higher incidence of theta waves, which scientists correlate with low emotional arousal and restfulness.

The Raindrop Effect

Have you ever seen a cartoon where one of the characters gets chased off a cliff and suddenly finds itself flailing in midair? It takes the character a few seconds to realize there is nothing beneath its feet before it panics and crashes to the ground.

This is an analogy I use in psychotherapy all the time. Sometimes a person doesn't even realize that he has run out of resources and support until he finds himself in midair with nothing to hold himself up.

My friend Frank Sesno grew up with a sister who had Down syndrome, which, as you may know, is a genetic disorder marked by severe mental disability and low IQ. His mother, who was a social worker, worked in a facility for people with disabilities, where a big part of her job was making sure her patients were well cared for. Frank, whom I have already introduced, recalls vividly how hard his sister's disability was on his mom. She didn't always handle it with grace either.

"I'd love to use the word empathy, but at times she wasn't all that nice or kind to my sister," he says.

Frank stresses that his mother loved her special-needs child as passionately as she loved all her other children. But long days, lack of help, and a difficult marriage left her burned out and weary. Even as a child, Frank sensed that his mother's emotional reservoir was often empty, leaving her with a short supply of patience. Sometimes this caused her to treat his sister harshly. He remembers hoping that she was giving better advice to her clients and their families than the example she was setting at home.

This scenario, where a caregiver acts poorly to the very person who depends upon her, is all too common. In surveys, people who choose caregiving professions are individuals who genuinely feel concerned for others but cite long hours, lack of sleep, and the high emotional demands of their jobs for sapping their empathic reserves. It's not that they aren't focused on the safety and well-being of their charges. Frank's mother certainly cared about her daughter. At some point they simply run out of emotional gas. His ability, as a journalist, to observe these dynamics from all the angles of his different family members surely contributed to his gift for perceiving others' perspectives.

Self-neglect over time blunts the ability to perceive or respond to the needs of other people because it diminishes the resources we have available for an empathic response. You have to help yourself before you can help others. When your own needs are attended to, you are less likely to be distracted. Tell me, how much empathy can you muster for someone—anyone—when you're feeling exhausted, hungry, burned out, and grumpy?

Empathy and compassion for others tend to be highest when the body is in a physiological state of balance that scientists refer to as homeostasis. In an ideal world, stress hormones like cortisol and adrenaline remain low until there is an emergency and we need to respond. But if cortisol and adrenaline levels are continually elevated by mental and physical stressors, it's as if we are operating in a state of emergency all the time.

With allostasis, the process by which the body responds to stressors in order to regain homeostasis, the brain is both the responder and target of stress. A high allostatic load when you are working hard all the time without getting back into balance means you are pumping out an excess of neurotransmitter and hormonal responses in everyday life, often more than is actually needed for the tasks at hand. This leads to a spike in inflammation of blood vessels in the heart and brain, which in turn puts you at risk for health problems such as elevated blood pressure, high cholesterol, and increased fat storage. Together these could explain the growing evidence for the connection between high stress, emotional disorders, and conditions such as heart disease, vascular disease, and other systemic disorders. With anxiety disorders, depressive illness, hostile and aggressive states, substance abuse, and posttraumatic stress disorder, the allostatic load is excessively high, and we also often see chemical imbalances and, in some cases, atrophy of brain structures.

Further, a high allostatic load can literally impact you at the cellular level and even the molecular level. Because genes are not static, their expression depends on how you interact with your environment through a process known as epigenetics. So for example, you may be born with genes for a degenerative disease, but they may never be expressed if you practice good health habits and take care of yourself, so the environment can affect gene expression. Those who experience constant stress and neglect their health habits place a high allostatic load on their cells. Studies suggest this leads to shortening of the end caps of the genes, known as telomeres. The research also suggests that shortened telomeres are associated with poor health and a shorter lifespan.

I often see a lack of self-awareness in those who suddenly realize they are like the cartoon character who has run off the cliff. Only when there is no air beneath their feet, and they view every request as a demand, taking on every responsibility even though it seems like another massive burden, do they start to notice that their interactions with the people they most love are fraying. This constant state of tension and stress is an indication that self-care is entirely lacking.

Feeling frazzled all the time is not a normal or healthy way for anyone to be showing up in the world. Not long ago I attended a self-care workshop at Kripalu Center for Yoga & Health in the Berkshires region of Massachusetts. I found myself surrounded by forty women who were juggling unbelievable workloads along with family responsibilities. All of us were stressed, burned out, and exhausted. It was a firsthand look at how critical it is for all of us to occasionally take time out and press the reset button. It was also a gateway to experience the joy of movement and to enhance our vitality by walking in nature and energizing our bodies through their exhilarating yoga dance program.

When irritability and a lack of endurance are the order of the day, it is a time to hold the mirror up to yourself and ask yourself if you have lost the ability to empathize with your own needs. Self-care not only promotes your own well-being and vitality; it can also make you more fun to be around and a better partner, friend, coworker, or parent. Once we learn to practice self-care and begin to be less harsh with ourselves, it creates a huge ripple effect. If you have greater awareness of what you are feeling and what you need, you'll be more likely to manage your needs for sleep, rest, exercise, movement, and food better than someone who is out of tune with himself. Being kind to yourself is the only way you can effectively practice empathy and compassion toward others.

One good thing to come out of Frank's story is that watching his mother helped him build an uncanny ability to empathize with others.

He grew up trying to understand the perspectives of all his family members without too much judgment. I believe this experience helped him become a world-class interviewer and storyteller because he developed a keen ability to walk in the shoes of others.

Mind Over Chatter

One of the biggest barriers to self-empathy is feeling so bad about yourself that you believe you are unworthy of kindness and compassion. This mind-set often leads to worry, anxiety, and self-doubt. Mindfulness helps combat negativity, segregating the self-critical default scripts that run through the brain until they can be evaluated and put into proper context.

While some people are born with a positive outlook on life and mindful thinking comes naturally to them, others dwell on the discouraging past and catastrophized future. Pessimistic tendencies are part of human nature. They are a holdover from our prehistoric past when it was more important to be on alert for danger than to stop and smell the flowers. This is why your heart hammers in your chest during an awkward social situation in the same way it would if you were being stalked by a tiger. In today's world most of the "tigers" we encounter are emotional rather than physical, but these threats coil through the psyche in exactly the same way. They represent peril and discomfort, signaling the amygdala and limbic system to release a flood of cortisol and other fight-or-flight neurochemicals.

If you had highly critical or harsh parents, the inner critics and bullies can be quite loud and demanding. You may even seek out bosses, jobs, or mates who echo what is in your own brain, unconsciously reinforcing that you aren't good enough. This insidious pattern may be repeated over a lifetime and perhaps passed down to the next generation. Though it may have started as a protective tactic—learning to be so self-critical that you beat the critics to the punch—the real problem with self-created criticism is that it outlives its usefulness and becomes harmful. While some negative self-talk may have helped you stay out of trouble as a child or work hard to overcome your imperfections, as an adult you have a *choice* to either listen to it or ignore it. If your inner critic is loud and relentless to the point of becoming an obsession, cognitive behavioral therapy is an excellent and proven form of psychotherapy that can reframe and restructure your thoughts. If the roots of your self-criticism lie in difficult childhood dynamics, psychodynamic psychotherapy is a form of treatment that helps you process your experience by remembering and grieving what didn't go right in the past in the context of a healing, therapeutic relationship; this helps you to heal and recover. Cognitive and emotional empathy are the foundations of psychotherapeutic interventions.

Separating your thoughts and feelings from who you are helps you stand up to those self-created critics and bullies. It teaches you to distance yourself from the messages they send about not being smart enough or good enough. When you choose not to take messages so personally, you may begin to process negativity and criticism with self-empathy on a deeper level and evaluate them in a nonjudgmental fashion. Rather than immediately going down the path of self-criticism, mindfulness teaches you to slow down, take a deep breath, and dispassionately examine your reactions.

I'll give you an example from my own experience.

One of the first professional lectures I ever gave was attended by a professor considered a giant in the field of psychiatry. He sat in the back of the room, and as soon as I started my presentation, he began squinting and frowning. His squirming and apparent displeasure at my presentation completely threw me off. My palms started to sweat, and I could feel my heart racing and my breathing quicken, all typical physiological flight-or-fight responses. Why was he making those faces? Did he think I had no idea what I was talking about? And for that matter, *did* I know what I was talking about?

Afterward he came up, congratulated me on "a very fine talk," and asked me to send him my slides. It turns out he had forgotten his glasses and couldn't see the screen.

The mind is quite a storyteller! I was just starting out my psychiatry teaching career, and this man was a respected pillar in my chosen field. I allowed myself to spin a tale based on the facial expressions of someone I did not know very well. Normally we have the ability to interpret face, body, and voice fairly accurately. They are the most valuable assets we have in shaping an empathic response. However, there are circumstances, especially in relationships with a power imbalance, where we may misinterpret the arch of a brow or the twitch of a lip. In this case, my perception of the professor's annoyed facial expression was correct, but my interpretation was not.

Worry is a form of ritualized reassurance. You imagine all the negative scenarios that can possibly occur and then all the ways to wiggle out of them. Anxious thinking is an attempt to calm the brain. The more you do it, the more you reinforce it as a cognitive habit. Some surveys suggest that approximately 85 percent of the time, what you worry about doesn't happen. Consider the waste of psychic energy. Among the many benefits of quieting the mind is diminishing all that self-defeating brain chatter. It flips the script—not by changing your thoughts but instead by changing your *relationship to* those thoughts.

Adopting a more self-forgiving approach allows you to mindfully stand apart from the emotional aspects of a situation and avoid the kind of emotional dysregulation that results in automatic negative analyses and maladaptive responses. As a recent Emory University study demonstrated, subjects who received mindfulness training improved in their ability to interpret eye contact and predict what others were thinking, both good tests of empathic accuracy.

If someone reacts badly to you or says something insulting, it can send your emotions skidding toward the negative and spin your thoughts into a self-critical hyper-loop. Mindful thinking counteracts automatic thinking, preventing you from jumping to conclusions. There are a lot of reasons someone might be unhappy that have nothing to do with you. Perhaps he is a critical person. Perhaps he is having a bad day or is preoccupied with something else. Or perhaps he simply has poor eyesight.

Forgiving yourself for things that didn't go right is one of the most powerful ways to let go of past hurts and grudges. Even when there is some accuracy to your critical thoughts, mindfulness teaches us that it shouldn't matter. There is no excuse for excessive self–trash talk. You can always find a kinder, gentler way to speak to yourself that avoids harsh labels and a self-destructive mind-set. It's okay to admit that you did something wrong. Just don't ignore what you did well or what you can do better next time. The worry-primed brain has not learned how to appreciate staying in the present moment and judging the self fairly. You can notice your thoughts. But *you are not your thoughts.* Learn to observe them from the balcony seat and choose how you will respond.

Where We Need to Go

In my own field of medicine, burnout has reached epidemic proportions, with more than half of doctors reporting at least one symptom of burnout such as exhaustion, depersonalizing others (viewing others more as objects than people), or loss of a sense of effectiveness in their work. Nurses report even higher rates of burnout. Preliminary data show that most people who enter medicine start out having an above-average level of empathy that diminishes while they are still in training. Studies have shown an alarming increase in burnout and decrease in empathy as early as the third year of medical school. However, one very recent study from the University of Chicago suggests that medical students seem to retain steady levels of cognitive empathy while their emotional empathy is chipped away under the intense rigors of training with few outlets to deal with the pressure and insufficient training in managing difficult human interactions.

Fortunately, the cognitive empathy of medical students seems to prevail, and most can persevere through their physical and emotional fatigue in order to provide compassionate care. After medical school, interns and residents continue to report an epidemic level of burnout, and even after completing their training, they don't rebound as completely as they once did. We know that the average resident now spends under two hours with their patients on a typical day—and nearly six hours interacting with data on the computer. Beyond the strain of so much computer time and the imperative to endlessly diagnose and treat complex medical conditions, excess focus on computerized records in patient exam rooms robs clinicians of valuable opportunities to practice the seven empathic keys.

Perhaps you have had the experience at a recent doctor's visit where you were asked a series of questions as the doctor recorded your responses. All the while as she sat tapping away on her keyboard, how many times did she glance up from her computer and look you in the eye or show that she understood your chief concern, and not only your chief complaint that day? Probably not often.

If this lack of eye contact or noticing your emotional concerns leaves you feeling more like a number than a patient, consider that the same effect is happening to your physician. Most physicians do not prefer to practice in this perfunctory way. When your doctor rushes through checklists and focuses exclusively on the problem that brought you in rather than hearing the whole person, both you and your doctor lose a bit of the humanity that once defined medical practice. You also both miss out on the burst of dopamine that comes with a satisfying interpersonal experience.

Electronic health records do have their good points, but they can act as a barrier between doctor and patient, stripping away eye contact, review of body language, and other empathic keys from the patient-doctor interaction. This is a bad experience for everyone involved. Doctors feel burnout and a mounting dissatisfaction with their work while patients increasingly report unsatisfactory interactions with the health-care system. More than 80 percent of malpractice suits are the result of poor communication and a perceived lack of empathy from the doctor by patients. Many efforts are underway to emphasize wellness practices and focus on expanding empathic capacity for the benefit of both patients and providers.

My friend Adi Haramati, whom I introduced earlier in the book, believes teaching medical students to become more mindful is an important part of the answer. In 2014 Adi helped found CENTILE, the Center for Innovation and Leadership in Education, at Georgetown's medical school, which runs programs for educators that focus on a variety of self-care and self-awareness techniques such as mindfulness meditation.

The results of CENTILE's mind-body classes to teach stress management and foster self-awareness are impressive. Students who participate in an eight-week program of mindful meditation and a variety of collaborative case study initiatives report what a powerful influence the course has been on their education. Before the class, two-thirds of the students report feeling empathy toward their classmates. By the end of the class, the percentage rises to 95 percent. Adi says letters pour into his office from medical students expressing gratitude for the experience and thanking the school for reminding them why they went into medicine in the first place.

This is the first program I'm aware of that paid attention to the emotional and allostatic load on medical students. As a physiologist, Adi understood that teaching about the physiology of the kidney, while important, was not imparting knowledge about how human physiological responses to stress during medical school can interfere with learning and stress management. By introducing mindfulness and meditation, once relegated to the realm of alternative and complementary medicine, self-care entered the world of the emerging physician. The lessons here are important for everyone: it is impossible to take care of others in an empathic and compassionate way if we neglect ourselves.

Fortunately, similar programs now have been adopted by medical schools around the country and internationally. A rapidly growing number of schools and training programs are adopting self-care practices into their curricula as essential teachings to prevent burnout. Rather than focusing the entirety of medical education on the care of the patient, medical schools are taking the "opportunity" of the current burnout crisis to steer the ship toward also emphasizing self-care for the caregivers. As we've seen throughout this book, empathy begets more empathy through shared brain mechanisms and trainings in self-care, empathy, and mindfulness. This emphasis on self-care and compassion is needed in all sectors of society.

Parents, educators, business leaders, health-care workers, attorneys, politicians, law enforcement officers, the legal system, and every worker who interacts with other people would be able to enjoy their roles and jobs much more while becoming more effective. When self-empathy and empathy for others are practiced with a foundation in the seven keys of empathy, we have hope to help shape a more civil society, respectful discourse, understanding of others, and a humane world.

Acknowledgments

This book would not have been possible without the warm and wonderful partnership with Liz Neporent. Liz helped bring to life decades of clinical and research experience in psychiatry, neuroscience, education, and empathy by synthesizing the stories behind them in a way that would engage you, the reader. We owe deep gratitude to Linda Konnor, of Konnor Literary Agency, for providing steady support, and to our sharp-eyed editor, Caroline Pincus, whose dedication and guidance were invaluable. Liz and I are deeply grateful to our families—Norm, Grant, and Claire Nishioka, and Jay and Skyler Shafran—for their curiosity, novel ideas, patience, and enthusiastic support.

My gratitude belongs to the psychiatry department at Massachusetts General Hospital (MGH) and Harvard Medical School, where the leadership of Drs. Ned Cassem, Jerry Rosenbaum, and Michael Jenike shaped my development as a psychiatrist, educator, and researcher. I am grateful for their support in founding the Empathy and Relational Science Program at MGH, the first hospital program of its kind.

Heartfelt thanks to my talented and dedicated colleagues and fellow researchers who have worked tirelessly on our many research projects in the MGH empathy program. Our work would not have been possible without the contributions of John Kelley, Gordon Kraft-Todd, Diego Reinero, Margot Phillips, Áine Lorié, Lidia Schapira, Rob Bailey, Lee Dunn, Tess Lauricella, Arabella Simpkin, Andrea Haberlein, and Joan Camprodan. Thanks also to the memory of our beloved colleague Lee Baer.

Thank you to my steadfast mentors and friends at Massachusetts General Hospital and Harvard Medical School, doctors Irene Briggin, Elizabeth Armstrong, Jon Borus, Michael Jenike, Elizabeth Mort, Maurizio Fava, Greg Friccione, John Herman, Christopher Gordon, Gene Beresin, Jim Groves, Margaret Cramer, Charlie Hatem, Carl Marci, Vicky Jackson, Juliet Jacobsen, Susan Edgman-Levitan, Tony Weiner, Beth Lown, David Eisenberg, Ed Hundert, Ron Arky, Rob Abernethy, Sherry Haydock, and Liz Gaufberg.

I'm grateful to the foundations that supported our research, especially the visionary Sandra Gold and the late Arnold Gold and Richard Levin of the Arnold P. Gold Foundation for Humanism in Medicine, The Josiah Macy Jr. Foundation for Medical Education, the Risk Management Foundation, and the David Judah Fund.

I continue to be inspired by the pioneers in the field of communication and mindfulness: Alan Alda, Don Berwick, Richard Chasin, Richard Davidson, Jean Decety, Paul Ekman, the late John O'Donohue, Ron Epstein, Dan Goleman, Dan Siegel, Baroness Sheila Hollins, Frank Sesno, and Tania Singer.

Special thanks to everyone who was interviewed and consulted for this book: Alan Alda, Caroline Abernethy, Frannie Abernethy Armstrong, Axelle Bagot, Susan Boisvert, Emile Boisvert, Richard Boyatzis, Christopher Gordon, Adi Haramati, Eric Kandel, Suzanne Koven, Lynn Margherio, Diane Paulus, Doug Rauch, Frank Sesno, Vicky Shen, Patty McLaughlin Simon, Dick Simon, and Renee Peterson Trudeau.

I'm grateful to all my colleagues and friends in the Consortium for Research on Emotional Intelligence in Organizations including cofounders Daniel Goleman and Richard Boyatzis, and Rick Aberman, Lauris Woolford, and Doug Lennick.

Above all I'm deeply grateful to all of the patients and families I've had the privilege to work with over the years. The power that is released in those who have the courage to know their own stories, to grieve and accept what didn't go right in their lives, and then emerge whole and emboldened to embrace life, has given strength and meaning to my life. The resilience of the human spirit never ceases to inspire me as you've changed your lives for the better and made the world a more peaceful and connected place.

Heartfelt thanks to my dear friends and colleagues who read portions of the manuscript and offered their invaluable insights. Thank you to Malcolm Astley, Leigh Divine, David Frankel, Melissa Kraft, Claire Nishioka, Grant Nishioka, Nancy Rappaport, Johanna Riess Thoeresz, and Christa T. Stout.

To all the people who made Empathetics, Inc. possible, I'm deeply grateful. Special thanks to Charlie MacCormack, former CEO of Save the Children and Middlebury College's Scholar in Residence, for his vision to spread empathy within and beyond health care. Deep gratitude to our board of directors—Joe Mondato, Pete McNerney, and Nathaniel Opperman—our advisory board, to Vance Opperman and the late Dr. Glen Nelson for their invaluable wisdom, guidance, and trust in Empathetics' potential, and to all of our dedicated leaders and staff, especially Diane Blake.

Thank you to my friends whose support was invaluable as I wrote this book: Melissa Kraft, Nan Stout, Wendy Gordon, Larry Rowe, Nancy Persson, Ruthann Harnisch, Eve Ekman, Sandy Honeyman, Frank Sesno, John Weinberg, Cathy Lee, Malcolm Astley, Pam Swing, Diane and Dean Goodermote, and Kim and Ernie Parizeau. Thank you to all the special women of Wayland who help balance my life and our kayak group: Jill Dalby Ellison, Anne Gilson, Annie Hollingsworth, Barb Burgess, Barb Fletcher, Bredt Handy Reynolds, Kim Wilson, Megan Lucier, and Nancy Osborn.

Sincere thanks to my parents, my brother, Victor, and to Jinny and Peter Bossart, for inspiring my love of classical music, art, photography, medicine, and faith that led to this book. Thanks to the amazing Nishioka family and especially my mother-in-law, Shizuye Nishioka, who exemplifies the principle that grace and dignity can prevail in spite of the most adverse circumstances. And special thanks to Adele Bargel, for living a life infused with empathy and who taught me about its power since early childhood.

Thanks to all who are not mentioned here but who have been an important part of this journey.

No one deserves more thanks than my sister, Johanna Riess Thoeresz, who has been my inspiration, role model, and best friend. Thank you.

References

Introduction

Borcsa, Maria, and Peter Stratton, eds. *Origins and Originality in Family Therapy and Systemic Practice*. New York: Springer, 2016.

Chasin, Richard, Margaret Herzig, Sallyann Roth, Laura Chasin, Carol Becker, and Robert R. Stains Jr. "From diatribe to dialogue on divisive public issues: Approaches drawn from family therapy." *Conflict Resolution Quarterly* 13, no. 4 (1996): 323–44. doi.org/10.1002/crq.3900130408.

Halpern, Jodi. *From Detached Concern to Empathy: Humanizing Medical Practice*. Oxford and New York: Oxford University Press, 2001.

Kelley, John Michael, Gordon Kraft-Todd, Lidia Schapira, Joe Kossowsky, and Helen Riess. "The influence of the patient-clinician relationship on healthcare outcomes: A systematic review and meta-analysis of randomized controlled trials." *PloS ONE* 9, no. 4 (April 2014): e94207. doi.org/10.1371/journal.pone.0094207.

Marci, Carl D., Jacob Ham, Erin K. Moran, and Scott P. Orr. "Physiologic correlates of perceived therapist empathy and social-emotional process during psychotherapy." *The Journal of Nervous and Mental Disease* 195, no. 2 (2007): 103–11. doi.org/10.1097/01.nmd.0000253731.71025.fc.

Marci, Carl D., and Helen Riess. "The clinical relevance of psychophysiology: Support for the psychobiology of empathy and psychodynamic process." *American Journal of Psychotherapy* 59, no. 3 (2005): 213–26.

Riess, Helen. "Biomarkers in the psychotherapeutic relationship: The role of physiology, neurobiology, and biological correlates of E.M.P.A.T.H.Y." *Harvard Review of Psychiatry* 19, no. 3 (2011): 162–74. doi.org/10.3109/08941939.2011.581915.

Riess, Helen. "Empathy in medicine—a neurobiological perspective." *Journal of the American Medical Association* 304, no. 14 (October 2010): 1604–5. doi.org/10.1001/jama.2010.1455.

Riess, Helen, and Carl D. Marci. "The neurobiology and physiology of the patient–doctor relationship: Measuring empathy." *Medical Encounter* 21, no. 3 (2007): 38–41.

Riess, Helen, John Kelley, Robert W. Bailey, Emily J. Dunn, and Margot Phillips. "Empathy Training for Resident Physicians: A Randomized Controlled Trial of a Neuroscience-Informed Curriculum." *Journal of General Internal Medicine* 27, no. 10 (October 2012): 1280–86. doi.org/10.1007/s11606-012-2063-z.

Chapter 1: Shared Mind Intelligence

Batson, C. Daniel, Bruce D. Duncan, Paula Ackerman, Terese Buckley, and Kimberly Birch. "Is empathic emotion a source of altruistic motivation?" *Journal of Personality and Social Psychology* 40, no. 2 (1981):290–302. dx.doi.org/10.1037/0022-3514.40.2.290.

Cartwright, Rosalind D., and Barbara Lerner. "Empathy, need to change and improvement with psychotherapy." *Journal of Consulting Psychology* 27, no. 2 (1963), 138–44. dx.doi.org/10.1037/h0048827.

Decety, Jean. "The neuroevolution of empathy." *Annals of the New York Academy of Sciences* 1231 (2011): 35–45. doi.org/10.1111/j.1749-6632.2011.06027.x.

Decety, Jean, and William Ickes, eds. *The Social Neuroscience of Empathy.* Cambridge, MA: MIT Press, 2011.

Decety, Jean, Greg J. Norman, Gary G. Berntson, and John T. Cacioppo. "A neurobehavioral evolutionary perspective on the mechanisms underlying empathy." *Progress in Neurobiology* 98, no. 1 (July 2012): 38–48. doi.org/10.1016/j.pneurobio.2012.05.001.

Ekman, Paul. *Emotions Revealed: Recognizing Faces and Feelings to Improve Communication and Emotional Life.* New York: Henry Holt and Co., 2007.

Harris, James. "The evolutionary neurobiology, emergence and facilitation of empathy." In *Empathy in Mental Illness*, edited by Tom F. D. Farrow and Peter W. R. Woodruff, 168–186. Cambridge: Cambridge University Press, 2007.

Karam Foundation. Accessed March 19, 2018. karamfoundation.org.

Knapp, Mark L. and Judith Hall. *Nonverbal Communication in Human Interaction.* 7th ed. Boston: Wadsworth, 2010.

Kohut, Heinz. "Introspection, Empathy, and Psychoanalysis: An Examination of the Relationship between Mode of Observation and Theory." *Journal of the American Psychoanalytic Association* 7, no. 3 (1959), 459–83. doi.org/10.1177/000306515900700304.

Lanzoni, Susan. "A Short History of Empathy." *Atlantic*, October 15, 2015. theatlantic.com/health/archive/2015/10/a-short-history-of-empathy/409912.

Mehrabian, Albert. *Nonverbal Communication.* Chicago: Aldine-Atherton, 1972.

Rankin, Katherine P., M. L. Gorno-Tempini, S. C. Allison, C. M. Stanley, S. Glenn, M. W. Weiner, and B. L. Miller. "Structural anatomy of empathy in neurodegenerative disease." *Brain* 129, no. 11 (November 2006): 2945–56. doi.org/10.1093/brain/awl254.

Riess, Helen. "Empathy in medicine—a neurobiological perspective." *Journal of the American Medical Association* 304, no. 14 (October 2010): 1604–5. doi.org/10.1001/jama.2010.1455.

Riess, Helen. "The Impact of Clinical Empathy on Patients and Clinicians: Understanding Empathy's Side Effects." *AJOB Neuroscience* 6, no. 3 (July–September 2015): 51. doi.org/10.1080/21507740.2015.1052591.

Rifkin, Jeremy. *The Empathic Civilization: The Race to Global Consciousness in a World in Crisis.* Cambridge: Polity, 2010.

Rogers, Carl R. *Client-Centered Therapy*. London: Constable & Robinson, 1995. First published 1951 by Houghton Mifflin (Boston, Oxford).

Shamay-Tsoory, Simone G., Judith Aharon-Peretz, and Daniella Perry. "Two systems for empathy: A double dissociation between emotional and cognitive empathy in inferior frontal gyrus versus ventromedial prefrontal lesions." *Brain: A Journal of Neurology* 132, no. 3 (March 2009): 617–27. doi.org/10.1093/brain/awn279.

Singer, Tania. "Feeling Others' Pain: Transforming Empathy into Compassion." Interviewed by Cognitive Neuroscience Society, June 24, 2013. cogneurosociety.org/empathy_pain/.

Vischer, Robert. "On the Optical Sense of Form: A Contribution to Aesthetics" (1873). In *Empathy, Form, and Space: Problems in German Aesthetics, 1873–1893*, edited and translated by Harry Francis Mallgrave and Eleftherios Ikonomou, 89–123. Santa Monica, CA: Getty Center Publications, 1994.

Wicker, Bruno, Christian Keysers, Jane Plailly, Jean-Pierre Royet, Vittorio Gallese, and Giacomo Rizzolatti. "Both of Us Disgusted in My Insula: The Common Neural Pathway for Seeing and Feeling Disgust." *Neuron* 40, no. 3 (October 2003): 655–64. doi.org/10.1016/S0896-6273(03)00679-2.

Chapter 2: How Empathy Works

Avenanti, Alessio, Domenica Bueti, Gaspare Galati, and Salvatore Maria Aglioti. "Transcranial magnetic stimulation highlights the sensorimotor side of empathy for pain." *Nature Neuroscience* 8, no. 7 (2005): 955–60. doi.org/10.1038/nn1481.

Bufalari, Ilaria, Taryn Aprile, Alessio Avenanti, Francesco Di Russo, and Salvatore Maria Aglioti. "Empathy for pain and touch in the human somatosensory cortex." *Cerebral Cortex* 17, no. 11 (November 2007): 2553–61. doi.org/10.1093/cercor/bhl161.

Decety, Jean, Greg J. Norman, Gary G. Berntson, and John T. Cacioppo. "A neurobehavioral evolutionary perspective on the mechanisms underlying empathy." *Progress in Neurobiology* 98, no. 1 (July 2012): 38–48. doi.org/10.1016/j.pneurobio.2012.05.001.

Ferrari, Pier Francesco, and Giacomo Rizzolatti. "Mirror neuron research: The past and the future." *Philosophical Transactions of the Royal Society of London B: Biological Sciences* 369, no. 1644 (2014): 20130169. doi.org/10.1098/rstb.2013.0169.

Hogeveen, Jeremy, Michael Inzlicht, and Sukhvinder Obhi. "Power changes how the brain responds to others." *Journal of Experimental Psychology: General* 143, no. 2 (April 2014): 755–62. doi.org/10.1037/a0033477.

Lamm, Claus, C. Daniel Batson, and Jean Decety. "The Neural Substrate of Human Empathy: Effects of Perspective-taking and Cognitive Appraisal." *Journal of Cognitive Neuroscience* 19, no. 1 (January 2007): 42–58. doi.org/10.1162/jocn.2007.19.1.42.

Miller, Greg. "Neuroscience: Reflecting on Another's Mind." *Science* 308, no. 5724 (May 2005): 945–47. doi.org/10.1126/science.308.5724.945.

Pelphrey, Kevin A., James P. Morris, and Gregory McCarthy. "Neural basis of eye gaze processing deficits in autism." *Brain: A Journal of Neurology* 128, no. 5 (2005): 1038–48. doi.org/10.1093/brain/awh404.

Preston, Stephanie D., and Frans B. M. de Waal. "Empathy: Its ultimate and proximate bases." *Behavioral and Brain Sciences* 25, no. 1 (March 2002): 1–20; discussion 20–71. doi.org/10.1017/S0140525X02000018.

Riess, Helen. "Empathy in medicine—a neurobiological perspective." *Journal of the American Medical Association* 304, no. 14 (October 2010): 1604–5. doi.org/10.1001/jama.2010.1455.

Riess, Helen. "The Science of Empathy." *Journal of Patient Experience* 4, no. 2 (June 2017): 74–77. doi.org/10.1177/2374373517699267.

Rizzolatti, Giacomo, Leonardo Fogassi, and Vittorio Gallese. "Neurophysiological mechanisms underlying the understanding and imitation of action." *Nature Reviews Neuroscience* 2, no. 9 (2001): 661–70. doi.org/10.1038/35090060.

Singer, Tania, and Claus Lamm. "The social neuroscience of empathy." *Annals of the New York Academy of Sciences* 1156 (March 2009): 81–96. doi.org/10.1111/j.1749-6632.2009.04418.x.

Zaki, Jamil. "Empathy: A motivated account." *Psychological Bulletin* 140, no. 6 (November 2014): 1608–47. dx.doi.org/10.1037/a0037679.

Zaki, Jamil, and Kevin N. Ochsner. "The neuroscience of empathy: Progress, pitfalls and promise." *Nature Neuroscience* 15, no. 5 (April 2012): 675–80. doi.org/10.1038/nn.3085.

Chapter 3: The Empathy Spectrum

Brewer, Marilynn B. "The social psychology of intergroup relations: Social categorization, ingroup bias, and outgroup prejudice." In *Social Psychology: Handbook of Basic Principles*, 2nd edition, edited by Arie W. Kruglanski and E. Tory Higgins, 695–714. New York: Guilford Press, 2007.

Dinh, Khanh T., Traci L. Weinstein, Melissa Nemon, and Sara Rondeau. "The effects of contact with Asians and Asian Americans on White American college students: Attitudes, awareness of racial discrimination, and psychological adjustment." *American Journal of Community Psychology* 42, nos. 3–4 (December 2008): 298–308. doi.org/10.1007/s10464-008-9202-z.

Ferrari, Pier Francesco, and Giacomo Rizzolatti. "Mirror neuron research: The past and the future." *Philosophical Transactions of the Royal Society of London B: Biological Sciences* 369, no. 1644 (2014): 20130169. doi.org/10.1098/rstb.2013.0169.

Goetz, Jennifer, Dacher Keltner, and Emiliana R. Simon-Thomas. "Compassion: An evolutionary analysis and empirical review." *Psychological Bulletin* 136, no. 3 (May 2010): 351–74. doi.org/10.1037a0018807.

Joseph, Chacko N, Cesare Porta, Gaia Casucci, Nadia Casiraghi, Mara Maffeis, Marco Rossi, and Luciano Bernardi. "Slow breathing improves arterial baroreflex sensitivity and decreases blood pressure in essential hypertension." *Hypertension* 46 , no. 4 (October 2005): 714–8. doi.org/10.1161/01 .HYP.0000179581.68566.7d.

Missouri State University. Orientation and Mobility Graduate Certificate Program website. Last modified January 16, 2018. graduate.missouristate.edu/catalog /prog_Orientation_and_Mobility.htm.

Orloff, Judith. *The Empath's Survival Guide: Life Strategies for Sensitive People.* Boulder, CO: Sounds True, 2017.

Phillips, Margot, Áine Lorié, John Kelley, Stacy Gray, and Helen Riess. "Long-term effects of empathy training in surgery residents: A one year follow-up study." *European Journal for Person Centered Healthcare* 1, no. 2 (2013), 326–32. doi.org/10.5750/ejpch.v1i2.666.

Radaelli, Alberto, Roberta Raco, Paola Perfetti, Andrea Viola, Arianna Azzellino, Maria G. Signorini, and Alberto Ferrari. "Effects of slow, controlled breathing on baroreceptor control of heart rate and blood pressure in healthy men." *Journal of Hypertension* 22, no. 7 (July 2004): 1361–70. doi.org/10.1097/01 .hjh.0000125446.28861.51.

Riess, Helen, John M. Kelley, Robert W. Bailey, Emily J. Dunn, and Margot Phillips. "Empathy Training for Resident Physicians: A Randomized Controlled Trial of a Neuroscience-Informed Curriculum." *Journal of General Internal Medicine* 27, no. 10 (2012): 1280–86. doi.org/10.1007 /s11606-012-2063-z.

Riess, Helen, John M. Kelley, Robert W. Bailey, Paul M. Konowitz, and Stacey Tutt Gray. "Improving empathy and relational skills in otolaryngology residents: A pilot study." *Otolaryngology–Head and Neck Surgery* 144, no. 1 (January 2011): 120–22. doi.org/10.1177/0194599810390897.

Singer, Tania, Ben Seymour, John P. O'Doherty, Holger Kaube, Raymond J. Dolan, and Chris D. Frith. "Empathy for pain involves the affective but not sensory components of pain." *Science* 303, no. 5661 (February 2004): 1157–62. doi.org/10.1126/science.1093535.

Singer, Tania, Ben Seymour, John P. O'Doherty, Klaas Enno Stephan, Raymond J. Dolan, and Chris D. Frith. "Empathic neural responses are modulated by the perceived fairness of others." *Nature* 439, no. 7075 (January 2006): 466–69. doi.org/10.1038/nature04271.

Slovic, Paul. "'If I Look at the Mass I Will Never Act': Psychic Numbing and Genocide." *Judgment and Decision Making* 2, no. 2 (April 2007) 79–95.

Slovic, Paul, Daniel Västfjäll, Arvid Erlandsson, and Robin Gregory. "Iconic photographs and the ebb and flow of empathic response to humanitarian disasters." *Proceedings of the National Academy of Sciences of the United States of America* 114, no. 4 (January 2017): 640–44. doi.org/10.1073 /pnas.1613977114.

Chapter 4: The Seven Keys of E.M.P.A.T.H.Y.®

Adams, Reginald B., Jr., Heather L. Gordon, Abigail A. Baird, Nalini Ambady, and Robert E. Kleck. "Effects of gaze on amygdala sensitivity to anger and fear faces." *Science* 300, no. 5625 (June 6, 2003): 1536. doi.org/10.1126/science.1082244.

Ambady, Nalini, Debi LaPlante, Thai Nguyen, Robert Rosenthal, Nigel R. Chaumeton, and Wendy Levinson. "Surgeons' tone of voice: a clue to malpractice history." *Surgery* 132, no. 1 (July 2002): 5–9. doi.org/10.1067/msy.2002.124733.

Boucher, Jerry D., and Paul Ekman. "Facial Areas and Emotional Information." *Journal of Communication* 25, no. 2 (June 1975): 21–29. doi.org/10.1111/j.1460-2466.1975.tb00577.x.

Bowlby, John. *A Secure Base: Clinical Applications of Attachment Theory.* London: Routledge, 1988.

Bowlby, John. *Attachment and Loss, Vol. I: Attachment.* New York: Basic Books, 1999. First published 1969 by Basic Books.

Chustecka, Zosia. "Cancer Risk Reduction in the Trenches: PCPs Respond." Medscape.com, October 25, 2016. medscape.com/viewarticle/870857.

Conradt, Elisabeth, and Jennifer C. Ablow. "Infant physiological response to the still-face paradigm: contributions of maternal sensitivity and infants' early regulatory behavior." *Infant Behavior & Development* 33, no. 3 (June 2010): 251–65. doi.org/10.1016/j.infbeh.2010.01.001.

Darwin, Charles. *The Expression of Emotions in Man and Animals.* 1872. Reprint, London: Friedman, 1979.

Decety, Jean, and G. J. Norman. "Empathy: A social neuroscience perspective." In *International Encyclopedia of the Social and Behavioral Sciences*, 2nd edition, vol. 7, edited by James D. Wright, 541–48. Oxford: Elsevier, 2015.

Decety, Jean, Kalina J. Michalska, and Katherine D. Kinzler. "The contribution of emotion and cognition to moral sensitivity: A neurodevelopmental study." *Cerebral Cortex* 22, no. 1 (January 2012):209–20. doi.org/10.1093/cercor/bhr111.

Dimascio, Alberto, Richard W. Boyd, and Milton Greenblatt. "Physiological correlates of tension and antagonism during psychotherapy: A study of interpersonal physiology." *Psychosomatic Medicine* 19, no. 2 (1957): 99–104. doi.org/10.1097/00006842-195703000-00002.

Ekman, Paul. *Emotions Revealed: Recognizing Faces and Feelings to Improve Communication and Emotional Life.* New York: Henry Holt and Co., 2007.

Ekman, Paul, Richard J. Davidson, and Wallace V. Friesen. "The Duchenne smile: Emotional expression and brain physiology II." *Journal of Personality and Social Psychology* 58, no. 2 (March 1990): 342–53. doi.org/10.1037/0022-3514.58.2.342.

Gauntlett, Jane. "The In My Shoes Project." Accessed March 19, 2018. janegauntlett.com/inmyshoesproject/.

Hatfield, Elaine, Christopher K. Hsee, Jason Costello, Monique Schalekamp Weisman, and Colin Denney. "The impact of vocal feedback on emotional experience and expression." *Journal of Social Behavior and Personality* 10 (May 24, 1995): 293–312.

Insel, Thomas R., and Larry J. Young. "The neurobiology of attachment." *Nature Reviews Neuroscience* 2 (February 2001): 129–136. doi.org/10.1038/35053579.

Jenni, Karen, and George Lowenstein. "Explaining the identifiable victim effect." *Journal of Risk and Uncertainty* 14, no. 3 (May 1997): 235–57. doi.org/10.1023/A:1007740225484.

Kelley, John Michael, Gordon Kraft-Todd, Lidia Schapira, Joe Kossowsky, and Helen Riess. "The influence of the patient-clinician relationship on healthcare outcomes: A systematic review and meta-analysis of randomized controlled trials." *PloS ONE* 9, no. 4 (April 2014): e94207. doi.org/10.1371/journal.pone.0094207.

Künecke, Janina, Andrea Hildebrandt, Guillermo Recio, Werner Sommer, and Oliver Wilhelm. "Facial EMG Responses to Emotional Expressions Are Related to Emotion Perception Ability." *PloS ONE* 9, no. 1 (January 2014): e84053. doi.org/10.1371/journal.pone.0084053.

Lieberman, Matthew D., Tristen K. Inagaki, Golnaz Tabibnia, and Molly J. Crockett. "Subjective Responses to Emotional Stimuli During Labeling, Reappraisal, and Distraction." *Emotion* 11, no. 3 (2011): 468–80. doi.org/10.1037/a0023503.

Lorié, Áine, Diego A. Reinero, Margot Phillips, Linda Zhang, and Helen Riess. "Culture and nonverbal expressions of empathy in clinical settings: A systematic review." *Patient Education and Counseling* 100, no. 3 (March 2017): 411–24. doi.org/10.1016/j.pec.2016.09.018.

Marci, Carl D., Jacob Ham, Erin K. Moran, and Scott P. Orr. "Physiologic correlates of perceived therapist empathy and social-emotional process during psychotherapy." *The Journal of Nervous and Mental Disease* 195, no. 2 (2007): 103–11. doi.org/10.1097/01.nmd.0000253731.71025.fc.

Mehrabian, Albert. *Nonverbal Communication.* Chicago: Aldine-Atherton, 1972.

Morrison, India, Marius V. Peelen, and Paul E. Downing. "The sight of others' pain modulates motor processing in human cingulate cortex." *Cerebral Cortex* 17, no. 9 (September 2007): 2214–22. doi.org/10.1093/cercor/bhl129.

Petrović, Predrag, Raffael Kalisch, Tania Singer, and Raymond J. Dolan. "Oxytocin attenuates affective evaluations of conditioned faces and amygdala activity." *Journal of Neuroscience* 28, no. 26 (June 25, 2008): 6607–15. doi.org/10.1523/JNEUROSCI.4572-07.2008.

Rabin, Roni Caryn. "Reading, Writing, 'Rithmetic and Relationships." *New York Times*, December 20, 2010. well.blogs.nytimes.com/2010/12/20/reading-writing-rithmetic-and-relationships/.

Riess, Helen. "The Power of Empathy." Filmed November 2013 at TEDxMiddlebury in Middlebury, VT. Video, 17:02. youtube.com/watch?v=baHrcC8B4WM.

Riess, Helen, and Gordon Kraft-Todd. "E.M.P.A.T.H.Y.: A tool to enhance nonverbal communication between clinicians and their patients." *Academic Medicine* 89, no. 8 (August 2014): 1108–12. doi.org/10.1097/ACM.0000000000000287.

Stephens, Greg J., Lauren J. Silbert, and Uri Hasson. "Speaker-listener neural coupling underlies successful communication." *Proceedings of the National Academy of Sciences of the United States of America* 107, no. 32 (August 2010): 14425–30. doi.org/10.1073/pnas.1008662107.

Chapter 5: Who's In, Who's Out

Brewer, Marilynn B. "The social psychology of intergroup relations: Social categorization, ingroup bias, and outgroup prejudice." In *Social Psychology: Handbook of Basic Principles*, 2nd edition, edited by Arie W. Kruglanski and E. Tory Higgins, 695–714. New York: Guilford Press, 2007.

Decety, Jean, and Jason M. Cowell. "Friends or Foes: Is Empathy Necessary for Moral Behavior?" *Perspectives on Psychological Science* 9, no. 5 (2014): 525–37. doi.org/10.1177/1745691614545130.

Decety, Jean, and Jason M. Cowell. "The complex relation between morality and empathy." *Trends in Cognitive Sciences* 18, no. 7 (July 2014): 337–39. doi.org/10.1016/j.tics.2014.04.008.

Fisman, Raymond J., Sheena S. Iyengar, Emir Kamenica, and Itamar Simonson. "Racial Preferences in Dating." *The Review of Economic Studies* 75, no. 1 (January 2008), 117–32. doi.org/10.1111/j.1467-937X.2007.00465.x.

Lamm, Claus, Andrew N. Meltzoff, and Jean Decety. "How Do We Empathize with Someone Who Is Not Like Us? A Functional Magnetic Resonance Imaging Study." *Journal of Cognitive Neuroscience* 22, no. 2 (2010): 362–76. doi.org/10.1162/jocn.2009.21186.

Lorié, Áine, Diego A. Reinero, Margot Phillips, Linda Zhang, and Helen Riess. "Culture and nonverbal expressions of empathy in clinical settings: A systematic review." *Patient Education and Counseling* 100, no. 3 (March 2017): 411–24. doi.org/10.1016/j.pec.2016.09.018.

Peters, William, dir. *The Eye of the Storm*. 1970; Filmed in 1970 in Riceville, Iowa, aired in 1970 on ABC. Video, 26:17. archive.org/details/EyeOfTheStorm_201303.

Petrović, Predrag, Raffael Kalisch, Mathias Pessiglione, Tania Singer, and Raymond J. Dolan. "Learning affective values for faces is expressed in amygdala and fusiform gyrus." *Social Cognitive and Affective Neuroscience* 3, no. 2 (June 2008): 109–18. doi.org/10.1093/scan/nsn002.

Piff, Paul K., Daniel M. Stancato, Stéphane Côté, Rodolfo Mendoza-Denton, and Dacher Keltner. "Higher social class predicts increased unethical behavior." *Proceedings of the National Academy of Sciences of the United States of America* 109, no. 11 (2012): 4086–91. doi.org/10.1073/pnas.1118373109.

Yiltiz, Hörmetjan, and Lihan Chen. "Tactile input and empathy modulate the perception of ambiguous biological motion." *Frontiers in Psychology* 6 (February 2015): 161. doi.org/10.3389/fpsyg.2015.00161.

Chapter 6: Growing Up with Empathy

Conradt, Elisabeth, and Jennifer C. Ablow. "Infant physiological response to the still-face paradigm: Contributions of maternal sensitivity and infants' early regulatory behavior." *Infant Behavior & Development* 33, no. 3 (June 2010): 251–65. doi.org/10.1016/j.infbeh.2010.01.001.

Cradles to Crayons. Accessed March 19, 2018. cradlestocrayons.org.

Fredrickson, Barbara. *Positivity: Groundbreaking Research Reveals How to Embrace the Hidden Strength of Positive Emotions, Overcome Negativity, and Thrive.* London: One World Publications, 2009.

Gladwell, Malcolm. *Blink: The Power of Thinking Without Thinking.* Boston: Little, Brown, 2005.

Hemphill, Sheryl A., Stephanie M. Plenty, Todd I. Herrenkohl, John W. Toumbourou, and Richard F. Catalano. "Student and school factors associated with school suspension: A multilevel analysis of students in Victoria, Australia and Washington State, United States." *Children and Youth Services Review* 36, no. 1 (January 2014): 187–94. doi.org/10.1016/j.childyouth.2013.11.022.

Kendall-Tackett, Kathleen A., and John Eckenrode. "The effects of neglect on academic achievement and disciplinary problems: A developmental perspective." *Child Abuse and Neglect* 20, no. 3 (March 1996): 161–69. doi.org/10.1016 /S0145-2134(95)00139-5.

Kendrick, Keith M. "Oxytocin, motherhood and bonding." *Experimental Physiology* 85, no. s1 (March 2000): 111S–24S. doi.org/10.1111 /j.1469-445X.2000.tb00014.x.

Kohut, Heinz. *How Does Analysis Cure?* Edited by Arnold Goldberg and Paul E. Stepansky. Chicago: University of Chicago Press, 1984.

Margherio, Lynn. "Building an Army of Empathy." Filmed November 2017 at TEDxBeaconStreet in Boston, MA. Video, 11:15. tedxbeaconstreet.com /videos/building-an-army-of-empathy/.

Open Circle learning program website. Wellesley Center for Women, Wellesley College. Accessed March 19, 2018. open-circle.org.

Piaget, Jean, and Bärbel Inhelder. *The Child's Conception of Space.* London and New York: Psychology Press, 1997.

Sagi, Abraham, and Martin L. Hoffman. "Empathic distress in the newborn." *Developmental Psychology* 12, no. 2 (March 1976): 175–76. doi.org/10.1037/0012-1649.12.2.175.

Warrier, Varun, Roberto Toro, Bhismadev Chakrabarti, The iPSYCH-Broad autism group, Anders D. Børglum, Jakob Grove, the 23andMe Research Team, David Hinds, Thomas Bourgeron, and Simon Baron-Cohen. "Genome-wide analysis of self-reported empathy: Correlations with autism, schizophrenia, and anorexia nervosa." *Translational Psychiatry* 8, no. 1 (March 2018): 35. doi.org/10.1038/s41398-017-0082-6.

Winnicott, Donald W. "The theory of the parent-infant relationship." *The International Journal of Psychoanalysis* 41 (Nov–Dec 1960): 585–95. doi.org/10.1093/med:psych/9780190271381.003.0022.

Chapter 7: The ABCs of Empathy in Education

Falk, Emily B., Sylvia A. Morelli, B. Locke Welborn, Karl Dambacher, and Matthew D. Lieberman. "Creating buzz: The neural correlates of effective message propagation." *Psychological Science* 24, no. 7 (July 2013): 1234–42. doi.org/10.1177/0956797612474670.

Farber, Matthew. *Gamify Your Classroom: A Field Guide to Game-Based Learning.* Rev. ed. New York: Peter Lang Publishing, Inc., 2017.

Hemphill, Sheryl A., John W. Toumbourou, Todd I. Herrenkohl, Barbara J. McMorris, and Richard F. Catalano. "The effect of school suspensions and arrests on subsequent adolescent antisocial behavior in Australia and the United States." *Journal of Adolescent Health* 39, no. 5 (November 2006): 736–44. doi.org/10.1016/j.jadohealth.2006.05.010.

Horn, Michael B., and Heather Staker. *Blended: Using Disruptive Innovation to Improve Schools.* San Francisco: Jossey-Bass, 2015.

Kidd, David Comer, and Emanuele Castano. "Reading literary fiction improves theory of mind." *Science* 342, no. 6156 (October 2013): 377–80. doi.org/10.1126/science.1239918.

Lieberman, Matthew D. "Education and the social brain." *Trends in Neuroscience and Education* 1, no. 1 (December 2012): 3–9. doi.org/10.1016/j.tine.2012.07.003.

Redford, James, dir. *Paper Tigers.* 2015; Branford, CT: KPJR Films. kpjrfilms.co /paper-tigers/.

Warrier, Varun, Roberto Toro, Bhismadev Chakrabarti, The iPSYCH-Broad autism group, Anders D. Børglum, Jakob Grove, the 23andMe Research Team, David Hinds, Thomas Bourgeron, and Simon Baron-Cohen. "Genome-wide analysis of self-reported empathy: Correlations with autism, schizophrenia, and anorexia nervosa." *Translational Psychiatry* 8, no. 1 (March 2018): 35. doi.org/10.1038/s41398-017-0082-6.

Chapter 8: Texts, Screens, and Digital Empathy

Berridge, Kent C., and Terry E. Robinson. "What is the role of dopamine in reward: Hedonic impact, reward learning, or incentive salience?" *Brain Research Reviews* 28, no. 3 (December 1998): 309–69. doi.org/10.1016/S0165-0173(98)00019-8.

Buckels, Erin E., Paul D. Trapnell, and Delroy L. Paulhus. "Trolls Just Want to Have Fun." *Personality and Individual Differences* 67 (September 2014): 97–102. doi.org/10.1016/j.paid.2014.01.016.

Buxton, Madeline. "The Internet Problem We Don't Talk About Enough." Refinery29.com, March 15, 2017. refinery29.com/online-harassment-statistics-infographic.

Dosomething.org. "11 Facts About Bullies." Accessed March 19, 2018. dosomething .org/us/facts/11-facts-about-bullying.

Keng, Shian-Ling, Moria J. Smoski, and Clive J. Robins. "Effects of mindfulness on psychological health: A review of empirical studies." *Clinical Psychology Review* 31, no. 6 (August 2011): 1041–56. doi.org/10.1016/j.cpr.2011.04.006.

Przybylski, Andrew K., and Netta Weinstein. "Can you connect with me now? How the presence of mobile communication technology influences face-to-face conversation quality." *Journal of Social and Personal Relationships* 30, no. 3 (May 2013), 237–46. doi.org/10.1177/0265407512453827.

Rideout, Victoria J., Ulla G. Foehr, and Donald F. Roberts. *Generation M2: Media in the Lives of 8- to 18-Year-Olds: A Kaiser Family Foundation Study.* Menlo Park, CA: Henry J. Kaiser Family Foundation, January 2010. kaiserfamilyfoundation.files .wordpress.com/2013/04/8010.pdf.

Schenker, Mark. "The Surprising History of Emojis." Webdesignerdepot.com, October 11, 2016. webdesignerdepot.com/2016/10/the-surprising-history-of-emojis/.

Steinberg, Brian. "Study: Young Consumers Switch Media 27 Times an Hour." Ad Age, April 9, 2012. adage.com/article/news/study-young-consumers-switch-media -27-times-hour/234008/.

West, Lindy. "What Happened When I Confronted My Cruelest Troll." *Guardian*, February 2, 2015. theguardian.com/society/2015/feb/02 /what-happened-confronted-cruellest-troll-lindy-west.

Wong, Hai Ming, Kuen Wai Ma, Lavender Yu Xin Yang, and Yanqi Yang. "Dental Students' Attitude towards Problem-Based Learning before and after Implementing 3D Electronic Dental Models." *International Journal of Educational and Pedagogical Sciences* 104, no. 8 (2017): 2110, 1–6. hdl.handle.net/10722/244777.

Chapter 9: Empathy, Art, and Literature

Alan Alda Center for Communicating Science. Accessed March 19, 2018. aldacenter.org.

Gauntlett, Jane. The In My Shoes Project. Accessed March 19, 2018. janegauntlett. infor/inmyshoesproject.

Kandel, Eric R. *The Age of Insight: The Quest to Understand the Unconscious in Art, Mind, and Brain, from Vienna 1900 to the Present.* New York: Random House, 2012.

Kidd, David Comer, and Emanuele Castano. "Reading literary fiction improves theory of mind." *Science* 342, no. 6156 (October 2013): 377–80. doi.org/10.1126/science.1239918.

Mazzio, Mary, dir. *I Am Jane Doe*. 2017; Babson Park, MA: 50 Eggs Films. iamjanedoefilm.com.

O'Donohue, John. *Anam Cara: A Book of Celtic Wisdom*, 25. New York: HarperCollins, 1997.

O'Donohue, John. *Beauty: The Invisible Embrace: Rediscovering the True Sources of Compassion, Serenity, and Hope*. New York: HarperCollins, 2004.

Rentfrow, Peter J., Lewis R. Goldberg, and Ran D. Zilca. "Listening, watching, and reading: The structure and correlates of entertainment preferences." *Journal of Personality* 79, no. 2 (April 2011): 223–58. doi.org/10.1111/j.1467-6494.2010.00662.x.

Rifkin, Jeremy. *The Empathic Civilization: The Race to Global Consciousness in a World in Crisis*. Cambridge: Polity, 2009.

Siegel, Daniel J. *The Developing Mind: How Relationships and the Brain Interact to Shape Who We Are*. 2nd ed. New York: Guilford Press, 2012.

Chapter 10: Leadership and the Politics of Empathy

Adams, Reginald B., Jr., Heather L. Gordon, Abigail A. Baird, Nalini Ambady, and Robert E. Kleck. "Effects of gaze on amygdala sensitivity to anger and fear faces." *Science* 300, no. 5625 (June 6, 2003): 1536. doi.org/10.1126/science.1082244.

Boyatzis, Richard, and Annie McKee. *Resonant Leadership: Renewing Yourself and Connecting with Others Through Mindfulness, Hope, and Compassion*. Boston: Harvard Business Review Press, 2005.

Buckner, Randy L., Jessica R. Andrews-Hanna, and Daniel L. Schacter. "The brain's default network: Anatomy, function, and relevance to disease." *Annals of the New York Academy of Sciences* 1124, no. 1 (March 2008): 1–38. doi.org/10.1196/annals.1440.011.

Cameron, Kim. "Responsible Leadership as Virtuous Leadership." *Journal of Business Ethics* 98, no. 1 (January 2011): 25–35. doi.org/10.1007/s10551-011-1023-6.

CNN Exit Polls, November 23, 2016, cnn.com/election/results/exit-polls.

DeSteno, David. *The Truth About Trust: How It Determines Success in Life, Love, Learning, and More*. New York: Hudson Street Press, 2014.

Fajardo, Camilo, Martha Isabel Escobar, Efraín Buriticá, Gabriel Arteaga, J. Umbarila, Manuel F. Casanova, and Hernán J. Pimienta. "Von Economo neurons are present in the dorsolateral (dysgranular) prefrontal cortex of humans." *Neuroscience Letters* 435, no. 3 (May 2008): 215–18. doi.org/10.1016/j.neulet.2008.02.048

Goleman, Daniel. *Emotional Intelligence: Why It Can Matter More Than IQ*. London: Bloomsbury, 2010.

Goleman, Daniel. *Social Intelligence: The New Science of Human Relationships*. New York: Bantam Books, 2007.

Goleman, Daniel, Richard Boyatzis, and Annie McKee. *Primal Leadership: Realizing the Power of Emotional Intelligence*. Boston: Harvard Business Review Press, 2002.

Grant, Daniel. "Artists as Teachers in Prisons." Huffington Post, July 6, 2010. Updated November 17, 2011. huffingtonpost.com/daniel-grant/artists-as-teachers-in-pr_b_565695.html.

Kraft-Todd, Gordon T., Diego A. Reinero, John M. Kelley, Andrea S. Heberlein, Lee Baer, and Helen Riess. "Empathic nonverbal behavior increases ratings of both warmth *and* competence in a medical context." *PloS ONE* 12, no. 5 (May 15, 2017): e0177758. doi.org/10.1371/journal.pone.0177758.

Kuhn, Daniel. *Dispatches from the Campaign Trail*. American University (2016), american.edu/spa/dispatches/campaign-trail/blog-two.cfm.

Lennick, Doug, and Fred Kiel. *Moral Intelligence: Enhancing Business Performance and Leadership Success*. Upper Saddle River, NJ: Pearson Education, 2008.

Lennick, Doug, Roy Geer, and Ryan Goulart. *Leveraging Your Financial Intelligence: At the Intersection of Money, Health, and Happiness*. Hoboken, NJ: John Wiley & Sons, Inc., 2017.

Maslow, Abraham H. "A theory of human motivation." *Psychological Review* 50, no. 4 (1943): 370–96. doi.org/10.1037/h0054346.

Peri, Sarada. "Empathy Is Dead in American Politics." *New York*, March 30, 2017. nymag.com/daily/intelligencer/2017/03/empathy-is-dead-in-american-politics.html.

Schwartz, Richard C. *Internal Family Systems Therapy*. New York: Guilford Press, 1994.

Sesno, Frank. *Ask More: The Power of Questions to Open Doors, Uncover Solutions and Spark Change*. New York: Amacom, 2017.

The Empathy Business, "Our Empathy Index." Accessed March 19, 2018. hbr.org/2015/11/2015-empathy-index.

"Transparency International—Bulgaria reports alarming rate of potential vote sellers." Sofia News Agency, October 19, 2011. novinite.com/articles/133068/Transparency+International-Bulgaria+Reports+Alarming+Rate+of+Potential+Vote-Sellers.

"The Trump Family Secrets and Lies." Cover story, *People*, July 31, 2017.

Valdesolo, Piercarlo, and David DeSteno. "Synchrony and the social tuning of compassion." *Emotion* 11, no. 2 (April 2011): 262–26. doi.org/10.1037/a0021302.

Chapter 11: Digging Deep for Empathy

Alda, Alan. *If I Understood You, Would I Have This Look on My Face?: My Adventures in the Art and Science of Relating and Communicating*. New York: Random House, 2017.

Arumi, Ana Maria, and Andrew L. Yarrow. *Compassion, Concern and Conflicted Feelings: New Yorkers on Homelessness and Housing*. New York: Public Agenda, 2007. publicagenda.org/files/homeless_nyc.pdf.

Baron-Cohen, Simon. *Autism and Asperger Syndrome*. Oxford and New York: Oxford University Press, 2008.

Baron-Cohen, Simon. *The Science of Evil: On Empathy and the Origins of Cruelty*. New York: Basic Books, 2011.

Baron-Cohen, Simon. *Zero Degrees of Empathy: A New Theory of Human Cruelty and Kindness*. London: Penguin Books, 2011.

Egan, Gerard. *The Skilled Helper: A Systematic Approach to Effective Helping*. 4th ed. Pacific Grove, CA: Brooks-Cole Publishing, 1990.

Final Report Draft (Washington, DC: The President's Commission on Combating Drug Addiction and the Opioid Crisis, 2017). whitehouse.gov/sites /whitehouse.gov/files/images/Final_Report_Draft_11-15-2017.pdf.

Wakeman, Sarah. *Journal of Addiction Medicine*. American Society of Addiction Medicine, 2017.

Yoder, Keith J., Carla L. Harenski, Kent A. Kiehl, and Jean Decety. "Neural networks underlying implicit and explicit moral evaluations in psychopathy." *Translational Psychiatry* 25, no. 5 (August 2015): e625. doi.org/10.1038 /tp.2015.117.

Chapter 12: Self-Empathy

Ekman, Eve, and Jodi Halpern. "Professional Distress and Meaning in Health Care: Why Professional Empathy Can Help." *Social Work in Health Care* 54, no. 7 (2015), 633–50. doi.org/10.1080/00981389.2015.1046575.

Epel, Elissa S., Elizabeth H. Blackburn, Jue Lin, Firdaus Dhabhar, Nancy E. Adler, Jason D. Morrow, and Richard M. Cawthorn. "Accelerated telomere shortening in response to life stress." *Proceedings of the National Academy of Sciences* 101, no. 49 (December 2004): 17312–15. doi.org/10.1073/pnas.0407162101.

Epstein, Ronald M. *Attending: Medicine, Mindfulness, and Humanity*. New York: Scribner, 2017.

Epstein, Ronald M. "Mindful practice." *JAMA* 282, no. 9 (September 1999): 833–39. doi.org/10.1001/jama.282.9.833.

Gazelle, Gail, Jane M. Liebschutz, and Helen Riess. "Physician Burnout: Coaching a Way Out." *Journal of General Internal Medicine* 30, no. 4 (December 2014): 508–513. doi.org/10.1007/s11606-014-3144-y.

Goleman, Daniel, and Richard J. Davidson. *Altered Traits: Science Reveals How Meditation Changes Your Mind, Brain, and Body*. New York: Avery, 2017.

Gračanin, Asmir, Ad Vingerhoets, Igor Kardum, Marina Zupčić, Maja Šantek, and Mia Šimić. "Why crying does and sometimes does not seem to alleviate mood: A quasi-experimental study." *Motivation and Emotion* 39, no. 6 (December 2015): 953–60. doi.org/10.1007/s11031-015-9507-9.

Hojat, Mohammadreza, Michael J. Vergare, Kaye Maxwell, George C. Brainard, Steven K. Herrine, Gerald A Isenberg, J. Jon Veloski, and Joseph S. Gonnella. "The devil is in the third year: A longitudinal study of erosion of empathy in medical school." *Academic Medicine: Journal of the Association of American Medical Colleges* 84, no. 9 (October 2009): 1182–91. doi.org/10.1097 /ACM.0b013e3181b17e55.

Kabat-Zinn, Jon. *Wherever You Go, There You Are: Mindfulness Meditation in Everyday Life*. New York: Hyperion, 1994.

Kearney, Michael K., Radhule B. Weininger, Mary L. S. Vachon, Richard L. Harrison, and Balfour M. Mount. "Self-care of physicians caring for patients at the end of life: 'Being connected... a key to my survival.'" *JAMA* 301, no. 11 (2009): 1155–64. doi.org/10.1001/jama.2009.352.

Linzer, Mark, Rachel Levine, David Meltzer, Sara Poplau, Carole Warde, and Colin P. West. "10 Bold Steps to Prevent Burnout in General Internal Medicine." *Journal of General Internal Medicine* 29, no. 1 (January 2014): 18-20. doi.org/10.1007 /s11606-013-2597-8.

Mascaro, Jennifer S., James K. Rilling, Lobsang Tenzin Negi, and Charles L. Raison. "Compassion meditation enhances empathic accuracy and related neural activity." *Social Cognitive and Affective Neuroscience* 8, no. 1 (January 2013): 48–55. doi.org/10.1093/scan/nss095.

Neff, Kristin D. "Self-Compassion: An Alternative Conceptualization of a Healthy Attitude Toward Oneself." *Self-Identity* 2, no. 2 (April 2003): 85–101. doi.org/10.1080/15298860309032.

Riess, Helen, and Gordon Kraft-Todd. "E.M.P.A.T.H.Y.: A tool to enhance nonverbal communication between clinicians and their patients." *Academic Medicine* 89, no. 8 (August 2014): 1108–12. doi.org/10.1097 /ACM.0000000000000287.

Riess, Helen, John M. Kelley, Robert W. Bailey, Emily J. Dunn, and Margot Phillips. "Empathy Training for Resident Physicians: A Randomized Controlled Trial of a Neuroscience-Informed Curriculum." *Journal of General Internal Medicine* 27, no. 10 (2012): 1280–86. doi.org/10.1007/s11606-012-2063-z.

Siegel, Daniel J. *The Mindful Brain: Reflection and Attunement in the Cultivation of Well-Being*. New York: W. W. Norton, 2007.

Shanafelt, Tait D., Sonja Boone, Litjen Tan, Lotte N. Dyrbye, Wayne Sotile, Daniel Satele, Colin P. West, Jeff Sloan, and Michael R. Oreskovich. "Burnout and satisfaction with work-life balance among US physicians relative to the general US population." Archives of Internal Medicine, 2012 Oct 8;172(18): 1377–85. doi: 10.1001/archinternmed.2012.3199.

Smith, Karen E., Greg J. Norman, and Jean Decety. "The complexity of empathy during medical school training: Evidence for positive changes." *Medical Education* 51, no. 11 (November 2017): 1146–59. doi.org/10.1111 /medu.13398.

Trudeau, Renée Peterson. *The Mother's Guide to Self-Renewal: How to Reclaim, Rejuvenate and Re-Balance Your Life*. Austin, TX: Balanced Living Press, 2008.

Index

About the Author

Helen Riess, MD, is a practicing psychiatrist, associate clinical professor of psychiatry at Harvard Medical School, and director of the Empathy and Relational Science Program at Massachusetts General Hospital (MGH). She is a core member of the Consortium for Research on Emotional Intelligence in Organizations. Dr. Riess developed an empathy training approach based on research in the neurobiology and physiology of empathy that has been rigorously tested in pilot studies and a randomized, controlled trial at MGH. She completed her residency and chief residency at MGH and Harvard Medical School. Dr. Riess has devoted her career to teaching and research in the art and science of the patient-doctor relationship. She is an internationally recognized educator, researcher, and speaker whose landmark article, "Empathy in Medicine—A Neurobiological Perspective," published in the *Journal of the American Medical Association* in 2010, transformed how physicians view empathy. Dr. Riess cofounded and serves as chief scientific officer of Empathetics, Inc., a platform that has trained thousands of medical professionals, educators, and leaders in empathic communication. She has received numerous awards for her groundbreaking research. Riess received her MD from Boston University School of Medicine and her BA from Wesleyan University.

About Sounds True

Sounds True is a multimedia publisher whose mission is to inspire and support personal transformation and spiritual awakening. Founded in 1985 and located in Boulder, Colorado, we work with many of the leading spiritual teachers, thinkers, healers, and visionary artists of our time. We strive with every title to preserve the essential "living wisdom" of the author or artist. It is our goal to create products that not only provide information to a reader or listener, but that also embody the quality of a wisdom transmission.

For those seeking genuine transformation, Sounds True is your trusted partner. At SoundsTrue.com you will find a wealth of free resources to support your journey, including exclusive weekly audio interviews, free downloads, interactive learning tools, and other special savings on all our titles.

To learn more, please visit SoundsTrue.com/freegifts or call us toll-free at 800.333.9185.